THE CIVILIZATION OF THE AMERICAN INDIAN SERIES

# THE CHIPPEWAS OF LAKE SUPERIOR

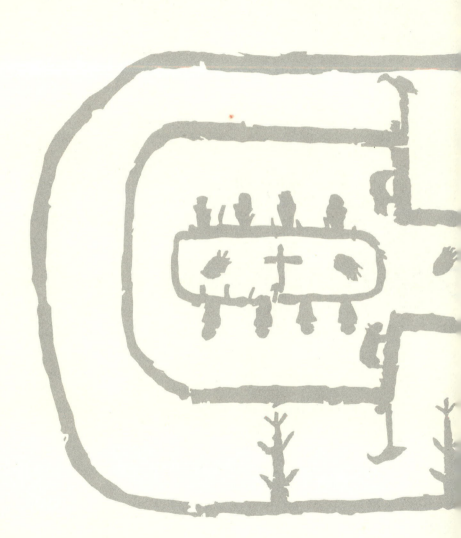

University of Oklahoma Press : Norman

# THE CHIPPEWAS
## OF LAKE SUPERIOR

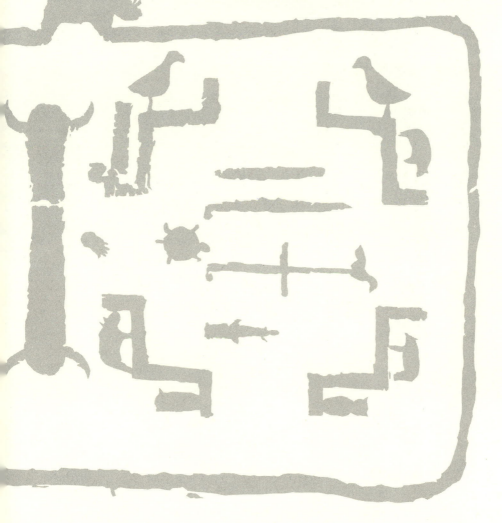

## By Edmund Jefferson Danziger, Jr.

By Edmund Jefferson Danziger, Jr.

*Indians and Bureaucrats: Administering the Reservation Policy
    During the Civil War* (Urbana, 1974)
*The Chippewas of Lake Superior* (Norman, 1979)

**Library of Congress Cataloging in Publication Data**

Danziger, Edmund Jefferson, 1938–
    The Chippewas of Lake Superior

    (The Civilization of the American Indian series; v. 148)
    Bibliography: p.
    1.  Chippewa Indians—History.  I.  Title.  II.  Series
E99.C6D25                        970'.004'97                        78-58130

*The Chippewas of Lake Superior* is Volume 148 in *The Civilization
of the American Indian Series.*

*For Allen, Esther, and all the Christys*

# Preface

This book tells the story of the Lake Superior Chippewa bands: their woodland life, the momentous impact of three centuries of European and American societies on their culture, and how the retention of their tribal identity and traditions proved such a source of strength for the Chippewas that the federal government finally abandoned its policy of coercive assimilation.

The Chippewa tribe, especially the Lake Superior bands, has been neglected by historians, perhaps because they fought no bloody wars of resistance against the westward-driving white pioneers who overwhelmed them in the nineteenth century. But historically, the Chippewas were one of the most important Indian groups north of Mexico. Their expansive north woods homeland contained valuable resources, forcing them to play important roles in regional enterprises such as the French, British, and American fur trade. Neither exterminated nor removed to the semiarid Great Plains, the Lake Superior bands have remained on their native lands and for the past century have continued to develop their interests in lumbering, fishing, farming, mining, shipping, and tourism.

Their history speaks to Americans today. Jim Hull, a Chippewa economic development specialist at Grand Portage reservation, believes that it is important for contemporary whites to understand their predecessors' greed and its effects on his people.[1] The average American neither knows nor cares about Indian history, asserts Frederick Dakota, tribal chairman of the Keweenaw Bay Indian Community. Although there is a great emphasis today on the schooling of Indians, those in real need of education are the non-Indians, he says. They should learn why tribes like the Chippewas were culturally assaulted. "It should be known that from the Indian point of view there was more than just one Hitler—several presidents of the United States have been Hitlers!"[2] Strong words. And it is time to listen. For centuries the Indian had no channel of communication with the dominant society; white Americans were too cocksure that the destruction of the Indians' woodland way of life and forced assimilation were justified. Now, by listening to what Native Americans say about their mistreatment, we can see ourselves more clearly. Moreover, as Commissioner of Indian Affairs John Collier suggested in the 1930's, Indian tribalism and the human values that tribes like the Chippewas understand have value for modern, industrialized, urbanized America.[3] If we listen.

Finally, this book will be of interest and use to the Chippewas at Keweenaw Bay, Bad River, Red Cliff, Lac du Flambeau, Lac Court Oreilles, Mole Lake, St. Croix, Fond du Lac, Grand Portage, and Nett Lake, as well as those living in urban areas. It tells them how previous tribal experiences have shaped reservation life in the 1970's. Perhaps it will be helpful also in charting a course for the future. St. Croix historian Lolita Taylor writes, "No one has a better right to earn a living in this land than we. No one has a better right to the pursuit of happiness here" in the land of the Chippewas.[4]

This book is not a retelling of the Great Lakes fur trade story nor an historical account of each of the ten reservations. With regard to the former, the reader is referred to several books and articles listed in the bibliography. Because of a determination to emphasize major themes for the entire sweep of Lake Superior Chippewa history, and to avoid weighing down the text with redundant detail, it was advisable at times to focus on one or two reservations to illustrate a point. Some readers might claim that such an overview is not wholly satisfactory—that each of the Lake Superior bands deserves fuller treatment, perhaps a monograph. Others may insist that the author's perspective (as a white historian) is limited, that Chippewas ought to be studying and writing about the past from their own unique points of view. Since the subject obviously is not exhausted, I heartily encourage both notions. There are other tribal divisions which merit greater attention from historians: the Southeast Chippewas of Michigan's Lower Peninsula and adjacent Ontario, the Southwest Chippewas of interior Minnesota, the Northern Chippewas of the Laurentian uplands above the Great Lakes, and the Plains Chippewas, or Bungees.

Completion of this book would not have been possible without special assistance. I would like to thank the staffs of the Bowling Green State University Library, the Houghton Library of Harvard University, the Washington National Records Center, the State Historical Society of Wisconsin, and the Minnesota Historical Society. Heartfelt thanks are extended to those employees of the Bureau of Indian Affairs (BIA) and Chippewas who graciously granted me interviews during the summers of 1974 and 1975. Robert Kvasnicka and Samella Anderson, of the National Archives; Elizabeth Trimmer and Bruce Harding, of the Federal Records Center at Chicago; and Michael Foley, of Georgetown University's history department— all deserve special acknowledgment. Data gathering was also facilitated by a grant from the Faculty Research Committee of Bowling Green State University. Two history department chairmen, William R. Rock and Gary R. Hess, encouraged this project in several ways, not the least of which was the arrangement of my schedule to allow adequate time for research. For Margaret, words will never suffice to thank her for the editorial skill, confidence, and understanding so freely given.

EDMUND JEFFERSON DANZIGER, JR.

*Bowling Green, Ohio*

# Contents

# Illustrations

# Maps

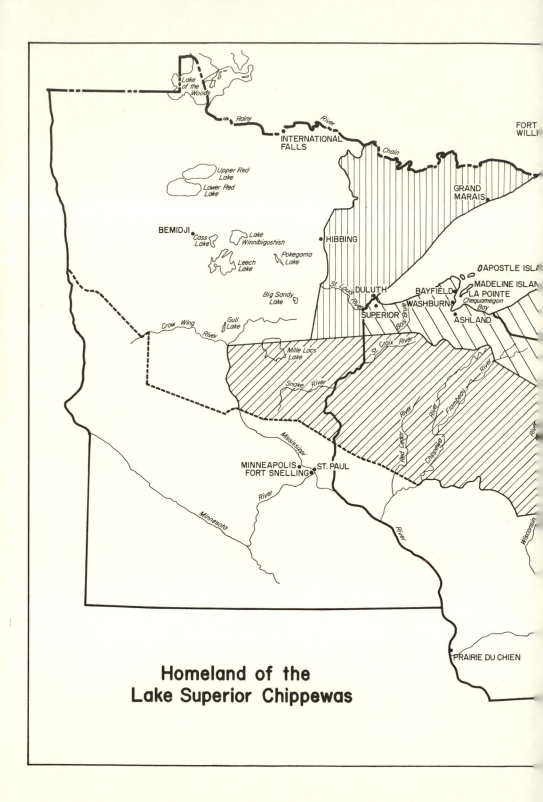

## Homeland of the Lake Superior Chippewas

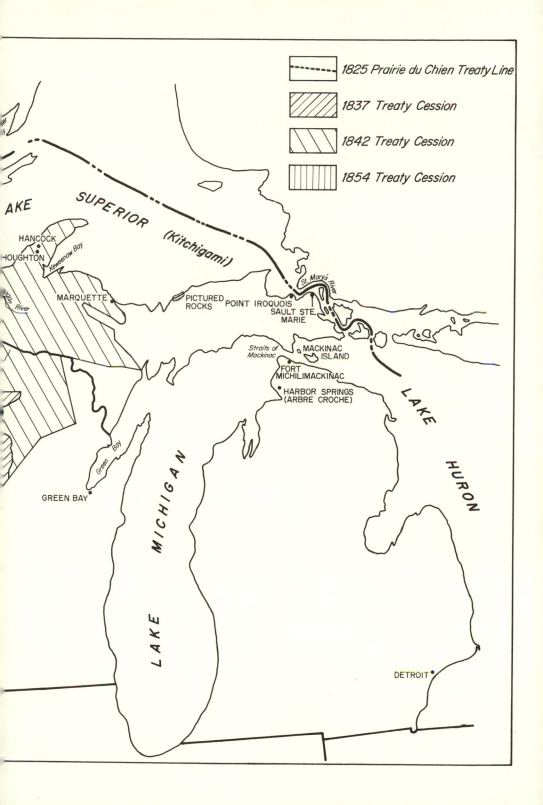

1825 Prairie du Chien Treaty Line

1837 Treaty Cession

1842 Treaty Cession

1854 Treaty Cession

LAKE SUPERIOR (Kitchigami)

HANCOCK
HOUGHTON
Keweenaw Bay
MARQUETTE
River
PICTURED ROCKS
POINT IROQUOIS
St. Mary's River
SAULT STE. MARIE
Straits of Mackinac
MACKINAC ISLAND
FORT MICHILIMACKINAC
HARBOR SPRINGS (ARBRE CROCHE)
Green Bay
GREEN BAY
LAKE MICHIGAN
LAKE HURON
DETROIT

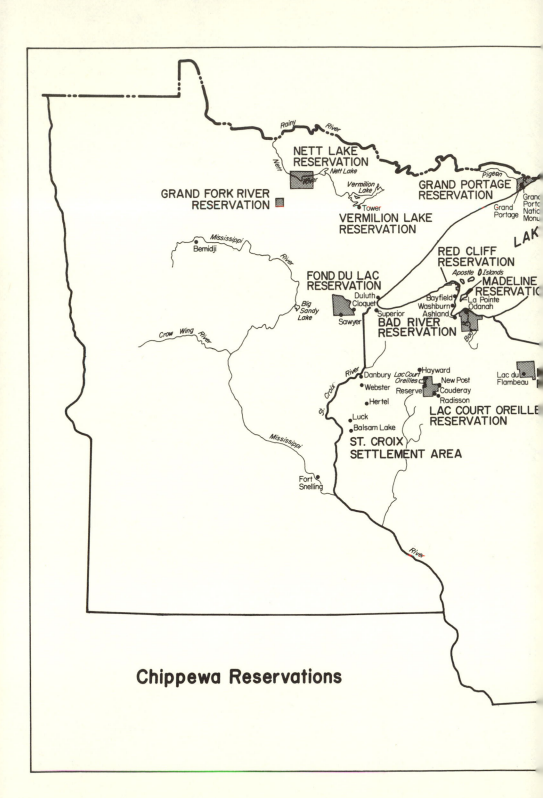

Chippewa Reservations

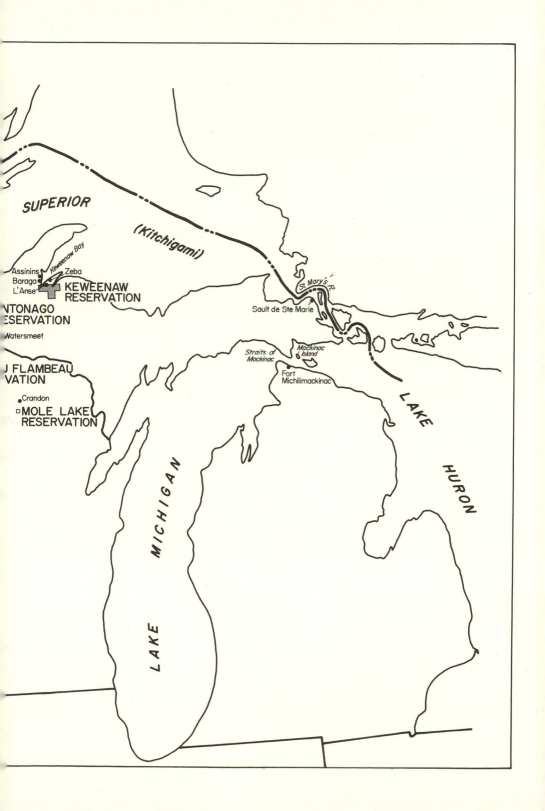

SUPERIOR

(Kitchigami)

Keweenaw Bay

Asginins　Zeba
Baraga
L'Anse　KEWEENAW
RESERVATION

NTONAGO
ESERVATION

Watersmeet

U FLAMBEAU
VATION

•Crandon

▫MOLE LAKE
RESERVATION

St. Mary's R.

Sault de Ste Marie

Mackinac
Island

Straits of
Mackinac

Fort
Michilimackinac

LAKE

HURON

LAKE

MICHIGAN

LAKE

# THE CHIPPEWAS OF LAKE SUPERIOR

# 1. 1854: The Turning Point

In August, 1854, Commissioner of Indian Affairs George W. Many-penny directed Agent Henry C. Gilbert of Detroit to arrange a treaty council with the Chippewa Indians to extinguish their titles to certain lands at the head of Lake Superior. The agent was also to establish reservations as future homes for the Lake Superior bands living along the shores of Michigan, Wisconsin, and Minnesota.[1]

Gilbert, head of the Mackinac Agency—which embraced all the Indians in Michigan as well as the Lake Superior Chippewas—dispatched a special messenger by way of Chicago and St. Paul to his Minnesota counterpart, Agent David B. Herriman, at Crow Wing. Gilbert asked Herriman to bring to the council ground a delegation of Mississippi River Chippewa chiefs and headmen who also claimed ownership to the lands in question. The Mackinac agent left Detroit on August 26 and arrived at La Pointe, Wisconsin, on September 1. Herriman joined him about two weeks later.[2]

The tiny village of La Pointe, on Madeline Island, offshore from Bayfield, Wisconsin, was an appropriate setting for treaty talks. La Pointe had been a focal point for white settlement on Lake Superior since the zestful days of French fur traders and missionaries. Thirteen miles long and about three miles wide, Madeline is the largest of the Apostle Island chain. Set against clear blue waters and skies, the rugged beauty of the island commands admiration. Red and brown sandstone shores loom wild and bold, while pleasant hills and stately elms, pines, and cedars suggest cool serenity. Before the founding of Superior, Wisconsin, and Duluth in 1853 and 1854, bustling little La Pointe, located on Madeline's southwestern tip, had been the only port of call on western Lake Superior. About four hundred Canadian, mixed-blood, and native inhabitants either worked for local traders or fished for a living in the perpetually cold waters off the coast. They lived in clusters of houses along Front Street, close to the lake shore. The large pier, a warehouse, and a row of one-story buildings had once been part of the American Fur Company complex. Other prominent La Pointe establishments included a hotel, Julius Austrian's store, and two churches.[3]

3

The Apostle Island–Chequamegon Bay area was once the seat of Chippewa power. During the early eighteenth century hunting parties in search of new resources emigrated to adjacent territories. Political ties atrophied, and local bands ripened into independent communities whose only sense of tribal unity came from language, kinship, and clan membership.[4] Those living in permanent lakeside villages depended on fishing for subsistence; the interior bands hunted, trapped, and harvested wild rice and maple sugar. For two hundred years after the arrival of the Europeans the Chippewa economy depended upon the fur trade.

Headmen who gathered at La Pointe in September, 1854, attested to the extent of their earlier dispersion: L'Anse, Vieux de Sert, and Ontonagon band members had journeyed from Michigan; the La Pointe (Bad River and Buffalo's), Lac du Flambeau, and Lac Court Oreilles, from Wisconsin; the Bois Forte, Grand Portage, Fond du Lac, and the Mississippi River bands, from Minnesota. Gilbert and Herriman estimated the assembled chiefs and their followers numbered about four thousand, all of whom expected to receive food and care from the United States commissioners.[5]

Jealousy and ill will between the lake and Mississippi River bands threatened to break up the council at La Pointe. The Mississippi bands would not even talk with their cousins to the east, much less agree to sell any mutually held lands. What averted a total breakdown in communications was the strong desire of all the Indians that the government apportion annuities between the two groups and distribute them at separate locations in the future. Taking advantage of their divisiveness, the commissioners asked that the bands first partition the lands they held in common west of Lake Superior. The Indians agreed and established their boundary at approximately the 93° meridian, which cuts through Minnesota just east of International Falls and west of Hibbing. Gilbert and Herriman, now able to deal separately with the lake bands, won a cession of the coveted north shore mineral range (Article I). Article VIII affirmed that the Lake Superior Chippewas were entitled to two-thirds of the benefits of former treaties and the Mississippi bands one-third.[6]

The commissioners agreed to the insistent demand of the lake Chippewas for permanent residence in their homeland. Otherwise, there simply would have been no treaty. Article II designated reservation lands to be set apart for the L'Anse and Vieux de Sert, Ontonagon, La Pointe, Lac du Flambeau, Lac Court Oreilles, Fond du

Lac, and Grand Portage bands. No portion of the lands was then occupied by whites except for the Reverend Leonard H. Wheeler's missionary complex at Bad River.[7] Article III of the La Pointe treaty gave the president the right to allot eighty-acre tracts to full-blood family heads or single adults. Also, the president was free to alter reservation boundaries if circumstances warranted. "All necessary roads, highways, and railroads" were given rights-of-way through reserved lands provided the Indians received proper compensation.[8]

In return for the cession of lands, Articles IV, V, and VI specified the annuities to be paid to the lake bands each year for two decades: $5,000 in coin; $8,000 in household goods; $3,000 in agricultural implements, cattle, and building materials; $3,000 for educational purposes. The United States further agreed to maintain a blacksmith and assistant on each reservation and to pay off $90,000 in Chippewa debts to traders. Article XII pledged to the impoverished Bois Forte who owned much of the ceded land on the north shore: $10,000 to meet "present just engagements" to traders and a similar amount in blankets, nets, guns, ammunition, and cloth. Upon selection of a reservation, the government offered them blacksmiths, smith-shop supplies, and two farmers.[9]

Madeline Island, September 30, 1854: After nearly two weeks of bargaining over endless issues, eighty-five Chippewa chiefs and headmen gathered on the lawn of the Charles Oakes house on Front Street to formally endorse the treaty. The United States Senate advised and consented a few months later, and President Pierce made proclamation of the treaty on January 29, 1855.[10]

Clearly, the treaty of 1854 played a vital role in the economic development of western Lake Superior. It secured north shore mineral resources, opened valuable pine timberland, and, by not displacing the native inhabitants along its shores, preserved an important labor supply for lumbering firms, lake shippers, miners, and railroad construction companies. Although it was not apparent for several decades, the 1854 agreement was also the most pivotal event in the history of the lake Chippewas following the coming of the white man. Henceforth they were to walk a new road.

Before accompanying the Chippewas down their pathway to the present, we ought first to take a look at the old road, the traditional Chippewa culture, and to examine to what extent it was modified by two centuries of direct European influence.

# 2. Traditional Culture of the Lake Superior Chippewas

The Great Lakes country forms the industrial hub of the world's mightiest nation. Nowhere else in the United States has the white man so transfigured the face of the land or displayed such an exploitative genius. Pioneer entrepreneurs felled seemingly boundless forests, turned the sod, gouged out fortunes in iron and coal and copper, bridged the rivers, and harnessed thundering waterfalls. Scores of towns and cities that sprang up during this age of enterprise are today united by a spiderweb of airlanes and shipping lanes, steel rails, and concrete roadways. Traditional lake Chippewa culture differed as much from this commercial scene as a backpacker's bivouac in the Superior National Forest differs from downtown Duluth. The lake country red man's lifestyle developed from an acceptance of his environment, not its transformation. He fished the streams rather than polluting them; he harvested the fruit of the land rather than mutilating mother earth; he refined the sap of maple trees rather than lumbering them for quick profits. At the heart of his woodland way of life was Kitchigami (Lake Superior), the sustainer of life, an object of wonder and worship.

Kitchigami originated during some past geological age from the collapsed shell of an extinct volcano. Then came the Ice Age. Glaciers perhaps thousands of feet thick gouged out its rocky basin and left the bottom 690 feet below sea level. Glaciation in the upper Great Lakes region also pulverized stone into fine sand and fertile soil, ground down the ridges of old mountains, and heaped rocks into mounds and hills. Ice and arctic air eventually fashioned a frigid wasteland devoid of life. The Wisconsin Glacier, the last of these great continental sheets, began its retreat about 11,000 B.C. and left in its wake lakes, ponds, swamplands, and glacial rivers which, in their search for outlets, dug drainage patterns for much of the Middle West and southern Canada. By 6000 B.C. the surface of Lake Superior was free of ice, the largest body of fresh water in the world, 383 miles long, 160 miles wide, 1,290 feet deep.[1]

With the withdrawal of the glaciers, living things once again entered the area. First came the plants which eventually were to blan-

ket the American shore with coniferous forests reaching heights of
65 to 125 feet. White, jack, and Norway pine grew in pure stands in
the sandy northern barrens; the better soils yielded northeast
hardwoods (birch, beech, maple, hemlock) or mixed forests of conifers
and hardwoods. Scattered among the evergreens were colorful pop-
lar, aspen, black and mountain ash, and pin cherry, while black
spruce, tamarack, and white cedar thrived in the dank swamplands.
Next came the animals which roamed throughout Kitchigami land:
bear, deer, wolf, coyote, fox, wolverine, and beaver, lynx, otter, and
muskrat, raccoon, porcupine, woodchuck, weasel, rabbit, mink, and
fisher. Abounding with such beasts, to which must be added the wild
fowl and fish, green-rimmed Lake Superior silently awaited the ad-
vent of human life—the American Indian.[2]

The Chippewas called themselves Anishinabe, meaning "first or
original man." Neighbors referred to them as the Ojibwa, probably
corrupted from o-jib-i-weg, meaning "those who make pictographs."
Engraved birch-bark rolls which held the records of the Midéwiwin
Society were a special feature of Chippewa culture, perhaps the
closest thing to written documents found among the Indians north of
Mexico. Ojibwa was later corrupted by the English into Chippewas,
the name by which they became commonly known. In its dealings
with these Indians during the last two centuries the United States
government has designated them Chippewas. So do modern eth-
nologists.[3]

Chippewa tradition relates that their people once lived near the
salt ocean—probably at the mouth of the St. Lawrence. In the late
sixteenth or early seventeenth centuries the Chippewas, along with
the Potawatomis and the Ottawas, journeyed west to Lake Huron in
search of new hunting grounds. At the Mackinac Straits the group
divided and pursued separate destinies, though a loose association
called "the three fires" was maintained. The Potawatomis migrated
into Michigan's Lower Peninsula; the Ottawas colonized the Lake
Nipissing region and several islands in northern Lake Huron. First
encountering the Chippewas at Sault Ste. Marie in the 1640's, the
French called them Saulteurs, "People of the Rapids."[4] Advance
guards of the Chippewas later inhabited both shores of Lake
Superior. In the eighteenth century they ousted the Santee Sioux
from northern Minnesota and helped themselves to the forfeited
hunting grounds and valuable rice lakes. By the early 1840's the
Chippewas numbered perhaps 30,000 and held sway over what is
today the northern two-thirds of Lake Huron, the American shore of

Lake Superior, northern Minnesota, parts of North Dakota, eastern
Montana, southeast Saskatchewan, and southern Manitoba, as well
as the lake country east of Lake Winnipeg extending almost to
James Bay.[5] At this point in Chippewa history, scholars discern five
tribal divisions: the Southeast Chippewas of Michigan's Lower
Peninsula and adjacent Ontario, the Chippewas of Lake Superior
(the subject of this book), the Southwest Chippewas of interior Minnesota, the Northern Chippewas of the Laurentian uplands above
the Great Lakes and the Plains Chippewas or Bungees. The first
four woodland groups followed a hunting-trapping-fishing-gathering
economy, with some local variations and emphases. By contrast,
the buffalo-hunting Bungees, the most far-ranging of the Chippewa
divisions, took on some cultural characteristics of the northern
plains tribes.[6]

So large a population, coupled with the resources of far-flung
hunting grounds, assured the Chippewas of a prominent role in the
history of America's heartland. Tribal attitudes toward the French,
the English, and later the Americans often determined when and
where the rich lake country would be exploited by white fur traders,
miners, lumberjacks, farmers, fishermen, and boatbuilders. An important Indian labor supply was preserved for these bocming
lakeside industries when the United States decided in 1854 not to
remove the Chippewas of Lake Superior. Outside of the Great Lakes
they were also well known by mid-century, thanks to the widely
read Chippewa cultural studies of Henry Rowe Schoolcraft, a long-
time federal Indian agent at Sault Ste. Marie. Henry Wadsworth
Longfellow's epic poem "Hiawatha," based on Chippewa stories first
recorded by Schoolcraft, further popularized the tribe.[7]

Beyond these relationships with the white community, the Chippewa people held fast to an intrinsic culture all their own: a woodland way of life remarkably and beautifully adapted to Kitchigami.
And, as one of the few prominent eastern tribes that was neither
exterminated nor removed to the semiarid plains, the Chippewas
who still reside on ancestral lands retain a unique and resilient
cultural heritage that neither intermarriage nor federal force has
been able to destroy.

Remarkably functional though it was, Chippewa culture at the
time of first European contact was static: archaeological records
reaching back two millennia suggest that technical knowledge was
passed from generation to generation with little change. An-
thropologists classify their way of life as early Neolithic, comparable

to the technological progress found in the eastern Mediterranean between 4000 and 3000 B.C.[8]

Dome-shaped wigwams ideally suited the seminomadic Chippewas of Lake Superior and were easily constructed with available materials in less than a day. First the men set peeled ironwood saplings in the ground in an elliptical pattern of approximately fourteen by twenty feet, then brought the saplings together in arches while the women bound the framework with green basswood fiber. Bark strips more than twenty feet long and about three feet wide were draped over the structure and secured by poles or weighted basswood cords. A hide covered the doorway. Bulrush mats served as flooring and as "tables" at meal times. Deer- or bearhide sleeping blankets were rolled up during the day and arranged along the walls for seating. Women gathered and hauled wood to stoke the open fireplace which heated and lit the wigwam. The finished home could comfortably house a family of eight. When a seasonal change signaled the start of a new phase of their economic year, the household simply left the ironwood frame and carried the rolled-up bark coverings to a new campsite.[9]

Wigwam life was particularly intimate when frosty winter weather drove the household (often comprised of two or three generations) indoors. When not out on the hunt, menfolk passed the daylight hours making and repairing snowshoes, traps, and other wooden implements; youngsters played in the center of the bark lodge so that adults could supervise their constant comings and goings; wives wove fishnets and mats or fashioned birch-bark containers (*makuks*) used each spring for collecting maple sap. Mothers prepared the meals and served the whole family. Nature's icebox temporarily safeguarded her food supply, part of which was kept near the door for the day's use, the remainder in a large cache. An adjacent storehouse held implements and extra clothing. Because firelight discouraged much eye-straining handwork on winter evenings, the Chippewas, whenever possible, visited neighbors or one of the band's many storytellers. At bedtime the family spread its blankets over cedar boughs and rush mats, loosened their clothing, slipped off moccasins, and slept with their feet near the fire.[10]

These denizens of the forest dressed in finely tanned hides and skins that the females fashioned into garments with wooden awls, thorn or bone needles, and thread made of nettle fiber or moose and deer sinew. Women outfitted themselves with nettle fiber undergarments, leggings, moccasins, and deerskin dresses belted at the waist; the men wore breechcloths, tight, hip-high leggings, and moccasins. Children's clothes were made from finely tanned fawn hides and the skins of beaver, squirrel, and rabbit. During the winter season family members added to their wardrobes heavy fur coats and moccasins lined with rabbit fur. Blackhaired youths and adults of both sexes usually wore their hair in a convenient braided arrangement that could be ornamented in various ways. Bear grease or deer tallow worked into the hair kept it smooth and in place.[11]

Efficient transportation was vital to the survival of the Chippewa family which, in quest of food, made a yearly circuit of its fishing and hunting grounds, wild rice field, berry patches, and sugar bush. A perfect partnership of form and function for the lake country, the graceful birch-bark canoe could be portaged easily across the countless watersheds and was even capable of voyages on the open waters of Kitchigami. Each family owned several such vessels of various sizes, ranging in weight from 65 to 125 pounds. Men and women worked together in their construction. Tough, yet light and easily peeled, birch bark was ideal for canoe shells, which the Chippewas sewed to frames with the roots of a species of spruce that would not rot in winter. Seams were sealed with spruce or pine gum. Native craftsmen thinned and shaped flexible pieces of white cedar into ribs and floorboards.[12] Equally satisfactory for winter travel were toboggans and racket-shaped snowshoes. The latter had ash frames which were criss-crossed with moosehide thongs. The toboggan transported heavy loads, pulled either by hand or by a team of three dogs. Harnessed in tandem with collars and side straps, dogs could average forty or fifty miles a day. They were the only domesticated animals known to the Chippewas prior to the coming of the white man. These Eskimo dogs also proved useful as camp guards and for tracking and treeing game.[13]

The subsistence level of the seminomadic Chippewas never encouraged a highly structured society or a large population. Their most important social subdivision was the rather permanent summer village of perhaps a dozen families who worked during the year within a radius of about a hundred miles. The society of the summer village offered a pleasant contrast to the isolation of winter wigwams. Chippewa families, whether in villages or on the move, shared still another social tie: a tribal-wide network of totemic clans. A clan was a group of persons who had a blood relationship traced through the father's line. The name of an animal, their totem, signified the clan's common ancestry. In the mid-nineteenth century the Chippewas of Lake Superior consisted of about fifteen or twenty clans, the principal ones being the crane, catfish, bear, marten, wolf, and loon. The only other particularly important functions of these consanguine groupings were at the time of marriage, when custom prohibited union between members of the same clan, or when Chippewa travelers made new acquaintances. Fellow clansmen, no matter where they met, regarded one another as close kinsmen.[14]

Before following a Chippewa family through an annual cycle of economic activity, some general characteristics of its livelihood ought to be reviewed. First of all, there was an unending struggle to satisfy elementary wants—particularly the need for food—which constantly drove the household from hunting ground to maple grove, from berry patch to rice bed. Yet even in a land of plenty these seasonal rovings could not stave off frequent winter starvation, because the women had no way of preserving large amounts of food for long periods of time. The cooperative spirit of the people partly mitigated the threat of famine. If a lucky family had more food than it could consume, the surplus was shared with the needy. A second notable feature of Chippewa economics was tribal self-sufficiency. Members fashioned all essential articles themselves: wooden ladles and bowls, containers of bark, large and small pottery vessels, and tools of chipped flint, bone, and stone. Families generally shunned close contacts with all but near neighbors, though hunters exchanged some moose and caribou hides for corn with agrarian tribes such as the Hurons. Finally, prior to the white man's arrival, the Chippewas had no such practice as individual ownership of land. Fishing and hunting grounds, maple groves, and rice fields were common property, though families customarily returned to the same areas year after year and their rights were respected.[15]

Freezing nights and mild days. Perfect weather for tapping trees. So in late March (Crusted Snow Supporting Man Moon) or early April (Putting Away Snowshoes Moon) the family moved to the maple grove to begin its economic year. Sap collected in birch-bark buckets was dumped into hundred-gallon moosehide vats which the women kept boiling day and night. The syrup gradually thickened, was strained and cooked some more, until it reached the proper consistency. Then the workers either transferred it to a trough to be worked by paddle and hands into granulated sugar, or poured it into molds if hard sugar was desired. Because the Chippewas had no salt, they used maple sugar as both a confection and as a seasoning for fruits, vegetables, cereals, and fish. After the lean winter months, sugar-making season was especially pleasurable. All ages enjoyed the accompanying dances and other leisure activities. Men played lacrosse or gambled with bone dice while the women chatted and cheered them on.[16]

When snow was off the ground in late May (Flowering Moon), families came together in villages near some clear body of water suitable for fishing and near traditional berry and garden patches. Men and women fished for immediate use almost all year with baited hooks, traps, and seines. In autumn they caught the winter supply of fish which was dried and stacked in the family cache. The men showed particular skill in spearing at night by torchlight and spearing through the lake ice after luring fish with decoys. They could also set fishnets made of bark fiber cord or nettle stalk twine under the winter ice to catch whitefish. After washing the nets the Chippewas sometimes dipped them in a liquid made from sumac leaves in order to kill any clinging odors which they believed scared off the fish.[17] In 1820, Schoolcraft viewed an elaborate weir located four miles up from the mouth of the Ontonagon River in Michigan's Upper Peninsula. Built of saplings, it extended from bank to bank, with a small opening on one side for spawning fish to pass upstream. In their descent, sturgeon were trapped and hooked by the Ontonagon band.[18] These and other Lake Superior Chippewas placed great reliance on fish for their subsistence.

Summer farming and berry picking were also important to their livelihood. Each family cultivated its own plot of ground. Corn planted in June (Strawberry Moon) was harvested in late summer, often while still green, because the climate did not allow it to ripen. Families dried part of each crop for winter storage. Women and older children with birch-bark baskets at their belts gathered the colorful varieties of wild berries that matured nicely in Chippewa country despite the brief summers. Succulent cranberries they ate fresh. Blueberries, chokeberries, and Juneberries they always dried. Juicy raspberries were boiled down into a thick paste. The Chippewas also concocted various hot and cold drinks by adding wild cherry twigs or wintergreen, raspberry, spruce, or snowberry leaves to water.[19]

Wild rice (really an annual cereal grass) grew in shallow lakes and streams, ripening in late summer—around mid-August (Blueberry Moon) or early September (Turning of Leaves Moon). At that time the villages broke up into smaller groups that went to family rice fields and prepared for work. While men poled canoes through the beds, women, who had tied the rice in bunches in mid-summer, bent the kernels over the canoe and knocked them off with a stick. When the canoe was full, the rice was taken to the shore and dried on birch-bark sheets or flat rocks. The Chippewas planted about a third of their harvest to ensure a yearly increase. "Nothing can equal the aroma of the ricing camp," writes Chippewa historian Lolita Taylor.

Wood fires burning, rice drying, and the dewy fresh air drifting in from the lake. A contented feeling of well-being filled the camp. The first grain of the season had been offered for a blessing from the Great Spirit. The time had come to partake of the gift. Boiled with venison or with ducks or rice hens it was nourishing and delicious.[20]

These lakeside rice camps ended the period, begun in early spring, when families worked in groups.

Families set out for their duck-hunting grounds in September and October (Leaves Falling Moon). The winter hunt began in November (Lake Freezing Moon). Hunters brought down plump waterfowl with blunt arrows; small animals such as mink, otter, muskrat, rabbit, fox, and beaver were trapped or snared. In hunting large game the Chippewas showed considerable ingenuity. For example, they drove deer down forest pathways into sapling-fenced traps. They were also caught in rawhide snares or shot at night by torch-light. Bears lumbered into deadfalls. Wolves impaled themselves while snatching hungrily at baited hooks suspended about five feet off the ground. As the source of essential food as well as clothing, the chase was a chief occupation of Chippewa men throughout the year.[21]

Within the seasonal cycle of economic activities just reviewed, Chippewa family members in their snug, oval wigwams personally experienced spring births, the maturity of summer, and the icy hand of death when winter touched their lives.

Springtime in the lake country is rich with promise. Green shoots that reach sunward through the melting snows and infant animals that totter from winter nests bear the future of their species. Chippewa children were likewise precious. Indulgent parents seldom reprimanded children with raised voices or corporal punishment. Neither did they lavish them with continuous praise or the promise of material rewards. To fit the child into the proper cultural pattern was the general goal of family educational practices. First, in order to establish good relations with the spirit world, parents demanded that boys and girls make prepuberty fasts, abstaining from food and drink and fixing their minds on the spirit world for one to ten days (depending on the child's endurance). This ritual was performed in hopes that thereby the youngster would acquire a guardian spirit— often visualized in the form of a person or animal—that henceforth would provide sound advice, knowledge, and even the power to influence the course of future events. Chippewa educational practices also were aimed at teaching the child the religious, economic, and political practices as well as the moral standards of the tribe. Lessons were learned from all members of the household—parents, grandparents, brothers, sisters—and from respected older members of the village.[22] Specifically, they taught boys to occupy themselves outside the home and to become brave warriors and successful woodsmen by mastering the bow and arrow, war club, spear, traps and snares, and particularly the ways of the forest and its creatures. Boys acquired both an appetite for praise—village-wide feasts celebrated their first successes at killing an animal and catching a fish—and the independence to follow lonely winter traplines for weeks at a time. Girls, on the other hand, learned to stay at home, converting the fruits of the hunter and fisherman into food and clothing. To make wigwams and other furnishings, to chop wood and gather berries and rice and medicinal herbs, to make birch-bark vessels and maple sugar, to dress skins and sew them into clothing, to bear children and cook meals—this was woman's role.[23] After puberty fasts and feasts, skillful boys and girls who had learned their lessons well could look forward to a good marriage. Their reputations would spread and young people of the opposite sex would seek them out.[24]

The promises of spring are fulfilled each summer when the ripened products of field and stream are harvested. This was also courting time for marriageable Chippewa youngsters, brought together once again by the formation of villages and the rounds of social activities. Parents arranged some marriages—always with tribesmen from different clans. More often a young warrior took the initiative and courted a maiden, under close supervision, in her family home. Modesty toward the suitor was expected from her. And the couple could not leave the wigwam together. If marriage was desirable, the hunter killed some large animal and presented it to the parents as evidence of his prowess and willingness to support their daughter. An invitation to share in the feast meant an acceptance of his proposal. No formal marriage ceremony occurred; the man simply moved his belongings in with the wife's parents, with whom they lived for about a year. Then they built a lodge of their own.[25]

Polygamy occurred only among extraordinary Chippewa hunters or chiefs and medicine men who could support several families. Apparently, plural marriage was one of the few opportunities for conspicuous display in a society that frowned on verbal boasting. Polyandry was not found among the Chippewas.[26]

Divorce eventually became nearly as common as marriage. For those Chippewas who changed partners, no special stigma was involved. When a couple no longer wished to share the same wigwam, the separation was about as unceremonious as the marriage: the wife simply went back to her people and the children were divided equally, if possible. Mutual friends did not feel any compulsion to try and save the union. If infidelity were involved, the separation might become violent, with the cuckolded husband biting off his wife's nose or killing her paramour.[27]

In the winter of their lives, the old warriors and women sat cross-legged in snowcovered wigwams, surrounded by children and grandchildren. Much respect and attention was bestowed upon them, and their advice was heeded, for they were the source of wisdom about herb medicines, religious ceremonialism, the education of youth, and the traditions of Chippewa forefathers. And, when their hearts beat no more, families mourned the loss.[28]

A deceased family member was usually buried before sunset on the day of death. First of all the corpse was readied to join the Dance of the Ghosts (Northern Lights) with hair freshly braided, dressed in his or her finest clothes, and arrayed in glittering ornaments. After a *Midé* priest conducted a type of funeral ceremony and a few eating utensils were placed with the body for the four-day journey to the hereafter, relatives wrapped it (in a fetal position) with thick bark and set it in a shallow grave facing west—the direction for the spirit's journey. Then the site was covered with weighted bark sheets or rush mats. Sometimes a family put the mummy-like remains on a high scaffold, perhaps because they lacked tools to excavate frozen winter ground. However, in 1826 one Chippewa chief explained that his band temporarily interred the dead on platforms because they did not wish to lose sight of them right away.[29]

Upon the death of a loved one, immediate expressions of grief varied among individuals and commonly included loud wailing to announce the fact to the village, and self-mutilation. Two year-long mourning customs were prescribed. Some outward sign of sorrow should be shown—a man might paint his face black, a woman cut her hair or wear ragged clothes. Since a widow was not permitted in any public place, she lived with her late husband's relatives and did their bidding. Each adult in mourning was also expected to keep a spirit bundle. Some remnant of the deceased, such as a lock of hair wrapped in birch bark, formed the nucleus of the bundle which was treated with much reverence, as though it actually housed the dead person's spirit. Apparently the Chippewas had differing views about whether the spirit lingered in such a bundle or departed to the west upon death. A widow added to her bundle the handcrafted items made during the year's isolation. If she behaved discreetly, the husband's relatives gave a feast at the end of the twelve months and presented her with new clothes and other gifts. She in turn unwrapped her bundle, distributing its contents among her former-in-laws. She was now free to marry again, if she chose.[30]

The Chippewas and six or seven kindred tribes in the Great Lakes area celebrated an annual Feast of the Dead, with participants alternating as hosts and guests. The host village resurrected the bodies of persons who had died since the last feast and reinterred them, perhaps with other remains brought by the visitors, in a common grave. Extensive gift giving by the host village as well as joint participation in dancing, feasting, and games of skill served as both a gratifying condolence rite and an instrument for creating and maintaining political alliances. The Chippewas gave up the Feast of the Dead after they migrated west to Lake Superior and became dependent on the French, who opposed the pagan practice.[31]

Visions of the afterlife differed among the Chippewas. Some believed souls remained in this world after death (perhaps living in a spirit bundle) and assisted friends in time of distress and danger. Others supposed that the souls of brave warriors and woodsmen went west to a camping ground of eternal bliss and carnal pleasures, while dissolute spirits wandered in darkness, exposed to the ravages of wolves, bears, and other flesh-eaters.[32]

From spring maple sugar camps to the winter deer hunt, from childhood to honorable old age, the Chippewa world was filled with a host of spirits (*manidog,* singular *manido*) which controlled the weather, lured game to the hunter, and affected his health. Consequently, Chippewa religious thought was focused on placating these supernaturals so that family members could satisfy their elementary economic needs and enjoy health and long life.[33]

Far away and at the head of this pantheon of spirits was Gitchi-manido—the supreme being and benevolent giver of life. Rather than participate directly in the affairs of the earth, he delegated responsibility to a host of subordinate deities (*manidog*). And to these lesser spirits the Chippewas directed their supplications. If the supplication involved the elements, they appealed to the four thunderbirds, which represented the cardinal directions and controlled the weather. The Chippewas attributed human characteristics to the sun (a man) and the moon (his wife). Snow was a man who came each winter and left each spring. Benign guardian spirits acquired during a youthful vision communicated warnings and advice directly to individuals via dreams. Yet the family's everyday life was also filled with fearsome spirits such as the Water Monster and the Windigo, a cannibalistic giant that haunted the winter woods. Caves, curious trees, waterfalls, and other remarkable features in the local landscape—the obvious abodes of *manidog*—were the objects of particular dread and veneration.[34]

Such organized religious activities as the *Midéwiwin* ceremonies were comparatively rare among the Chippewas, to whom the establishment and maintenance of close, friendly relations with the spirits was primarily an individual affair of regular communication with *manidog* in one's immediate area.[35]

A Chippewa family member never undertook an important action without first invoking the aid of a local good spirit or trying to ward off an evil one. Before beginning a journey, he might kill a dog and throw it into a lake or stream as a sacrifice to the *manido* of the waters. If he suffered from bad luck out on a hunt, he assumed the *manido* of the game was angry, and made an offering to it. With the first preparations of seasonal foods, individual families and sometimes entire villages made the Offering of the First Fruits or Game.[36] For woodland tribes like the Chippewas, the most important medium for communication between frail humanity and the *manidog* was tobacco, believed to be especially pleasing to the spirits, which could only get it from man. Tobacco was used in all feasts and before all religious ceremonies; pinches of it were thrown on the waters each day before the rice was harvested; it was placed at the base of a tree or shrub from which medicine was to be gathered. Tobacco even sealed treaties between tribes and agreements between individuals.[37]

Another way the Chippewas sought control over their environment was the inducement of dreams and power visions. From these mental images came wisdom and knowledge. The ability to dream was cultivated early, with childhood fasting and isolated meditation. Hunger not only helped to induce dreams that portended good or bad fortunes but aroused the pity of the *manidog,* which brought forth power-giving visions.[38]

Lesser *manidog* might also assist a person in time of adversity if he utilized a medicine bag. Preserved with great care in these containers were herbs, roots, feathers, wooden images, minerals, and other objects which were revealed to its owner in a vision or by a medicine man, and which possessed supernatural powers. A Chippewa carefully guarded his medicine bag and displayed its contents with much ceremony.[39]

Family survival likewise depended on the good health and long life of its members. Kitchigami land was nature's cornucopia: woods rustling with game, marsh grasses heavy with rice, waters alive with fish and wildfowl; yet such abundance was useless to a Chippewa too sick to harvest it. A family's first line of defense was the employment of accepted hygienic practices such as wrapping infants in cradleboards for warmth and protection, frequent bathing in lakes and rivers (in winter, rubbing faces and hands with snow), washing dishes and clothes in a lye solution made from hardwood ashes, regular airing of clothing and bedding, keeping the wigwam swept clean, and feeding refuse to the dogs. Colds, cuts, and bruises they accepted as eventualities in a life filled with physical activity and exposure to the elements. More serious illness or injury had supernatural origins. Perhaps a spirit was offended, or some resentful tribesman had hired a shaman to produce the malady.[40] Whichever the case, an ailing father or mother had several curative methods from which to choose.

Upon entering a wigwam-like sweatlodge, an ailing Chippewa was enveloped by eye-stinging steam from a pile of hot stones in the center of the floor upon which had been sprinkled a liquid concocted from boiled bark and evergreen boughs. Removing deerskin leggings and breechcloth, he squatted naked amidst glistening fellows who were also taking the cure for a bad cough, asthma, rheumatism, or pneumonia. Doubtless some were there just to relieve mental or physical fatigue in the miraculous mists of the sweatlodge. The drowsy, copper-skinned figures lingered just long enough to tone their bodies or relieve the pulmonary distress. Then, depending on the season and the seriousness of the illness, the bathers groped their way out through the hide-covered doorway and plunged into a nearby stream or lake, or wrapped up in a moosehide robe to rest for several hours.[41]

A Chippewa in poor health could also apply a curative charm to the injured or diseased part of his body. More than any other tribe, the Chippewas believed in the magical power of such objects to stimulate love, attract worldly wealth, insure a successful journey, bring misfortune to another, or counteract an evil. Usually purchased from a fellow tribesman, charms consisted either of special herbs or some representation of the individual to be affected—perhaps a figurine or piece of clothing.[42]

If a malady was believed to be the work of a human enemy, a shaman (medicine man) was hired to find the culprit, cure the patient, and then redirect the sickness back to the sender. Conjurors and sucking doctors treated a client on the psychological level by startling, stimulating, terrifying, or amazing him. The former specialized in consultations with the spirits about the causes of diseases—frequently sorcery or the breach of a taboo—which were then cured by magic. Sucking doctors used tubular bones to "draw out" a disorder for the patient to see. This might be a bug or a particle of hair. Incantations, songs, drum beating, and rattle shaking were also part of such psychological treatment. A second group of medicine men, many of whom were members of the Midéwiwin Society, had a practical knowledge of medicinal herbs, barks, and roots. They administered compounded medicines and intoned special songs that released the power of the remedies. Village shamans were greatly feared and respected because of this power for good and evil, which they obtained in a vision quest.[43]

The Midéwiwin (Mystic Doings) Society incorporated many of these individual relations with the *manidog* into a set of religious ceremonials conducted by an organized Chippewa priesthood. Anthropologist Harold Hickerson dates its origin soon after confederated clans migrated to the Chequamegon Bay area in the late seventeenth century. Amidst their great social stress the Midéwiwin emerged as the guardian of traditional cultural forms—a nativist ceremonial in the same class as the Ghost Dance of the western tribes two centuries later, the Handsome Lake religion of the Iroquois, and the cult of the Shawnee Prophet.[44] Midé priests, besides being important repositories for tribal folk history, preserved a knowledge of medicines used for healing the sick. For a Midé the key to long life was proper personal conduct and the appropriate use of herbal medicines and music. Men should neither lie nor steal. They should be moderate in speech and manner, and should respect women. To cure a malady, the priest mixed various substances from his Midé bag and sang the special song which made it potent—then sold it to the sick person.[45] The society was highly institutionalized, with a limited membership (usually men) ranked in four degrees. Each grade had to be taken in succession, and each required a large payment as well as the mastering of certain knowledge. New members received individual instruction in healing and religious ceremonies. For example, a first degree Midé priest learned the names and uses of a few common herbs and the songs that went with them. He then collected and kept these items in his Midé bag. The higher ranks were taught the mysteries of the Midéwiwin as well as the properties of the rare herbs and even the nature of vegetable poisons. Ritual songs and other instructions for new members were recorded on birch-bark Midé scrolls with engraved pictures which suggested the ideas to be remembered down through the generations.[46] In late spring or early summer annual meetings took place in a special lodge called the Midéwigan. The four days of feasting, dancing, drum beating, singing the Midé songs, and sacrificial offerings infused spirit power into new members and renewed it in older ones.[47]

Like religious thought and practice, folklore was interwoven into the fabric of traditional Chippewa culture, revealing much about attitudes toward life and the *manidog*. Storytellers used folk history to emphasize such religious and ethical values as courage, daring, and right action—not just to entertain children and adults on long winter nights. Midé priests believed that merely telling the creation story released powers helpful in warding off evil. Aside from *adizoke* (fairy tales) told purely for the amusement of youngsters, traditional tribal stories and legends fell into two classes. One concerned the first earth and its red inhabitants who so angered Gitchi-manido that he unleashed a deluge. Only the intercession of Wenebojo (a demigod and Chippewa culture hero) saved them and allowed them to live on the earth. Later he taught the Chippewas how to farm, hunt, and cure the sick. He also gave them tobacco and a religious code (Midéwiwin) by which they could communicate with the offended Great Spirit. A culture hero of this sort, who played the dual role of trickster and benefactor, is found in the folk history of most woodland tribes. And stories about the adventures of Wenebojo con-

stitute a second class of folk tales. The oft-repeated humorous portions of Wenebojo stories always produced laughter from Chippewas
who probably identified with his human characteristics and failings.
Though his tricks often made Wenebojo look foolish in the end, the
tales contained important morals about conduct.[48] One delightful
story concerned ten men who went to talk with Wenebojo:

Finally one man heard a voice say, "Well, well, my uncle; come in if you
want to see me. Don't stand out there." (This was the voice of Winabojo.)

The man who heard the voice went and told the rest of party. Each had a
present for Winabojo. They went into the lodge and had the presents on
their backs and in their arms and hands. Winabojo shook hands with them
and they all sat down. There was absolute silence.

Beside the door was a stump overgrown with moss. After a while a voice
came from this stump saying, "Why don't you speak to your uncle? When we
were on earth we talked to our relations." (This was the voice of Winabojo's
grandmother.)

Winabojo replied, "I am just thinking what to say. I will talk to our
relations. If we are to follow the custom of the place they came from, we
must give them food. They must be hungry."

In stories about Winabojo when he was on earth it is always said that he
carried his lunch in a bag on his back. This bag still stood there, and in it
were bones of bear, deer, and other animals. He had eaten the meat and put
the bones back in the bag.

Winabojo got up on his knees, put his hand in the bag, and happened to
take out the bone of a bear's foreleg. He threw it in front of them, and it
became a bear. It was almost dead, and he told them to kill it and take it to
their camp, saying they would find a big kettle there. The men killed the
bear and dragged it to their camp. They cooked enough for one meal. It was
greasy and there was a great deal of nice broth. When the meat was ready
two men took the kettle on a stick and set it before Winabojo.

Winabojo lived with his grandmother. His daughter had grown up and
lived in another lodge. He told his daughter to bring wooden dishes and
spoons. She came bringing the dishes and spoons. She was very beautiful
and wore a red sash. The men had their feast and took the kettle back to the
camp. They had come to ask favors, but they decided to wait until the next
day.

They went to Winabojo on the following day, and he said, "You have come
to ask favors. I will do what I can for you."

One man said, "I have come to ask you to give me a life with no end."
Winabojo twisted him around and threw him into a corner and he turned
into a black stone. Winabojo said, "You asked for a long life. You will last as
long as the world stands."

Another man gave Winabojo a present and said, "I have come to ask for
unfailing success and that I may never lack for anything." Winabojo turned
him into a fox, saying, "Now you will always be cunning and successful."

The others saw what was happening to these men and they became frightened. They decided to ask for one thing together, so they asked that they might have healing power in their medicine.

Winabojo put some medicine in a little leather bag and gave it to each man. He said the others had asked so much that they had failed, but that he had given these eight men the real success. He said, "I have given you this medicine. Use it sparingly. When it is gone your power will also be gone." Then he said: "Ten men came to see me. Two made bad requests, and will never get home. The medicine I have given you will not last forever, but I will give my daughter to you. Do not approach her until you get home, then one of you may take her for his wife. She is to be the means of keeping up the power of medicine among men."

They started the next day, and Winabojo said, "I want my daughter to go back, for she is human. Protect her until you get home, then select one of your number to marry her, otherwise she will return here and you will lose the power of your medicine."

So they started; she sat in the middle of the canoe. They went across to the mainland and made a camp for the night. She cooked for them and had her camp at some distance from the rest of the party. It was necessary to camp three nights. All went well until the last night, when the men started a discussion as to which should be her husband. One said: "I suppose she knows which she wants. I will go quietly and ask her." All were watching as this man went and sat down a little distance from the girl's camp. He asked which one of them she would select for her husband if she had her choice. There was no reply. He came back and reported to the others. Then another man said he would go and would say a little more than the first had said. He thought he would say that she could have her choice. So he went toward the girl's camp, but she was gone. They had lost her.

The men felt very, very badly. They realized that a wrong had been done to the world, as her medicine would have been a benefit to the whole race.[49]

Chippewa art was utilitarian and an integral part of everyday life. Men produced several types of useful objects ranging from simple wooden bowls embossed with human and animal figures to the complex and handy birch-bark canoe. Women excelled in such decorative arts as weaving, leatherwork, and quill work. They also engraved attractive silhouette patterns on birch-bark *makuks*. A non-functional art form unique to the Chippewas was dental pictographs. Craftsmen folded thin sheets of birch bark in two and bit designs into them with their canine teeth.[50]

Every phase of Chippewa life was expressed in another functional art form—music. Songs entertained children and accompanied games, the courting of lovers, preparations for war, Midéwiwin rites, treatment of the sick, and ceremonies for the dead. Except for the lovers' flute, musical instruments (drums and rattles) only accompanied the human voice. Chippewa singers, who frequently used the vibrato (a sign of musical expertise) had a certain throaty quality to their voices. Their music lacked a definite system of notation and thus a standard of exactness. Melody and rhythm conveyed a central idea rather than reflecting individual words. Sometimes only one or two words occurred in a piece, for the singer derived supernatural power from rhythmic repetition.[51]

Bands of three or four hundred people constituted the basic unit of the rather informal Chippewa political structure, in which individual families and villages maintained much autonomy. Early in the eighteenth century Sieur d'Aigrement, subdelegate of the Intendant for New France, noted that Chippewa chiefs "can not say to them: 'Do this and so,' but merely—'it would be better to do so and so.'" Quite true. A band civil chief had no coercive force. Control over affairs depended entirely on his personal prestige and the demands of the moment. Nor could a war chief compel band members to join an expedition. Civil chiefs could help to settle certain internal disputes, since rule by law was virtually nonexistent among the Chippewas. Bands sanctioned the adjustment of most injuries by the ancient practice of "an eye for an eye, a tooth for a tooth." Only murders were brought to public attention, and in most instances the chief left it up to the nearest relative of the deceased to gain satisfaction—though he might shield a criminal if he learned that a killing was provoked.[52] Civil chiefs, usually men who inherited their position, also presided at band councils and represented their people at common and grand councils. All men and women past puberty were included in the open discussions of the band council, which was called by the civil chief to make decisions affecting the general welfare. Shamans and the war chief exercised a great deal of *de facto* power in such a meeting. Since there was no one political leader for all the Chippewa bands, tribal policies regarding land divisions and sales or business transactions with other tribes were set by a common council of band chiefs and principal men. General councils deliberated on matters of interest to several tribes, all of whom sent representatives.[53]

Even with general councils, unbroken harmony in intertribal relations was unattainable, especially with the Iroquois and the Sioux. Warfare thus became an important feature of traditional Chippewa culture. The bloody killing and capturing of enemy warriors was in part a psychological release for the pent-up bitterness and frustration of dealing with not-so-benign medicine men and *manidog*. Men also waged war to avenge the combat deaths of fathers, brothers, and uncles, or to annex new hunting grounds. Villages offered new social status for daring young men who could boast of bravery and extraordinary exploits on the battlefield. A particularly gory encounter, on the other hand, might cripple a village by destroying a tenth or more of its fighting men. Perhaps because of this possibility, as well as the problems of distance and slow communications, the risky business of warfare was often an individual matter. One autonomous village might be locked in combat while a neighboring one remained at peace.[54]

A war party into enemy country could be led by any fighting man with a sufficient reputation for wisdom, skill, and bravery to attract followers. First he sent a messenger with tobacco to nearby villages, asking for volunteers. Once assembled near the leader's lodge, the buckskin-clad warriors, well armed with bows and arrows, spears, knobbed wood clubs, and moosehide shields, learned of the expedition's purpose. Braves indicated their decision to join by puffing on the leader's colorfully decorated stone pipe when it was offered. Among them would doubtless be the civil and war chiefs, bent on boosting their prestige with even more enemy scalps. Each night until the campaign began, shrieking warriors danced themselves into a delirium of valor to the accompaniment of turtle-shell rattles and pounding drums. Squatting around the big war drum, they also listened to their leader discuss detailed war plans, and absorbed confidence from his personal tales of mighty deeds and his assurances of their safe return. Just before leaving for battle the warriors shared a dog's head feast—a final pledge of their readiness to face death. Anxious wives then sang songs of farewell and escorted the war party to the village outskirts.[55]

While on the march the leader maintained strict discipline, for secrecy, caution, skill, and his intimate geographical knowledge of the country were the keys to an expedition's success. Because the enemy was also clever and perceptive and usually on the watch—as a wolf is for its prey—border raids rarely involved lengthy battles at close quarters. The leader of a war party often preferred a modest victory—catching the enemy unprepared and with little loss of life to his own followers. Once they discovered an Iroquois or Sioux position, like hunters the stealthy Chippewas stalked their prey. At the proper moment they screamed into the enemy camp, indiscriminately tomahawked men, women, and children, tore off a few scalps and, before their opponents could counterattack, quickly retreated with their grisly trophies and raced back along their forest trails to boast of brave and honorable actions to their admiring families.[56]

Chippewa villagers lavished their greatest praise on the leader of a successful war party and those who distinguished themselves in battle. Highlighting the victory celebration was a scalp dance. Songs and shouts from Indians of all ages intermingled with the incessant sounds of drum and rattle. Women danced for days while above their bobbing heads fluttered the new collection of enemy scalps, already stretched over wooden hoops and attached to five-foot poles. During brief pauses, wives and mothers of slain warriors received numerous presents, including captured women and children, whom they could dispose of as they saw fit. After the dancing, villagers planted the scalp poles on the nearby graves of fallen fighting men.[57]

Governed largely by the ecology of Kitchigami land, the lake Chippewas evolved a culture that gave them a reasonably satisfying life. Traditional activities, institutions, and beliefs were family-centered and tied to the rhythms of the seasons. Self-sufficient households, often isolated, lived in a loosely related political and social world of villages, clans, bands, and tribes. Their spiritual world was one of sorcery and medicine men. With rather crude Stone Age tools, men and women produced such utilitarian articles as bulrush mats, fishnets, *makuks,* traps, weapons, animal-skin clothing, wigwams, musical instruments, and the birch-bark canoe.

Then the Europeans came and catapulted them into the Age of Iron.

# 3. The Coming of the French to Lake Superior

In early September, 1641, the Huron Indians invited the Chippewas and other confederated Algonquian nations of the Great Lakes to Georgian Bay to celebrate the Feast of the Dead. As the guests arrived, their canoe flotillas formed a long line in order to make an imposing entry into the harbor adjacent to the feast ground. Before reaching shore, the visitors threw beaver skins, porcelain beads, hatchets, and dishes overboard to their Huron hosts. The two thousand celebrants feasted, danced, played games of skill, gave more gifts, and participated in religious ceremonies. During the festivities the Chippewas met the Jesuit missionaries to the Hurons and asked them to visit their own country at the outlet of Lake Superior. The "blackrobes," as the Indians called them, accepted.[1]

Fathers Charles Raymbault and Isaac Jogues departed in late September on the seventeen-day voyage to the Chippewa settlement of about two thousand inhabitants on the St. Mary's River. Villagers encouraged the visitors to reside with them as brothers, so that the Indians could profit from their teachings, but Raymbault and Jogues declined the offer until, with the help of more missionaries, they could first convert the eastern tribes.[2] During this first European visit to the Chippewa country of which we have a definite description, the two Jesuits named the St. Mary's Rapids (*Sault de Sainte Marie*), where Superior's waters tumbled twenty-one feet into Lake Huron. Henceforth Frenchmen called these Indians the Saulteurs—People of the Rapids.[3]

The Saulteurs were probably an advance band of the westward-expanding Chippewa hunter-nomads, who soon settled along the St. Mary's River and in Michigan's Upper Peninsula, attracted there by its abundant fisheries, game resources, and its remoteness from their Iroquois enemies south of Lake Ontario. A growing population and need for additional hunting grounds generated new Chippewa settlements along the south shore of Lake Superior, which they appropriated from the Fox and the Santee (Eastern) Sioux Indians by the end of the seventeenth century.[4] The most important was on Madeline Island in Chequamegon Bay.

Tribal tradition relates that the Chippewas first occupied the island two centuries earlier. By the close of the 1500's, their growth had exceeded area resources. Tribal medicine men resorted to cannibalism, and children, especially young girls, were sacrificed until outraged parents finally revolted and killed the shamen. Terrified of the ghosts of slain youngsters who supposedly stalked the dark woods, they abandoned the island and went east to the St. Mary's River. Anthropologist Harold Hickerson claims that historical evidence contradicts this tradition.[5]

The Indian settlement at Chequamegon Bay, established in the late seventeenth century and about which we have ample documentation, flourished during what may be called the Chippewas' golden age. A 1736 French census reported 150 resident warriors, indicating a total population of about 1,000. Chequamegon's commanding geographical position made it the seat of power and activity center for Lake Superior Chippewas. Subsequent migrations into the interior radiated out from this metropolis, and to a lesser extent from the village at Keweenaw Bay. Until the interior camps became permanent, all the lake Chippewa bands returned yearly to Chequamegon to trade and for the national Midéwiwin rites.[6]

The sphere of European influence touched the Chippewas even before the Jesuit visit in 1641. Huron middlemen had been taking French trade goods to the northern and western tribes for several years. Of particular interest to the Chippewas were the weapons, tools, and utensils of the Iron Age Europeans. One Huron hostage, who was taken to France as a living curiosity of the New World, later reported to his tribesmen about the variety of Old World oddities, such as the French king who whirled along the trails in a golden cabin dragged by "eight moose without horns." Superior French technology by no means undermined Indian feelings of self-worth and of cultural superiority. Indeed, many regarded the avaricious, bearded, curly-haired, and white-skinned Europeans as both unsightly and uncouth.[7]

The reports of missionaries and other early visitors to the upper Great Lakes evoked visions of vast economic opportunities in that area. Yet for nearly two decades after Raymbault and Jogues arrived at Sault Ste. Marie, the fur trade languished because the Iroquois Confederacy, whose New York homeland was trapped out, stepped up its assault on the Huron middlemen. By 1650 they succumbed to the Iroquois juggernaut. Villages on Georgian Bay lay smashed and smoldering, the inhabitants killed or scattered, the

Jesuit missionaries fiendishly tortured and martyred. New France's economic revival occurred when French entrepreneurs went to Lake Superior and traded directly with native trappers.

Two unlicensed traders, Médart Chouart, Sieur des Groseilliers, and his younger brother-in-law Pierre-Esprit Radisson, embarked on a bold westward expedition in 1659. They paddled their canoes along the picturesque south shore of Lake Superior, portaged across the Keweenaw peninsula and arrived at Chequamegon Bay by the fall of 1659. In a log hut they built on the mainland between the present towns of Washburn and Ashland, they cached most of their trade goods while they made a winter trek to the Ottawa camp at Lac Court Oreilles. Sometime later, at the invitation of the Santees, the partners followed the overland trail from the head of Lake Superior to their villages in eastern Minnesota. Radisson and Groseilliers finished trading early in 1660 and returned to Quebec with an immense harvest of furs, only to have the French governor confiscate their illegal cargo.[8]

The successful operations of Radisson and Groseilliers enticed bands of red men and French traders to the Sault, Keweenaw, and Chequamegon. In 1659 Chequamegon Bay was fairly deserted. When Jesuit missionary Claude Allouez arrived six years later he found its shores peopled by Ottawas, Chippewas, Potawatomis, Kickapoos, and others who had come to trade, fish, hunt, garden, and enjoy this refuge from Iroquois and Sioux war parties.[9]

When Radisson and Groseilliers later deserted to the British, thereby threatening the Northwest fur trade, Quebec officials consolidated their hold on Lake Superior. In June, 1671, at the invitation of French trader Nicolas Perrot, fourteen tribes of the upper Great Lakes attended a great council at the St. Mary's rapids—the westernmost foothold of New France. A young nobleman, Simon François Daumont, Sieur de St. Lusson, negotiated a treaty of friendship with the Indians and, with much pageantry and gift giving, annexed their bountiful homeland for the Sun King.[10] Later in the decade Governor Frontenac gave tacit permission to Daniel Greysolon, Sieur de L'hut, to trade on Lake Superior, effect a peace among various warring tribes, and explore unknown country. (Finding a route to the Pacific was the burning ambition of Duluth, as he was later called.) His party wintered at the Sault in 1678–79. The following spring they journeyed to western Lake Superior and built a trading post on Thunder Bay. During the next two years Duluth and his cohorts secured French control of Kitchigami land. They built more forts, made alliances with important tribes, annexed the Sioux country for Louis XIV, reconciled the Sioux and Assiniboins—enemies for thirty years—and established a new route to the Mississippi via the Brule and St. Croix rivers.[11] Lake Superior thus became an integral part of the French Empire during the 1670's and 1680's; its native inhabitants confederated with the government, its tributaries were mapped, its natural resources tapped. Along its southern and western shores, mission stations and trading posts proliferated.[12]

In 1693 French officer Pierre Le Sueur arrived at Chequamegon Bay with orders to develop the fur trade. He chose the southwest corner of Madeline Island as a convenient location for conducting business, safe from Sioux raids, and there his detachment of troops and traders built Fort La Pointe, the first permanent settlement on Madeline Island. So large was the volume of Lake Superior furs that French prices plummeted by 1698, and for the next twenty years official operations above the Sault were suspended. In 1718 the *fleur-de-lis* once more fluttered over La Pointe. Captain Paul le Gardeur, Sieur de Saint Pierre, reconstructed the post at a nearby site and revived the legitimate Indian trade. Here, until the fall of Quebec in 1759, a series of commanders supervised the traffic in furs.[13]

French military presence on Lake Superior was vital to the imperial struggle for North American riches, but this handful of soldiers had little direct contact with the thousands of nomadic Chippewa families. A far greater influence was exercised by fur traders and Jesuit missionaries.

Simply stated, the goals of the blackrobes in the Northwest were to preserve the pine forests and native inhabitants in their rustic seventeenth-century state and to Christianize the Indians. Civilization and assimilation policies always seemed to lead to debauchery with liquor and white men's vices and to exploitation by unscrupulous traders. Jesuits therefore did not introduce red men to the French language, French customs, French habits, or to Frenchmen (including *coureurs de bois*—or woods rangers—and commandants), except for themselves, of course, whom they regarded as the eventual supreme authorities on the upper Great Lakes.[14]

The first Jesuit to visit the homeland of the Lake Superior Chippewa was feeble, fifty-six-year-old Father Réné Ménard, one of the survivors of the decimated Huron mission and an expert in Indian languages. He accompanied Groseilliers on his return trip to Kitch-

igami in the fall of 1660. Shortly thereafter he perished on a chari-
table trek south to rescue some starving Hurons on the Black River.
In the mid-sixties another bold Jesuit, Allouez, built a bark chapel
and cabin on Chequamegon Bay just south of modern Washburn.
After three years of spiritual toil and few converts, he left to labor
among the Indians on Green Bay and in Illinois and Michigan, until
his death in 1689. Father Jacques Marquette, a young Jesuit from
Laon, France, who later won great fame as an intrepid explorer,
took charge of the Chequamegon mission in 1669. The most important decade of French mission activity on Lake Superior soon ended
when an intensification of the Sioux–Chippewa war drove the
priests east to the Sault.[15]

There were few conversions of Northwest red men during the
following century of religious activity. A shortage of priests followed
the decline in French enthusiasm for the mission effort. This coin-
cided with Louis XIV's struggle with Rome over the autonomy of the
national church and the cessation in 1673 of the stimulating published volumes of *Jesuit Relations,* our best historical source for the
French missions on Lake Superior. The resistance of self-satisfied
and self-reliant northwestern tribesmen to such a major cultural
change as Christianization was a second, and by far a more important, reason for the Jesuits' marked lack of success. Headmen noted
the obvious differences in customs and beliefs, but generally felt
their own ways were superior. Moreover, the conflicting ideals of red
man and blackrobe led to incompatibility, distrust, and sometimes
to persecution. A young Chippewa male, for example, who planned
to become a great hunter and warrior, was required to be independent, hate his enemies, and reject any sort of submission. Little
wonder the mass-saying, book-reading, baptising, patient Jesuit
elicited the warrior's scorn. Little wonder that the aloof missionary,
unlike the unlicensed, gregarious *coureurs de bois,* remained outside the Indian world: neither a comrade nor a counselor, and certainly not a father image.[16]

Despite these failures, the Jesuit missions should not be termed
worthless. Their presence on Lake Superior restrained the illegitimate activities of *coureurs de bois*. They were also effective liaison
agents between various native bands and the governor at Quebec.
Finally, their detailed and scholarly treatises on Indian languages
and cultures are invaluable aids for the historian, anthropologist,
BIA bureaucrat and modern-day missionary.[17]

Of far greater importance to French officials was the lucrative

Lake Superior fur trade. Wisconsin woods and waters teemed with fur-bearing animals when the Chippewas and French settled the snug shores of Chequamegon Bay in the late seventeenth century. Beaver hats were fashionable in Europe, and the international market for prime north country otter, marten, beaver, fox, mink, wolf, and bear pelts seemed unlimited.[18]

Chippewa hunters modified their traditional economic pursuits more readily than their religious practices and beliefs. The availability of white men's metal guns, hatchets, knives, traps, kettles, awls, needles, multicolored blankets, and clothing—as well as their tasty wines and brandies—lured more and more natives to the hunt for bear and beaver. Soon the Indians were not just engaged in the fur trade; they depended on it. Accordingly, Indian material culture was revolutionized and certain habits of life were altered. Men ceased to hunt just for immediate food needs. As game grew scarce, winter trappers ranged farther and farther from their homes for the choicest pelts. Summers were wasted hanging around trading posts.[19]

Their dependence on European goods at times produced tragic results. In 1718, when Captain St. Pierre arrived at Madeline Island to revive the fur trade after a twenty-year absence of licensed traders, he discovered starving, ragged Indians who obviously had forgotten the traditional skills of making stone, bone, and wood substitutes for worn-out or lost iron and brass weapons, tools, and utensils.[20]

Two programs to regulate the fur trade were initiated by the French, partly at the urging of the Jesuits. By the mid-eighteenth century the army had built wilderness forts at La Pointe, La Baye (Green Bay), Michilimackinac (at Mackinac Straits), and at approximately two dozen other far-flung Great Lakes locations, to enforce the trading laws. French forts also safeguarded the loyalty of neighboring tribes, reduced intertribal warfare, and warded off British traders and their Iroquois allies.[21] Scattered outposts obviously could not control the whole Northwest, yet the local dominance of Fort La Pointe, which commanded the Lake Superior river routes to interior Wisconsin and influenced the powerful south shore Chippewa bands, cannot be denied. In 1698 Louis XIV further ruled that henceforth all Indians must trade at authorized trading centers rather than with roving licensed traders (*voyageurs*) or *coureurs de bois*. The Indians ignored the ruling. Following the king's death in 1715, Quebec again allowed the licensing of *voyageurs*.[22]

Chippewa association with *voyageurs* and *coureurs de bois* was far
more complex than the pat picture of social wickedness presented by
outraged French missionaries. One level, the business relationship,
induced the Indian economic dependency noted above. Tribesmen
living near a trading center, usually a warehouse and trader's
dwelling, dealt directly with the merchant. Those in the interior
bartered with *voyageurs* and *coureurs de bois* who paddled, poled,
and portaged their canoes, loaded with seventy-five-pound packs of
trade goods, along various waterways to their villages. Transactions
were on a credit basis. Early in the fall Chippewa hunters and trappers outfitted themselves with traps, ammunition, food, and clothing, which were charged to their accounts by the trader, who kept
pictographs of each man's purchases. At season's end the merchant
received Indian pelts, also pictured in his ledgers, and settled each
account.[23] Bad hunting and trapping seasons as well as the Indians'
growing desire for manufactured consumer goods—encouraged, no
doubt, by clever traders—soon bound the Chippewas to sizeable
debts. Although the red man lost much economic independence, he
was never in a state of peonage. He remained a free trapper, similar
to the later Jacksonian mountain man of the Far West.

Besides the obvious economic relationship, white merchants exercised considerable political influence with some Chippewa bands,
especially in the selection of chiefs. It could be argued that the
natives' reliance on French traders in effect made them subjects of
the French king and his allies in wartime. Yet white traders bent on
the main chance were unruly subjects at best; they sold to the highest bidder when possible and maintained much political autonomy.[24]

Widespread social repercussions of the fur trade are difficult to
assess. The trading center was an important focal point for community activities when a Chippewa band camped nearby. The Indians
relied so heavily on supplies that if a trader moved his place of
business, they of necessity followed him. Also, the similarities between the Chippewa people and the isolated, crafty, adaptable, and
present-minded French woodsmen led to social mixing, including
intermarriage and the raising of large half-breed families who remained in the Lake Superior country.[25]

In summary, Chippewa economic and perhaps psychological reliance on the French fur trader cannot be denied. Access to European trade goods often meant the difference between starvation and
survival. Yet dependence had its limits. Historical evidence suggests that the Chippewas maintained their sociopolitical autonomy;

that the network of native social ties, such as the family structure, remained unaltered by Frenchmen. Indeed, many Frenchmen became a part of it.[26]

The great expansion of aboriginal hunters and trappers into the interiors of Michigan, Wisconsin, and Minnesota was another important phase of Chippewa history after the coming of the French to Lake Superior. The lake bands' involvement with the fur trade was the motive for their expansion. As the fur-bearing animals on traditional lands grew scarce, the need for new hunting and trapping grounds drove energetic woodsmen deeper and deeper into the forests and swamplands.[27]

Early in the eighteenth century, Chippewa invaders from Chequamegon Bay thrust southward into the great midland country lying between Lake Superior and the Mississippi River. The Fox, weakened from warring on the French, relinquished the headwaters of the Ontonagon, Wisconsin, Chippewa, and St. Croix rivers and sought sanctuary among the Sauks around Green Bay. The menace of lingering Fox and Sioux war parties forced Chippewa hunters to return each spring to La Pointe, where they bartered their winter pelts and participated in unifying Midéwiwin rites. About 1745 the first permanent interior village was started on the shores of Lac Court Oreilles, at the head of the Chippewa River. Numbering forty lodges within twenty years, this settlement became the source for further migrations. The next important interior colony was settled on Lac du Flambeau at the head of the Wisconsin River. Eventually the two villages assumed sufficient independence from the parent settlement at Chequamegon Bay to observe the Midéwiwin rites within their own districts.[28]

Meanwhile, a second splinter group from the south shore surged west. Their village on the Vermilion River, southeast of Rainy Lake, became the nucleus for additional Chippewa pioneer settlements as far west as Lake of the Woods, as the Crees withdrew in search of better trading opportunities among French explorers to the northwest. Once entrenched in the border lakes region the Chippewas pushed south against rugged Sioux resistance into Minnesota's interior rice lands, and settled at Leech Lake by 1780.[29]

Expansion and Indian–white relations were but two features of early lake Chippewa history. Associations with aboriginal neighbors were likewise notable. The Iroquois, whose ferocious warriors overran the Huron country by 1650, broke the Huron's Great Lakes fur trade monopoly and shoved the survivors nearly to the Mis-

sissippi River. Bloody wars with the Five Nations Confederacy pro-
foundly affected the affairs of New France. Jesuit missions were
decimated and economic development of the Northwest dwindled as
central Algonquian fur trappers such as the Ottawas, Potawatomis,
Sauks, Fox, Illinois, Kickapoos, and Mascoutins sought asylum beyond Lake Michigan, in Wisconsin's pine forests and tangled
swamplands. In their wake the plumed and painted Iroquois came to
conquer the refugees and appropriate their hunting grounds.[30]

In 1662 there occurred perhaps the most glorious and bloody event
in Chippewa military history.[31] An Iroquois war party, looking "for
a village to eat," camped on a point fifteen miles above the Sault.
According to Perrot,

They were confident that, having carried terror among all the other savages, whom they had driven from their native lands, they would make
themselves feared as soon as they came in sight. The hundred Irroquois men
who composed this party . . . descried fires along the high hills at the north,
not far distant from them; they sent scouts in that direction, to ascertain
who might be there.

Some Saulteurs, Outaoüas [Ottawa], Nepissings [Nipissing], and
Amikouëts [Amikoue] had left their settlement and come hither to hunt elk
in the neighborhood of this Sault, and to carry on their fishing for the great
whitefish, or salmon, which they catch there in abundance, in the midst of
the boiling waters of those rapids. . . . These people were scattered about,
hunting, when one of them perceived the smoke from the camp of the Irroquois. They gave warning to one another, and rallied together to the
number of a hundred men. They elected for chief of their party a Saulteur,
who well deserved to be thus honored; for he had a thorough knowledge of
the region where they were, having lived in it before the war with the
Irroquois.

. . . The Saulteurs advanced, and proceeded as far as the camp of the
Irroquois without being discovered; a very dense forest favored them, so
that they had opportunity to count the enemy and the women whom they
had with them. The intention and plan of the people who were encamped
there was, to carry away the [inhabitants of the] villages, one place after
another, remaining in each [long enough] to consume the provisions which
they would find there, and doing the same with regard to the others.

The scouting party of the Saulteurs, having succeeded therein, returned
to their camp to report the discovery that they had just made. Their people
immediately embarked, and proceeded all night without being able to
reach the place where the Irroquois were; they passed it, however, in a
very thick fog, without being perceived by any one. They had gained knowledge of a little cove, quite deep, the head of which was in the rear of the
[Iroquois] camp; they gained that location, and concluded that they must
defer the attack of the enemy until the next day. During the night they
made their approaches, and posted themselves on a small but steep bank of

earth, some five or six feet high, at the base of which were the tents of the Irroquois, who were sleeping very tranquilly. Their dogs, scenting the ambushed Saulteurs, were beguiled by a little meat that was thrown to them, in order to prevent them from barking; and when the light of day began to appear sufficiently for discharging their arrows with effect, the assailants uttered their usual war cries. The Irroquois awoke, and, trying to hasten to seize their arms, they were pierced by the shots that were fired at them from every side, and were forced to face about by the enormous number of arrows that were showered upon them. When the Saulteurs had finished shooting them (I mean the men), they leaped down from the bank, [and] entered the tents of their enemies, with clubs in their hands. It was then that the Saulteur youth gave way, and fled toward their canoes, while the men dealt their blows everywhere, and one could know by their yells whenever they killed an Irroquois. Those who tried to flee toward the shore were fiercely attacked; the Saulteur youth, who had not seconded their elders in the fight, regained their courage when they heard the cries of victory uttered by the latter, and rushed to meet those Irroquois who had been routed, and finished the slaughter, none of the enemy escaping. You see how complete their victory was.

The Irroquois who had been sent out as scouts returned to their camp a few days after this defeat, expecting to join their people there; but when they found only headless corpses on the ground, and the bones of those whose flesh had been eaten, they made diligent haste to carry back to their own country this dismal news.[32]

The site of this gory encounter is now known as Point Iroquois. Its Indian name, Nadoueuigoning, means "the place of the Iroquois bones."[33]

The Iroquois were thwarted on Lake Superior because the French, who followed the uprooted Algonquians to Wisconsin in the 1650's and 1660's, located strategic forts on the upper Great Lakes and forged a native alliance that finally withstood attack. In fact, by the close of the century, Frenchmen and their western Indian allies had invaded New York. So the Iroquois wars ended in 1701.[34] No longer need the western-driving Chippewas fear a stab in the back.

As the Iroquois danger subsided, the Chippewas became the sole occupants of Superior's south shore, except for a portion of the Michigan-Wisconsin border shared with the usually friendly and distantly related Menominees. To the west, and not nearly so amicable, were the Sioux settlements, separated from the Chippewas by a kind of no-man's-land buffer zone.

If struggles against the Iroquois characterized Chippewa intertribal relations in the 1600's, the next century and a half was dominated by the Sioux. The Chippewa called them Na-dou-esse, meaning "snake in the grass." French traders spelled it Nadouesioux, later shortened to Sioux.[35]

Duluth's general peace council at the western end of Lake Superior in 1679 temporarily alleviated the hostilities between the two tribes struggling for control of the south shore. Because the Chippewas remained neutral during the Sioux wars against the Crees and Assiniboins, which Duluth's truce did not long forestall, the Chippewa–Sioux rapprochement ripened into a mutually profitable commercial alliance which continued until the 1730's. The Chippewas bartered French products, their own manufactures, and probably instructed the Sioux—widely known as poor trappers—in woodland skills. In addition to trading profits, Chippewa hunters and trappers gained peaceful access to the Sioux country. One group, as we have seen, pushed westward from the Sault and planted permanent settlements at Keweenaw and at Chequamegon.[36]

Ironically, French imperialists who had forged the Chippewa-Sioux trade alliance provoked the breach in the 1730's. Chippewa trappers and hunters, goaded by competitive Canadian traders, pushed farther into Wisconsin and Minnesota. The rivalry between Chippewa and Sioux males thus intensified. French entrepreneurs such as Pierre Gautier de Varennes, Sieur de la Vérendrye, also had expansionist ambitions. In return for the promise of a direct trade, the Crees and Assiniboins permitted him to explore the border lakes region to Lake Winnipeg and beyond. To appease the Sioux, enemies of the Crees and Assiniboins, the French established a large trading post and mission station at Lake Pepin, on the upper Mississippi. Unfortunately for the cause of peace, this direct trade did not placate the Sioux and, even worse, usurped the very basis of Chippewa-Sioux commerce. Now the tribes were full-fledged economic competitors, both needing the hunting grounds they had shared for half a century.[37]

Smoldering hostility erupted into bitter warfare in 1736. A Sioux war party in search of Cree scalps near Lake of the Woods massacred twenty-one Frenchmen, including a son of La Vérendrye, to demonstrate their animosity toward French trade with their Indian enemies. On the pretext of avenging these deaths, Chippewa braves attacked the Sioux at Lake Pepin. In reality they were also showing displeasure with French policy. Denis La Ronde, the commandant at Fort La Pointe, urged the Chippewas to mend the Sioux alliance, but the motivation for cooperation was gone.[38]

Chippewa bands, armed and adventurous, allied with the Crees and Assiniboins against the Sioux. War raged from northern Wisconsin to the Dakotas. By the mid-1740's Chippewa hunters had driven the Sioux out of the Lac Court Oreilles and Lac du Flambeau districts and founded permanent villages of their own. In Minnesota they first assaulted the enemy stronghold at Mille Lacs. The turning point came about 1750, with a Chippewa victory in the three-day battle of Kathio, which forced the first of a series of Sioux evacuations—from Mille Lacs, and then from Sandy, Cass, Winnibigoshish, Leech, and Red lakes. Not a single Sioux village existed east of the Mississippi above the Falls of St. Anthony by the close of the American Revolution.[39] By sheer force the Chippewas had extended their domain over the northern forests and interior lakes, which earlier they had shared with the entrenched Sioux, thereby tipping the balance of power in their favor.

Detailed descriptions of the Sioux–Chippewa warfare would not be useful, since our sources for this period are riddled with discrepancies and the number of large campaigns and pitched battles were few. The struggle for eastern Sioux lands can best be characterized as a series of forays by bold, independent raiding parties bent on getting revenge and scalps and military experience—as well as enemy territory.[40]

Why were the Chippewas so successful in dislodging the Santee Sioux? To begin with, they were better equipped with European weapons and were peerless woodsmen. Their light birch-bark canoes, for example, far surpassed the enemy's awkward dugouts. Secondly, and doubtlessly as decisive, the Sioux had already begun migration westward, attracted by trading posts established for them in the lower Minnesota Valley and by the horse-buffalo culture which reached the northeast Plains by the mid-eighteenth century. Probably only 300 Sioux warriors remained in the lake country when the Chippewa wars began in 1736.[41]

The wars generated important consequences for Sioux and Chippewas. By uprooting the Santees and driving them west, their transformation from an eastern woodland to a prairie-plains culture was accelerated.[42] Occupation of their abandoned domain south and west of Lake Superior fragmented the Chippewas. Gone forever was the close ceremonial, economic, and political cooperation at Chequamegon Bay that characterized their early years on Lake Superior. Instead, independent bands of about twenty hunter-warriors and their dependents became the basic socio-economic groups.[43] For France, Chippewa abandonment of the hunt for beaver in order to chase the Sioux meant a precipitous decline in the Northwest fur harvest and reduced defenses against the British.

The prolonged Anglo-French struggle for hegemony on the rich North American continent began in 1689. To protect the trading network which provided them with indispensable European manufactures, the Chippewas supported the French. Not that the British had been unwilling to compete for Indian furs and military support. Indeed, British traders had superior merchandise at better prices than the French, as illustrated by some statistics from about 1720:[44]

| For: | Indians Paid in Beaver Skins to the | |
|---|---|---|
| | English | French |
| 8 pounds of powder | 1 | 4 |
| 1 gun | 2 | 5 |
| 40 pounds of lead (for bullets) | 1 | 3 |
| 1 blanket (red or white) | 1 | 2 |
| 6 pairs of stockings | 1 | 2 |
| 4 shirts | 1 | 2 |

Britain's predicament was geographical. Traders from Hudson's Bay, New York, and Pennsylvania lacked easy access to the Lake Superior country, and Chippewa flotillas would not hazard a journey to such distant posts.[45] It should also be noted that most Northwest tribes had a personal preference for the French, especially the lusty *coureurs de bois* and *voyageurs* dwelling among them. This affection, the lure of plunder, and the need to preserve their economic lifeline to Montreal prompted the Chippewas to join the battle against British intruders moving into the unfortified upper Ohio Valley in the mid-eighteenth century.

Armed conflict began in June, 1752. An unauthorized French expedition, which included a few whites and 240 Chippewas and Ottawas from the Mackinac region, led by the young Canadian half-breed Charles Langlade, fell upon the unsuspecting Miami Indian village at Pickawillany, center of British commercial activity south of Lake Erie. Langlade's party killed one trader and captured five others, together with £3,000 in merchandise. Thirty Miamis also were slaughtered, including Chief "Old Britain," whose body was boiled and eaten. France was not officially involved in the incident, but it marked the beginning of resolute military resistance to British inroads among the western Indians.[46] By the mid-1750's France had erected Fort Duquesne at the forks of the Ohio River, as well as a chain of garrisons stretching north to Lake Erie. In 1755, Chippewa, Ottawa, Potawatomi, Menominee, Winnebago, and Huron tribesmen, led by Langlade, helped the French defeat British General Edward Braddock's regiments which had marched from Virginia to capture Fort Duquesne. Two years later, again hundreds of miles from their homeland, Lake Superior Chippewas fought beside the French at Lake Champlain. They were also with Montcalm on the Plains of Abraham when Quebec fell in 1759. In the same year the *fleur-de-lis* was hauled down at Fort La Pointe—the last French stronghold on Lake Superior— and the troops recalled.[47] Montreal surrendered in 1760, which ended France's rule in North America. In the Treaty of Paris, France ceded to Great Britain the vast Canadian territories and all her lands east of the Mississippi River except a small strip around New Orleans.

The loss of the Lake Superior country alone was substantial. Since the days of Radisson and Groseilliers, French traders had profitably tapped its vast supplies of fur-bearing game. Wilderness-trained *voyageurs* and *coureurs de bois* explored the hinterlands, built trading centers, and incorporated Indian trappers into the system. Montreal merchants developed European markets for the rich fur harvest channeled down the St. Lawrence River from the upper Great Lakes. Yet France left no physical imprint on Kitchigami land after a century of administration, except for a few abandoned military and commercial posts. There were no permanent white settlers above the Sault.[48]

A peaceful exploitation of the fur trade had been the goal of France's Indian policy; more than any other major European power in North America, she minimized the uprooting of Indian tribes and incursions on their cultures. The deep roots of native traditional life—languages, religious rites, tribal customs—were relatively unaltered. Nevertheless, France had a notable impact on the red men of the upper Great Lakes. By about 1760, all the tribes had scrapped their woodland material cultures for the superior tools, weapons, ornaments, and liquor introduced by the ingenious French traders. The economy of New France caused mass tribal migrations, and involved Indian fur trappers in numerous intertribal border wars as well as in the Anglo-French struggle for the Ohio country.[49]

By the mid-eighteenth century the Lake Superior Chippewas had become the major Indian beneficiaries of the French trading empire, despite tribal dependence on European goods. Their scattered bands controlled the rich region west of the Keweenaw Peninsula as far as the upper Mississippi Valley, but they had to fight to keep it. There followed another century of bloody skirmishes with the hostile Minnesota Sioux. To the east, British businessmen and bush rangers replaced the French at Montreal and Mackinac. Whether they were friend or foe, only time would tell.

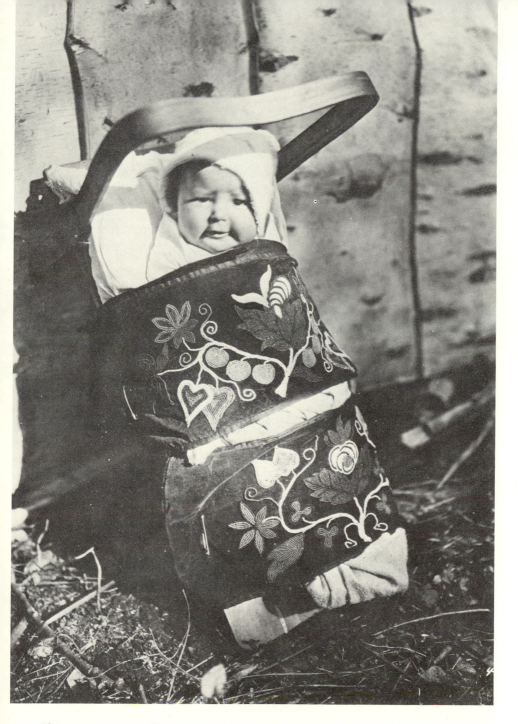

Chippewa papoose. *Courtesy Minnesota Historical Society.*

Chippewa Indians gathering wild rice. *Courtesy Minnesota Historical Society.*

Building a birch-bark canoe in Chippewa Indian camp. *Courtesy Minnesota Historical Society.*

Chippewa Indians on snowshoes hunting deer. *Courtesy Iconographic Collection, State Historical Society of Wisconsin.*

43

Chippewa Grand Medicine Lodge Midé scroll. *Courtesy Minnesota Historical Society.*

Chippewa Scalp Dance, from watercolor by Peter Rindisbacher. *Courtesy Iconographic Collection, State Historical Society of Wisconsin.*

The Witch Tree, Grand Portage Reservation. This weather-beaten cedar is a recognized shrine of the Chippewas, who for hundreds of years have left offerings at its base to appease Lake Superior's "storm Spirits". *Collection of the author.*

Midéwiwin wigwam. *Courtesy Iconographic Collection, State Historical Society of Wisconsin.*

Chippewa Indian graves and mourners. *Courtesy Public Archives of Manitoba, Canada.*

Bishop Frederick Baraga. *Courtesy Iconographic Collection, State Historical Society of Wisconsin.*

Chief Buffalo, head chief of the La Pointe Band and a signatory to the 1854 treaty. *Courtesy Iconographic Collection, State Historical Society of Wisconsin.*

Chippewa annuity payment, ca. 1860's. *Courtesy Minnesota Historical Society.*

Ashland, Wisconsin, February 26, 1867, and Apostle Islands. *From* Frank Leslie's Illustrated Newspaper, *courtesy Iconographic Collection, State Historical Society of Wisconsin.*

Chippewa Indian Drum Ceremony, Hayward, Wisconsin, 1925. *Courtesy Minnesota Historical Society.*

Reserve, Wisconsin, June 19, 1919. Chippewa Indians and returned soldiers at victory celebration. Ira O. Isham, Chippewa interpreter in foreground. *Courtesy Iconographic Collection, State Historical Society of Wisconsin.*

Bad River Reservation Agricultural Fair, 1918. *Courtesy National Archives.*

Exhibits at the Bad River Reservation Agricultural Fair, 1918. *Courtesy National Archives.*

# 4. Redcoats, Nor'westers, and Red Men

The Chippewas of Lake Superior were lucky that the British, like their French predecessors, were interested in the Northwest chiefly as a source of furs; the British tried to protect the traditional culture, which had made the Indian such an efficient hunter and trapper, by regulating Indian-white relations and discouraging intertribal warfare. During the closing years of the French regime, Britain divided the frontier at the Ohio River into northern and southern departments. Sir William Johnson of New York, appointed commissioner for the north in the spring of 1856, was empowered to make treaties and to buy Indian lands no longer needed as hunting grounds. During the following decade he took control of Indian trade. To convince hostile Northwest tribesmen and westward-driving white pioneers that London was sincere about peaceful settlement and trade relations—devoid of treaty-ground trickery and forced land sales—the king proclaimed in October, 1763, a temporary but official dividing line between British settlers and the Indian country west of the Appalachian Divide.[1]

Before the proclamation was initiated, western Indians launched a widespread rebellion. At the root of their discontent was the fact that Sir Jeffrey Amherst, commander-in-chief of British forces in North America, had discontinued the popular French practice of entertaining Indians lavishly with rum, presents, and ammunition.[2] In 1761 a group of sixty Mackinac Chippewas, led by Chief Minavavana, remarked to Alexander Henry, a trader:

> Englishman, your king has never sent us any presents, nor entered into any treaty with us, wherefore he and we are still at war; and, until he does these things, we must consider that we have no other father, nor friend, among the white men, than the king of France; . . .[3]

Pontiac's bloody rebellion eventually reached the Chippewa country. Fort Michilimackinac, entrepôt for the upper Great Lakes fur trade, stood on the south shore of the straits between Lakes Huron and Michigan. Cedar pickets and bastions enclosed two acres of land at the water's edge; inside, thirty buildings housed traders, mainly French-Canadian, and the thirty-five troops commanded by Captain George Etherington. There was also a Catholic chapel with a resident Jesuit missionary, Father Jonois. On a pleasant day in early June, 1763, some neighboring Chippewas and visiting Sauks began a game of baggattaway (lacrosse) near the stockade. Unaware of the expanding Indian war, the uniformed soldiers gathered to watch.[4] Historian Francis Parkman vividly recreates the scene:

It is easy to conceive, with sufficient accuracy, the appearance it must have presented on this eventful morning. The houses and barracks were so ranged as to form a quadrangle, enclosing an extensive area, upon which their doors all opened, while behind rose the tall palisades, forming a large external square. The picturesque Canadian houses, with their rude porticoes, and projecting roofs of bark, sufficiently indicated the occupations of their inhabitants; for birch canoes were lying near many of them, and fishing-nets were stretched to dry in the sun. Women and children were moving about the doors; knots of Canadian voyageurs reclined on the ground, smoking and conversing; soldiers were lounging listlessly at the doors and windows of the barracks, or strolling in careless undress about the area.

Without the fort the scene was of a very different character. The gates were wide open, and soldiers were collected in groups under the shadow of the palisades, watching the Indian ball play. Most of them were without arms, and mingled among them were a great number of Canadians, while a multitude of Indian squaws, wrapped in blankets, were conspicuous in the crowd.[5]

Amidst the excitement, several women carrying concealed tomahawks entered the stockade. About noon a baggattaway ball was sent soaring toward the gate. Hundreds of players rushed after it— then into the fort. Seizing weapons from their women, they shouted a war-whoop and set upon the bewildered British. Lieutenant Jamet, fifteen soldiers, and a trader were killed instantly; the other soldiers became prisoners, while the French-Canadians retired unmolested to their homes.[6] Henry, hiding in the garret of one such house, observed:

The dead were scalped and mangled; the dying were writhing and shrieking, under the unsatiated knife and tomahawk; and, from the bodies of some, ripped open, their butchers were drinking the blood, scooped up in the hollow of joined hands, and quaffed amid shouts of rage and victory.[7]

The captives escaped the dreadful tortures planned for them only because of the intercessions of Father Jonois and Charles Langlade and the arrival two days later of the Ottawas from nearby l'Arbre Croche (Harbor Springs), angered because they had missed the raid on British trade goods and military supplies from Fort Michilimack-inac. After a nasty debate the Ottawas were awarded Captain Eth-erington and twelve of the prisoners. When Ottawa tempers cooled the following month the soldiers were set free. Etherington's command, accompanied by an Ottawa escort and Lieutenant James Gorell's small garrison recalled from the fort at Green Bay, journeyed via the Ottawa River to the safety of Montreal.[8] Thus were the upper Great Lakes cleared of British troops.

Pontiac and a Mackinac Island chief sent wampum belts of war to La Pointe and other principal Chippewa villages in the Lake Superior country. Except for a few warriors who might have participated in the bloodshed at Fort Michilimackinac, the Lake Superior and Minnesota Chippewas did not ally with them. Their neutrality was attributable to the strong influence of Jean Baptiste Cadotte, interpreter for the French at the Sault. Unlike so many Canadians, he stood firmly against any attack on the British. And he spoke with authority. His Chippewa mother had married a French officer named Cadeau, who had come to the Sault in 1671 with Saint-Lusson. Jean Baptiste married into the same tribe. To the headmen he said that the king of France had not just "fallen into a drowse"; his power was gone forever from the Chippewa country. They must accommodate the British and their traders or risk military reprisals and the loss of London trade goods.[9]

Cadotte was right; Indian warriors could not for long hold off the westward-driving Englishmen. Pontiac raised the siege of Detroit late in 1763. The following year the formidable Indian uprising was suppressed.

General Amherst's refusal to offer presents had sparked a dangerous rebellion, which began a grinding and bloody shift of gears in the Northwest from the French to the British regime. The experience taught red man and white valuable lessons; by 1764 both were ready to work out a new *modus operandi* so that the fur trade could flourish once more.

Johnson invited the Western tribes to a great peace council that summer. Henry noted the dramatic arrival of Sir William's envoy to the Chippewas at Sault Ste. Marie. "My friends and brothers," he said,

I am come, with this belt, from our great father, Sir William Johnson. He desired me to come to you, as his ambassador, and tell you, that he is making a great feast at Fort Niagara; that his kettles are all ready, and his fires lit. He invites you to partake of the feast, in common with your friends, the Six Nations, which have all made peace with the English. He advises you to seize this opportunity of doing the same, as you cannot otherwise fail of being destroyed; for the English are on their march, with a great army, which will be joined by different nations of Indians. In a word, before the fall of the leaf, they will be at Michilimackinac, and the Six Nations with them.[10]

More than two thousand Indian deputies from the Six Nation Confederacy and the Western Confederacy met Johnson and Colonel John Bradstreet, British commander for the Western District, in July, 1764, at Fort Niagara.[11] On the thirteenth, Johnson conferred separately with the Chippewas. One chief, who spoke for bands living on Lake Superior and around the Sault, addressed Sir William:

Brother
   We are to assure You that on $y^e$ breaking [ ... ] of this War We present were so much shocked at it $y^t$. we were afraid & ashamed to lift our heads, as the Earth, Trees & Waters seemed all in motion & angry, & more so as we found that the Chiefs who ought to suppress such, were fomenting it. . . .

Brother
   We are a poor & foolish People, You are wise — $Y^r$. Speeches good, We have on our way hither cleared the road, & settled everry thing, so that the Trees are not tossed about & blown down therein as of late. We left home in a great hurry in order to come & hear what you would say to us, so that we might bring $y^r$. words to our Nations, we have now shaken hands with you, and as soon as we hear you shall return. . . .

Brother
   we are Indians, & very poor being in want [ ... ] necessarys of life, & unless allowed Trade & Amunition [ ...] & our Families must inevitably suffer, wherefore hope [ ... ] be allowed us, We were formerly told by $y^r$. People that they could, & would always Supply us with goods for our furs & we now beg it may be so, as we have nothing ill in our hearts towards You.

Brother
   we again beg to have liberty to trade as formerly, & that you will let the Rum run a little as our People will expect on our return to taste $y^r$. Water $w^h$ they like above all things.[12]

At a general session Johnson scolded those guilty of warring against the British. He then negotiated separate treaties with each tribe, in which the Indians (as Johnson recalled) "promised not only to get all

the Prisoners out of the Enemys Hands but also to procure restitu-
tion for the Traders losses, they have likewise agreed to the reestab-
lishing a Post at Michilimacinac." To protect tribesmen against the
unscrupulous traders, a list of trade goods prices, in terms of beaver
skins, was agreed to.[13]

With peace restored in the Northwest, the fur trade entered its
period of greatest prosperity. Happily, from the Chippewa point of
view, British businessmen modified traditional bartering procedure
only slightly. Indian bands still dealt directly with Canadian hire-
lings, whose activities were as difficult for the British to regulate as
they had been for New France. The rich harvest of furs still was
convoyed down the St. Lawrence to Montreal, though its ultimate
destination was London, not Paris. Hundreds of *voyageurs* and
British traders flocked to the upper Great Lakes to turn a handsome
profit from the Indians' dependence on white men's goods. As loaded
canoes converged upon the Mackinac Straits, Captain William
Howard, commanding Fort Michilimackinac, was pressured into
granting a few licenses to barter for furs in the interior, even though
it violated the orders of General James Murray, governor of Canada,
that trade be confined to garrisoned posts. Thus, Alexander Henry of
New Jersey, who had entered into a partnership with Cadotte of
Sault Ste. Marie, became the first post-war British trader on Lake
Superior.[14]

At Fort Michilimackinac Henry purchased trade goods priced at
ten thousand pounds of "good and merchantable beaver"—beaver at
this time being worth two shillings and sixpence per pound. Cred-
itors also accepted other types of furs, which were calculated according to their value relative to beaver. Specie was so scarce at the fort
that "in going to a cantine, you took with you a marten's skin, to pay
your reckoning."

Each of Henry's thirty-six-foot canoes was capable of carrying four
tons. For the journey to Lake Superior they carried, in addition to
merchandise, fifty bushels of provisions (maize), purchased at ten
pounds of beaver per bushel, and a crew of twelve *voyageurs,* each
hired at one hundred pounds of beaver per year. Henry's party embarked on July 14, 1765, and reached Point Iroquois on the twenty-
seventh.[15]

After entering Superior, Henry counciled with some Chippewas
who agreed to trap for him and sell him additional supplies in exchange for trade goods. Together they paddled westward skirting
the rugged shores of Kitchigami. Beyond the mouth of the Ontona-

gon Henry outfitted more Chippewa beaver hunters on the following terms:[16]

| For Trade Goods Sold on Credit | Indians Must Pay in Beaver Skins |
| --- | --- |
| Stroud blanket | 10 |
| White blanket | 8 |
| Pound of powder | 2 |
| Pound of shot or ball | 1 |
| Gun | 20 |
| One pound ax | 2 |
| Knife | 1 |

At Chequamegon Bay Henry found a Chippewa village of fifty lodges. His first impressions were quite favorable:

The Chipeways of Chagouemig are a handsome well-made people, and much more cleanly, as well as much more regular in the government of their families, than the Chipeways of Lake Huron. The women have agreeable features, and take great pains in dressing their hair, which consists in neatly dividing it on the forehead and top of the head, and in plaiting and turning it up behind. The men paint as well their whole body as their face; sometimes with charcoal, and sometimes with white ochre; and appear to study how to make themselves as unlike as possible to anything human. The clothing, in which I found them, both men and women, was chiefly dressed deer-skin, European manufactures having been for some time out of their reach.

But the residents were actually in precarious circumstances, because of the interruption of the French trade by the colonial wars and Pontiac's rebellion. Henry had to advance them credit worth three thousand beaver skins before their families were secure enough to be left for the duration of the hunt.[17]

Most of the Chippewa hunters accompanied Henry's clerk to Fond du Lac at the southwestern tip of Lake Superior; the *voyageurs* remained on Madeline Island, where they built snug winter quarters and, for subsistence, caught two thousand trout and whitefish. In mid-December the bay froze over. Henry spent the frigid months spearing twenty-pound trout through the ice.[18]

Chequamegon Bay ice broke up on April 20, 1766. A month later, a flotilla of native canoes appeared, overloaded with furs. A war with the Sioux had prevented them from harvesting even more. When accounts were settled Henry netted 150 packs of beaver and 25 of otter and marten. (Each pack weighed 100 pounds.) Henry did not have enough trade goods to purchase the entire catch, so 50 Chippewa canoes, with 100 unsold beaver packs, joined him on the circuitous return journey to the straits.[19] Their exciting appearance at Fort Michilimackinac confirmed the hopes of traders: on the shores of Kitchigami was an abundance of fur-bearing animals, just ripe for the taking. Chippewa trappers were ready to do the taking as soon as whites displayed the trade goods.

During the 1770's, the Henry-Cadotte partnership tapped the wealthy region west of Lake Superior. Grand Portage became their base, rather than Madeline Island, because of its access to the Pigeon River and the Rainy Lake chain. Also significant for the Chippewas was the expiration of Henry's exclusive franchise. Sir William Johnson opened Superior to other licensed and bonded Mackinac traders, most of whom, like Henry, allied with French-Canadian partners. Brisk competition and attractive profits brought many trading posts to the major lakes and waterways of northern Wisconsin and Minnesota.[20]

The American Revolution did not interrupt the upper Great Lakes fur exchange. In fact, the Superior-Montreal-London trade route remained so firmly in British hands that by 1778 Lake Superior entrepreneurs, who employed five hundred persons, were yielding £40,000 annually, more profit than in the prewar years. Nor did the Chippewas suffer from lack of European merchandise and from military losses as they did during the French-English conflict; tribesmen were too busy trapping the north woods to skirmish with George Rogers Clark in the Ohio country. French-Canadians, who sympathized with the Americans but were also cut off from the south, remained nominally loyal. To insure that valuable trade goods did not fall into rebel hands, Major Arent Schuyler DePeyster, British commandant at Fort Michilimackinac, sent a military escort each year with merchants outbound to Lake Superior.[21]

Because the Northwest fur trade produced such handsome profits, Canadian traders came to fear cutthroat competition and the powerful Hudson's Bay Company far more than the Americans. Therefore, several ambitious and foresighted independent merchants, backed by Montreal capital, formed an informal commercial alliance in 1779 called the North West Company. For the next thirty-five years this unincorporated partnership controlled the Lake Superior fur trade and was a formative force in Chippewa history.

Rebel arms were defeated in the Ohio country and did not even penetrate the upper Great Lakes, yet American and British peace

commissioners meeting in Paris in 1782 set the western frontier of
the United States at the Mississippi, and its northern boundary
through the Great Lakes, Lake of the Woods, and beyond. Twenty-
five unsuspecting Indian tribes, including the Lake Superior Chippewas, were thereby turned over to the United States. The surrender of Detroit, Michilimackinac, and Grand Portage also vitiated the
Canadian fur trade, at least on paper. The protests of Canadian
merchants and their London suppliers were loud but unheeded.[22]
Soon it became evident, however, that the Treaty of Paris would not
mean the immediate destruction of the British regime in Kitchigami land. It would be another thirty years before the young repub-
lic was strong enough to break the iron grip of the North West
Company on the Great Lakes.

In the mid-1780's, when it became obvious that London would
not deliver up her Great Lakes posts to the Americans, ingenious
Nor'Westers vigorously embarked on an expansion program and
systematized their operations. Shipments of trade goods to the
Grand Portage emporium were increased by 20 per cent for the
1783–84 season. Annual returns averaged £200,000 sterling. The
energetic cartel also tightened its grip on native peoples south and
west of Lake Superior, and at the same time demanded that employees, who had signed contracts called *engagements,* do its bidding. Smaller competitors, south of Superior, were sidetracked,
eliminated, or, as with the Henry-Cadotte partnership, absorbed by
the parent organization.[23] None could deny that enterprising fur
trade interests dominated the land of the Chippewas.

During the 1790's the Canadian fur trade network expanded still
farther. In the Jay Treaty of 1794 Britain agreed to remove its
troops from the American Northwest, yet the agreement's reciprocal
clauses permitted British merchants to cross the border, which they
did in ever-increasing numbers—building new posts, hiring more
*engagés* and, with the help of the Canadian government, lavishing
enough gaudy presents upon the Chippewas to keep them within the
economic sphere of the Union Jack. Cadotte's two sons, Michel and
Jean Baptiste, managed the company's south shore trading centers
at La Pointe on Madeline Island and at Fond du Lac.[24] Grand Portage, thanks to the opening of new regions in the Far West, became
the most important entrepôt beyond the Sault. Each summer, according to William Whipple Warren,

The partners and clerks of the company, who passed the winter amongst the inland posts, collected their returns of fur, and were met -ts[at Grand Portage] by the partners from Montreal with new supplies of merchandise. These yearly meetings were enlivened with feastings, dancing, and revelry, held in the great hall of the company. In the style of feudal barons of old, did these prosperous traders each year hold their grand festival surrounded by their faithful and happy "coureurs du bois" and servitors.[25]

Certainly the Nor'Westers earned the annual carnival at Grand Portage; they had battled the elements in the north woods—pesky insects, swamplands, perilous rapids, rocky portages, sub-zero temperatures—and wrested a handsome profit for themselves. However, their good fortune with the Chippewas did not go unchallenged. By the turn of the century they faced bitter intertribal warfare, new trading rivals and the expanding authority of the United States government.

The incessant Chippewa-Sioux hostilities persisted under the British. The Canadian fur trade suffered greatly and Montreal merchants feared the loss of all trade on the Mississippi above the mouth of the Illinois River. On April 4, 1786, a memorial sent by thirty-five of them (Henry included) to Sir John Johnson, Superintendent General of Indians for Quebec Province, revealed the powerlessness of local traders and military to reconcile the warring nations.[26] On April 13, the merchants sent Johnson a memorandum with supplemental details about each of the warring nations, which included the Chippewas, Sioux, Menominees, Winnebagos, and Sauks and Fox. Notations about Lake Superior Chippewas testify to their importance in the fur trade:

A few of them are around Lake Huron & at Michilimackinac but by far the most numerous and warlike part (and to whom the present remark more particularly alludes) inhabit the south side of Lake Superior, from the Falls of St. Mary to the west end of that Great Lake with the Country adjacent and a very numerous tribe of them occupy the sources of the Mississippi with all the Country on the East side of that famous River. . . . This tract cannot be surpassed or perhaps equalled by any in the Upper Country for the fine furrs it produces, but owing to the vicinity of the Scioux and the constant war between these rival Nations, the Traders, do not procure from it one forth part of the furrs, which it is capable of producing annually.[27]

In October, 1786, Johnson's deputy, John Dease, took charge of Indian affairs at Michilimackinac and arranged for a great council at Mackinac Island the following summer. Nearly two hundred delegates from the warring tribes arrived in August amidst much ceremony and lavish British gift giving. The chiefs and headmen promised to treat white traders more hospitably and to keep their young men off the warpath. For more than twenty years the pledges were honored, except by the two most important tribes, the Chippewas and the Sioux.[28] Their bloody skirmishes lasted another seventy years.

Competition from the X Y Company, a coalition of rival traders formed in 1798, further damaged efficient North West Company operations. X Y employees trailed Nor'Westers, built posts near their traders and dispensed rum and presents on favorable enough terms to secure much of the Chippewa peltry.[29] Francois V. Malhiot, a French-Canadian clerk who managed a North West Company post on the north shore of Lac du Flambeau, noted in his 1804 journal just how pernicious this rivalry was for red man and white:

> ... [Simon] Chorette [an able X Y employee also stationed at Lac de Flambeau] gives a brasse of cloth for a bear skin. Rum flows like water on both sides, but Chorette is beginning to complain and I still have seven kegs of mixed rum. I have hardly any more tobacco and fear I shall have none at all before I leave. My supply of goods will also fail. ... For eleven years that I have been wintering among the Savages I have never known a competitor trade as cheaply as Chorette. I think Lucifer brings him his goods from London as he needs them.
>
> 26th [May] Friday. The son of "La pierre à Affiler," Chorette's brother-in-law, came here last night and made me a present of an otter skin, 15 musk-rat skins and 12 lbs of sugar for which I gave him 4 pots of rum. He went to drink it at Chorette's with "l'Ours" and "La Petite Racine." When they were quite drunk they cleared the house, nearly killed Chorette, stabbed Lalancette and broke into the storeroom. They took two otter skins, for which I gave them some more rum in the morning not knowing that they had stolen them. All this row happened because Corette had promised them rum for their skins and had none to give them.
>
> They came here tonight intending to get me to give them liquor, but we drove them away by striking them with poles from the top of the Fort. In their fury they went for their guns but did not venture to fire them and went away with the shame of not having succeeded in doing anything.
>
> I thank God every day for having inspired me with the idea of making so good a fort, impregnable to bullets and to all attacks.[30]

Eventually, Malhiot and other clerks despised the large number of debauched Chippewas which their own cutthroat competition had created:

> There are some others whom I might include in the number of good Savages, but, as a rule, if I could put them all in a bag and know that Lucifer wanted them, I would give them all to him for a penny.... If they were lambs formerly, today they are rabid wolves and unchained devils. As a rule

they possess all the vices of mankind and only think they are living well, when they live evil lives.[31]

In November, 1804, the Nor'Westers united with the X Y Company, thus ending the bitter rivalry and its corrupting influence upon the Chippewas.

The United States government, having achieved internal stability during Washington's presidency, quickly extended its jurisdiction into the Great Lakes region and became a far greater threat to Nor'Westers than the X Y Company or intertribal warfare. In 1795 Anthony Wayne made peace with the Western Indian Confederacy (Chippewas, Wyandots, Delawares, Shawnees, Ottawas, Potawatomis, Miamis, Eel-rivers, Weas, Piankashaws, Kickapoos, and Kaskaskias). His treaty, signed at Greenville, Ohio, established a general boundary between the lands of the United States and tribesmen of the Northwest. The federal government accordingly relinquished claim to native possessions south and west of the upper lakes and east of the Mississippi; future Indian land sales, however, could only be made to the United States, whose guardianship the chiefs acknowledged.[32] The following summer Britain surrendered its posts south of the Canadian border, under the terms of the Jay Treaty.

In the 1790's the United States also established a factory system of trading posts, where merchandise was sold to the tribes at cost. The purpose was to preserve Indian friendship and simultaneously draw them away from private British traders on the upper Great Lakes and Spanish merchants in the Southwest.[33] Forced to deal on a cash-and-carry basis, stationary American factors could not compete with enterprising Nor'Westers, who pushed into the heart of Kitchigami land and extended liberal credit to Chippewa trappers. Moreover, United States government goods were often ill-suited to Indian needs. Joseph B. Varnum wrote bitterly from the Mackinac factory in September, 1810:

... Our steal traps are also an article so miserably made that they will never sell for one half what they first cost; I have even offered them at that and have not been able to vend one of them; in fact they are not worth anything more than so many pounds of Old Iron Hoops; of which they are in part manufactured. The price of a first rate Trap in Montreal is generally from seven to eight shillings Halifax Currency; more than one hundred per cent less than ours cost in the States, consequently they would not sell even if they were of quality, much less in their present state. . . .
... Our copper Kettles will not sell for much more than first cost, they are

to be sure well made, strong and heavy, well calculated for the use of white
people; but they are too thick, too heavy in proportion to their size; in short,
they are too good for Indians; which makes them so high they cannot afford
to buy them. . . .

. . . Ear Bobs for instance are charged 40 Cents per pair, and when the
percentage required is added it will bring them at 66⅔ Cents per pair; a
price so far beyond anything heretofore given for silver trinkets only weighing 6½ Cents (for they weigh no more) that the natives even laugh when the
price is mentioned. Our arm and wrist bands, Broaches and Crosses are
about one hundred per cent too heavy for their size, they being only calculated for a temporary ornament.[34]

Operating at such a disadvantage, factories could not control nearby
natives. Yet they were the first serious challenge by the United
States to British dominance of the lucrative Northwest fur trade.

In February, 1806, the Chippewas counseled with American
Lieutenant Zebulon Montgomery Pike on the upper Mississippi.
Pike's twenty-man party had orders to regulate British trading activities, explore the Mississippi to its source, select suitable sites for
military forts along its route, and make alliances with local aboriginees.[35] The previous September the lieutenant had met some
Sioux chiefs at the confluence of the Minnesota and Mississippi rivers. He bought a tract of land for army purposes, and also induced
the red men to stop fighting with the Chippewas.[36] Pike's party then
pushed farther up the Mississippi, asserting American authority
over what is today northern Minnesota. In the February conference,
Pike ordered the Chippewas to give up medals and flags received
from the British. He also banned rum from their villages; drunken
Indians neglected their families and got involved in too many quarrels and murders. Pike further informed the headmen that the
Sioux, "have agreed to lay by the hatchet, smoke the calumet, and
become again your brothers, as they were wont to be."[37] The Chippewas agreed to the cease-fire. Pike explained his success, as follows:

. . . the British government, it is true, requested, recommended, and made
presents; but all this at a distance; and when the chiefs returned to their
bands, their thirst of blood soon obliterated from their recollection the lectures of humanity, which they had heard in the councils of Michilimackinac. But, when I appeared amongst them, the United States had lately
acquired the jurisdiction over them, and the names of the Americans (as
warriors) had frequently been sounded in their ears; and when I spoke to
them on the subject, I *commanded* them, in the name of their great father,
to make peace; and offered them the benefit of the mediation and guarantee
of the United States: and spoke of the peace, not as a benefit to us, but a step

taken to make themselves and children happy. This language held up to both nations, with the assistance of the traders; a happy coincidence of circumstances; and (may I not add?) the assistance of the almighty, affected that which had long been attempted in vain. But I am perfectly convinced, that, unless troops are sent up between those two nations, with an agent, whose business it would be to watch the rising discontents; and check the brooding spirit of revenge: that the weapons of death will again be raised, and the echoes of savage barbarity will resound through the wilderness.[38]

Pike was right, of course; shortly after he departed the Lake Superior country in April, 1806, the Sioux-Chippewa truce was broken. Also, the Union Jack waved again over the trading posts of the Nor'Westers.[39] Neither the Pike expedition nor the Mackinac factory could control Chippewa or British behavior.

About the turn of the century white frontiersmen surged onto Indian land in the Northwest. By 1810, Ohio had a population of 230,000, and Governor William Henry Harrison of Indiana was busily acquiring more and more rich Indian land as far as the Mississippi.[40]

The Chippewa and other Great Lakes tribes, apprehensive about these intruders, were susceptible to any plan or idea which promised riddance of the whites. The Shawano cult offered one such promise.

Two Shawnee brothers mobilized Indian resistance to land-hungry white settlers. Tecumseh formed an Indian confederacy; Lalawethika, known as the Prophet, urged red men to discard all white influences and return to the old ways. The Prophet's Code was carried with much success to other Great Lakes tribes.[41]

During the summer of 1808, Lalawethika's messengers with their faces painted black brought the good tidings of a new religion to the Chippewas. The visitors performed special new ceremonies and told how the Great Spirit, through the medium of a Shawnee prophet, had come to deliver the red race. They asked the Chippewas to live the simple and self-sufficient lives they all once enjoyed and to renounce corrupt European merchandise, especially liquor. They commanded that no skins or furs be bartered, no intertribal battles fought. They forbade certain traditional religious practices, such as the use of medicine bags; this struck at the root of the Midéwiwin, which the Prophet claimed had lost its original purity. Lastly, the messengers urged the Chippewas to go to Detroit, where the Prophet would explain his revelations from the "Great Master of Life."[42]

The Shawano cult spread rapidly, touching even the remotest hunting grounds. Disciples of the new religion plundered the fur trading post at Lac Court Oreilles in 1808. Many others gathered at

Chequamegon, where they threw their midé bags into the bay and held religious ceremonies for several days. About 150 canoes of Shawano followers started for Detroit, carrying the body of a dead Lac Court Oreilles child, for the Prophet had also claimed that he could raise the dead. Michel Cadotte met them near Pictured Rocks and convinced most of the Indians that the Prophet was a fraud who was mainly interested in forming a large army to fight the white man.[43]

The Shawano cult, though it soon disappeared, was not without significance. John Tanner, a white man who lived among the Chippewas west of Lake Superior at the time, recalled in 1830:

... The influence of the Shawnee prophet was very sensibly and painfully felt by the remotest Ojibbeways of whom I had any knowledge,... For two or three years drunkenness was much less frequent than formerly, war was less thought of, and the entire aspect of affairs among them was somewhat changed by the influence of one man. But gradually the impression was obliterated, medicine bags, flints, and steels, were resumed, dogs were raised, women and children were beaten as before, and the Shawnee prophet was despised. At this day he is looked upon by the Indians as an imposter and a bad man.[44]

In theory, the Prophet's Code could have created real Indian solidarity and crippled the fur trade. But it came much too late. Northwest tribesmen by 1812 were too dependent on white traders. Later in the century, frantic Sioux Ghost Dancers learned the same bitter lesson: appeals to their gods would not bring back "the good old days." The white man had come to stay.

Unlike the Shawano cult, political unity and military opposition to Americans preached by Tecumseh had little appeal to isolated Lake Superior Chippewas. Their long dependence on the Canadian fur trade doubtless made them pro-British, but neither the destruction of Tecumseh's village after the battle of Tippecanoe in November, 1811, nor British appeals could arouse them to war on the United States. A chief of the Pillager Chippewa band replied to a British messenger seeking an Indian alliance during the War of 1812:

When I go to war against my enemies, I do not call on the whites to join my warriors. The white people have quarreled among themselves and I do not wish to mingle among their quarrels, nor do I intend ever to be guilty of breaking the window of glass of a white man's dwelling.[45]

The only Chippewas south of the border to enter the war were small bands confederated with the Ottawas or scattered about Michigan's southern peninsula. Soon after the United States declared war, these Indians joined a British expedition led by Captain Charles Roberts, which captured the vital American stronghold on Mackinac Island without a shot being fired.[46] Of far greater historical significance to Kitchigami land was the peace treaty signed at Ghent in December, 1814. By making no changes in prewar boundaries, diplomats conceded eventual American occupation of the Northwest. Britain's hegemony on the upper Great Lakes was forever broken.

Like the French regime, British rule was nothing more than a "vast commercial enterprise controlled by Montreal traders" interested solely in procuring furs. For more than fifty years these entrepreneurs prospered. They protected traditional native cultures (which produced skillful hunters and trappers), minimized Indian-white contact, discouraged intertribal wars and slowed American advances into the Northwest. The physical impact of the British regime on the Lake Superior country was minimal; by 1814 there were no permanent settlements. Canadian traders came, made their profits, and left. The Chippewa way of life was altered little by all of this; technological acculturation simply progressed a little farther than under the French regime. However, by 1815 the Chippewas must have been uneasy about the new American "father," since the bands had been taught by the British to fear and distrust the settlers from the south.[47] And for good reason. A nationalistic, imperialistic United States was determined to extend its authority over the Northwest.

# 5. The Chippewas and their White American Neighbors, 1815-1854

In August, 1815, chiefs of the Chippewa, Ottawa, Potawatomi, Wyandot, Delaware, Seneca, Shawnee, and Miami tribes from the state of Ohio and the territories of Michigan and Indiana journeyed to Spring Wells, near Detroit. They met in council with United States Commissioners William H. Harrison, Duncan McArthur, and John Graham until September 8, when a treaty was signed. The agreement established peaceful relations between them and the United States, and restored to them the possessions and rights to which they were entitled prior to the War of 1812. The Treaty of Greenville and all subsequent treaties also were confirmed.[1]

For forty years following the Spring Wells treaty the Chippewas dealt with two powerful but different groups of white Americans. Traders employed by John Jacob Astor's American Fur Company, following in the footsteps of the French and British, fought successfully until the early 1840's to preserve a south shore wilderness sanctuary so that the profitable fur trade with the lake Chippewas could continue. Meanwhile, agents of civilization—white miners, lumbermen, farmers, townbuilders—sought to subdue Kitchigami land.[2] Led by the copper miners, these whites elbowed the natives off most of their hunting grounds and had them assigned to small reservations where they would be forcibly acculturated by BIA bureaucrats and missionaries. By 1854 the heyday of the fur trader and Chippewa trapper was over.

Following the War of 1812, Congress enacted two laws which greatly helped Astor to dominate the fur trade and, consequently, the native peoples of the upper lakes and upper Mississippi region. An April, 1816, bill permitted only American traders to be licensed; others were forbidden south of the international border, except at the discretion of the president.[3] Convinced that publicly operated frontier trading houses were woefully inefficient and no longer needed, since Britain's influence over most of the American Indians had been broken, legislators abolished the factory system in May, 1822, thereby shutting out another group of Astor's competitors.[4]

From New York, Astor exported Great Lakes furs to London and imported Indian trade goods—cloth, woolens, utensils, tools, guns—which were shipped west each spring to Ramsay Crooks and Robert Stuart, experienced traders in charge of American Fur Company field operations. Headquartered on beautiful Mackinac Island, the company's Northern Department embraced the upper lakes and upper Mississippi valley. It was divided into outfits according to geography and Indian bands, each outfit headed by a trader. During the summer visit to Mackinac, fur packs were unloaded and the trader selected merchandise for restocking his posts. Some of the men were independents, sharing costs and profits with the company; others were salaried.[5]

By 1818, American Fur Company outfits covered most of the Chippewa country. In the Keweenaw region John Holliday traded six thousand dollars worth of goods annually during the early 1820's. Across the lake, Astor purchased the North West Company's Grand Portage post as well as several other forts in the rugged boreal woodlands to the west. Yet many of the red men sold their furs to the British, who were located conveniently across the international border at Fort William and offered better prices and more whiskey than the Americans. Astorians at Grand Portage prospered nonetheless. By 1810 they had an impressive complex of family dwellings, bachelors' quarters, a store, a barn, and a root house for storing more than two hundred bushels of potatoes grown by employees. The cooper's shop and fish store were used in an important subsidiary operation of the company, developed by Crooks. Bountiful catches of fresh Lake Superior fish were brought in during the off-season and packed in barrels for export.[6]

In 1816, the American Fur Company also took over North West posts in the lake country west of present-day Duluth—a zone so rich in fur-bearing animals that the British had once employed 109 men at Sandy, Mille Lacs, Rice, Gull, Pokegama, and Leech lakes. To exploit the area as far as the Mississippi, the Astorians divided it into several sub-outfits and built a headquarters fort twenty miles up the St. Louis River at Fond du Lac. William A. Aitkin, an experienced Scotch trader, commanded the Fond du Lac outfit during much of the 1820's and 1830's. He supervised each sub-outfit, sold supplies to traders, and acted as their banker. Men like Aitkin also exercised considerable influence over Chippewa affairs, especially among the growing number of mixed bloods, offspring of intermarriages between Indian women and French-Canadian, Scottish, and American traders.[7]

Between the Fond du Lac and Keweenaw outfits was an equally rich region which stretched south from the lake shore to the ricelands at the head of the St. Croix, Red Cedar, Chippewa, and Flambeau rivers. In 1818, Truman Abraham Warren and Lyman Marcus Warren, New England brothers and independent traders, arrived on the south shore and entered into brisk competition with the Lac Court Oreilles, Lac du Flambeau, and St. Croix sub-outfits of the American Fur Company. Fair dealings with the Chippewas won respect for the Yankees, who shrewdly marketed their fur packs with the North West Company across the international border. Astorian Michel Cadotte of La Pointe, supervisor for the whole region (the northern outfit), recognized the brothers' competence and hired them as company traders at La Pointe. By 1821 each had married one of Cadotte's two daughters. Lyman Warren bought out his father-in-law three years later and became chief factor, a post he retained until 1838. Meanwhile, the northern outfit absorbed those at Keweenaw, Fond du Lac, and Grand Portage. It traded $50,000 worth of goods annually, employed 154 men and gathered the finest furs in the United States.[8]

During the years of Lyman Warren's prominence, La Pointe prospered because of its good harbor and central geographical location. Conspicuous village buildings included the American Fur Company's red store and warehouse, a large fish house (La Pointe, like Grand Portage, was a fishing center), Protestant and Catholic missions, and the ninety scattered shacks and wigwams which housed the permanent residents. These included several hundred *voyageurs,* mixed bloods, and Chippewas. Most had Indian wives and, as Crooks observed, as many children as they could afford to feed.[9]

In 1825 a son, William Whipple, was born to Lyman and Marie Cadotte Warren. He grew up on Madeline Island, where his mother's Chippewa blood tie and his father's important commercial position gave him access to Canadian social circles and Chippewa council fires. To further broaden the youngster's knowledge, his father sent him East for a formal education. By the early 1840's William had returned to La Pointe and had become an interpreter for the federal Indian subagent there. In August, 1843, young Warren married Matilda Aitkin, daughter of the Fond du Lac trader, thereby merging two influential south shore families shortly after the American Fur Company brought all its Lake Superior outfits under the supervision of the La Pointe factor. Considered an authority on the Chippewa language and various historical legends of the lake bands, William Whipple Warren completed his valuable *History of the Ojibway Nation* in 1853, a year before his death. It detailed his personal experiences in tribal affairs and preserved a wealth of Chippewa traditions about the pre-reservation years.[10]

Astor sold the La Pointe complex and other American Fur Company holdings in 1834 to a New York firm headed by Crooks. During the next decade the fur trade entered upon hard times. Crooks was a masterful, aggressive leader, but even his valiant efforts could not save the company from the depression of the late 1830's, cutthroat competition in the new raccoon trade, and the collapse of the world fur market. In September, 1842, the American Fur Company slid into bankruptcy.[11]

Astorians had influenced Chippewa affairs in a variety of ways. A keen observer of the American fur trade's economic impact on native people was Lieutenant James Allen of the Fifth United States Infantry. He commanded the military escort on Henry R. Schoolcraft's expedition to the upper Mississippi during the summer of 1832 and kept a daily journal about the condition of various tribes encountered en route. Visits with the south shore bands convinced him that they had become dangerously dependent on American Fur Company traders. Indians in the Keweenaw region, for example, survived the summer months by eating the plentiful whitefish, herring, and trout taken from the bays with gill nets and spears; but there was little food for their families in the winter because of the depletion of bear, deer, and other large game. Provisions were procured from their trader, John Holliday. By 1832, more than half of the trading stock he brought out from Mackinac was foodstuffs and clothing.[12] Other lake bands as far west as Fond du Lac were in a similarly "deplorable" condition—poor and getting poorer. The Indian population increased as the number of furred and large game animals dwindled. Each spring there were fewer furs with which to buy necessities. The lake bands seemed unaware that they were headed toward economic calamity; therefore, Allen asserted, "humanity" must convince them to take up agriculture and support themselves. Kitchigami land could sustain ten times its present population if the Chippewas could cultivate the soil and abandon their "established and peculiar habits of living."[13]

The Chippewas did indeed suffer serious economic dislocation following the flush times of the fur trade. Yet this does not necessarily mean that the fur trade was bad for them. A review of the two hundred years prior to Allen's south shore visit shows that when these isolated, Stone Age aboriginees bartered furs for European goods—trinkets, tools, utensils, yard goods, and guns—a technological renaissance occurred which raised the material standard of living for all the tribes of the upper Great Lakes. Moreover, Chippewa unemployment in the late 1830's was not unique—this was a depression era—and their future was not totally bleak just because the game supply had been exhausted. Cutthroat competition, exploitation of natural resources, and depressions characterized American economic history as a whole—not just that of the Great Lakes—well into the twentieth century. Economic booms eventually followed the busts, and the Chippewas, having been brought by the fur trade into the white economic stream, could profit with the development of each new industry—lumbering, farming, fishing, mining, and tourism. The north woods still had abundant resources worth the taking.

In addition to providing economic necessities to the Lake Superior Chippewa bands, the American Fur Company traders counseled their customers about political matters and often acted as liaisons with the United States government prior to the establishment of a federal Indian agency on the south shore. Evidence that Indian headmen and federal treaty commissioners accepted this function may be found in the agreements which traders helped to negotiate. In the land cession treaties of 1837 and 1842, for example, the Chippewas sold the northern half of Wisconsin. From the proceeds of the land sales they granted debt claims to traders of $70,000 and $75,000.[14]

Anthropologist Victor Barnouw also discerned a Chippewa psychological dependence on their trader, who was addressed as "father" because of his dominant position. One behavioral manifestation of this father-child relationship was a deep-seated inhibition of aggressive feelings the Chippewas had toward the whites in general. Resentment and hostility toward white encroachers was usually expressed orally. Unlike the plains tribes, these woodland warriors—even when intoxicated—rarely attacked frontier families. Barnouw further argues that psychological dependency on the trader was important because it was a model for later Chippewa dealings with federal Indian gents, to whom they likewise looked for fatherly leadership, political advice, and economic support.[15]

The Astorians' insatiable demands for furs and the Chippewa's dependence on trade goods aggravated such perpetual problems as Indian drunkenness and intertribal warfare. Federal statutes forbad the sale of intoxicants to Indians. Nevertheless, alcohol was liberally dispensed by Hudson's Bay men just across the border and by unscrupulous American hucksters, whose activities in this vast domain could not be supervised once they left the immediate vicinity of a United States military post or Indian agency office. Ramsay Crooks insisted for years that his company tried to keep Indians sober and was responsible for much of the Chippewa's relative economic progress as well as their peaceful relations with white neighbors. Eventually even the American Fur Company was forced by its competitors to use whiskey in exchange for Indian furs.[16] War was as bad for business in the mid-nineteenth century as it had been in 1786, when Montreal merchants called on Sir John Johnson to stop the Great Lakes wars. Though peace among the various tribes in the Northwest was promoted by the Astorians, the same sorts of financial necessities which drove white traders into bitter confrontations also intensified the Sioux-Chippewa struggle for control of Kitchigami land and its game resources.

Fighting over hunting grounds was one cause of intertribal warfare south and west of Lake Superior. There were other motives too. Warren wrote that ambitious warriors were incited by "blood and renown." Taking a Sioux scalp while on the warpath greatly enhanced the stature of a Chippewa male in the eyes of village maidens and the ruling council. The victim might be a Sioux hunter, but the scalp of a woman or child was equally treasured. If Sioux raiders killed a Chippewa villager, the female relations blackened their faces, tore at their hair, mutilated themselves and cried out in pitiful tones until the rest of the relatives took revenge.[17] Nothing could stop this; both Sioux and Chippewas believed that this sort of satisfaction was a duty. So keen was intertribal hatred that histories of enemy actions were passed from father to son. Revenge thus became hereditary. It also merged with religious thought. The large Leech Lake band was the vanguard of the advancing Chippewas; it lived closest to the Sioux, hated them the most, fought them most frequently. In July, 1832, at a meeting with Schoolcraft and Allen, Chief Flat Mouth of the Leech Lake band summed up the feeling: "it was decreed by the Great Spirit that hatred and war should ever exist between the Sioux and themselves; that this decree could never be changed; and the Chippewas must ever act accordingly."[18]

Sioux war parties frequented the Chippewa border country in such numbers, Warren wrote, that a tribesman

moved through the dense forests in fear and trembling. He paddled his light canoe over the calm bosom of a lake or down the rapid current of a river, in search of game to clothe and feed his children, expecting each moment that from behind a tree, an embankment of sand along the lake shore, or a clump of bushes on the river bank, would speed the bullet or arrow which would lay him low in death.[19]

Eventually Kitchigami land was scarred with battle sites where Sioux and Chippewa warriors had met. In refusing to relinquish his people's land, one headman remarked that "the country was strewn with the bones of their fathers, and enriched with their blood."[20] By the 1830's the lake bands no longer participated regularly in the bloody feud with the Sioux; this freed them from the constant anxiety and alarm felt by Chippewa bands along the Mississippi and at Leech and Red lakes. Still, eastern villages sent a few war parties to the borderlands and runners kept their chiefs informed of Sioux whereabouts.[21]

Warfare west of Lake Superior was mainly waged by small raiding parties sent out from scattered villages of two or three hundred inhabitants. As in the eighteenth century, combatants lacked political unification, transportation, and supply systems to carry on sustained campaigns. The loss of life was minimal, and a retaliatory foray was successful if just one enemy scalp was lifted. Most alliances among two or more villages were short-lived wartime expediencies.[22]

Intertribal warfare often thwarted the "civilization" and Christianization of the Chippewas. The fate of one borderland village in Minnesota on the Snake River, a branch of the St. Croix, was typical. In August, 1840, the Reverend Frederick Ayer reported that the alarmed inhabitants, fearing a Sioux attack, had abandoned their gardens and mission schools and fled to some remote, wooded sanctuary. The following year, as many of the villagers gathered early in the summer to start their gardens, an enemy war party struck without warning; two Chippewas were killed and four or five wounded. The survivors fled. Agency farmer J. Russell believed the cowered Chippewas would never return; nor would it be easy to find them a secure townsite.[23] These destitute families, as well as other displaced villagers and their missionaries, thus retreated toward Lake Superior in the early 1840's. As long as they wandered about the borderlands in search of fish and game, white agents of "civiliza-tion" and Christianization had no hope for success.[24]

For more than half a century white Americans tried to stop the intertribal warfare. Early Lake Superior traders like Jean Baptiste and Michel Cadotte took the lead in promoting peace, but the truces they forged rarely lasted as long as a year. Federal intervention was eventually necessary when many traders and white settlers moved into the tribal battle zones in Wisconsin and Minnesota. First, forts were built and garrisoned at Green Bay, Prairie du Chien, and at the junction of the Minnesota and Mississippi rivers to protect white farmers and to regulate traders.[25] The BIA then invited several nearby tribes to a grand conference at Prairie du Chien in August, 1825, to terminate hereditary hostilities and settle land claims.

William Clark of Missouri and Lewis Cass of Michigan, both ter-ritorial governors and ex officio superintendents of Indian affairs, conducted negotiations and arranged for several thousand dollars worth of food and gifts for the Indian delegates. The Chippewa, Sioux, Potawatomi, Winnebago, Sauk and Fox, and Iowa tribes were represented by more than 1,000 headmen and their families. Sault Ste. Marie Agent Schoolcraft arrived with a party of 150 Chippewas and an escort of 60 soldiers. From Fond du Lac, Mille Lacs, Cass, Leech, and Red lakes came still more Chippewa chiefs. Nearly 400 Sioux and Chippewas from southern Minnesota, accompanied by their agent Major Lawrence Taliaferro who was stationed at Fort Snelling, made a rather dramatic entrance to the council ground:

There was a halt before entering the town, at the "Painted Rock," where, after attending to their toilet and appointment of soldiers to dress the col-umns of boats, the grand entry was made with drums beating, many flags flying, with incessant discharges of small arms. All Prairie du Chien was drawn out, with other delegations already arrived, to witness the display and landing of this ferocious looking body of true savages.[26]

During the course of the conference, which lasted from August 5 to August 20, Clark and Cass worked out compromise boundary settlements. The most important dividing line was between the Sioux and Chippewa lands; it ran in a southeast direction across Minnesota and into Wisconsin (see map), and tribes could cross it only on peaceful missions. The Sioux and the federal negotiators thereby recognized as belonging to the Chippewas those hunting grounds which they captured east of the line during the previous century. All the Indian delegates seemed satisfied when they signed the peace treaty of Prairie du Chien, which involved no land cessions to the white man. Commissioners Cass and Clark believed that there was a spirit of fellowship, although minor violations were expected from headstrong young men.[27] Cass further strengthened the bonds of friendship when he and Commissioner of Indian Affairs Thomas L. McKenney met with several other Chippewa headmen from western Lake Superior at Fond du Lac in August, 1826, and won their full acceptance of the Prairie du Chien peace.[28]

Peace was short-lived. Indeed, during the same summer as the Fond du Lac council, the Sioux ambushed a Chippewa party on the east bank of the Mississippi, within view of Fort Snelling. One witness wrote that "Men, women, and children were indiscriminately butchered." Within a year or two, full-scale warfare raged on either side of the compromise dividing line, which the federal government did not even survey until 1835.[29] In May, 1827, Chief Flat Mouth and about thirty Chippewa men and their families visited Agent Taliaferro and camped near the walls of the fort. Nine seemingly friendly Sioux shared a meal there with them and smoked the peace pipe. After dark, they sneaked back and attacked the unsuspecting Chippewas. Colonel Josiah Snelling caught the culprits and delivered them to the Chippewas for punishment. One of the Sioux who was executed had many powerful friends and relatives; thus the vicious cycle of revenge continued.[30]

The BIA, disgusted with the general unrest on the Lake Superior frontier, ordered Agent Schoolcraft to warn the Chippewa chiefs in northern Michigan and northern Wisconsin that intertribal hostilities would not be tolerated. During the summer of 1831 Schoolcraft's small party traveled over two thousand miles halting warfare in that region. In 1832, Schoolcraft spent four months on a similar trip to talk with Chippewa bands in northern Minnesota. At Leech Lake, Flat Mouth scolded the president of the United States for not fulfilling government promises made at Prairie du Chien and Fond du Lac. Sioux raiders had recently killed many Chippewas, including the chief's son. His people had no choice but to fight the Sioux. They had lost respect for the white Americans; their letters of advice and their gifts—medals, ribbons, flags, wampum—were now covered with Chippewa blood. Flat Mouth threw down several medals at Schoolcraft's feet, asking that he wash the stains away and "make them again bright." In a final report, Schoolcraft claimed to have won promises of peace from several bands. With regard to Flat Mouth, he urged the construction of new forts at strategic locations and an immediate survey and marking of the Chippewa-Sioux boundary line.[31]

The War Department carried out Schoolcraft's recommendations, but the decade closed with a spectacular bloodletting during the summer of 1839. The Kopozha and Minnesota River Mdewakanton Sioux attacked a party of Chippewas who had come to Fort Snelling for annuities, killing one hundred and losing twenty-three of their own warriors. Intertribal fighting continued until the 1850's; by then the Santee Sioux were confined to reservations in southwest Minnesota, and white farmers had bought up ceded lands separating the warring tribes.[32]

The BIA also exercised increasing control over the annuity bands through its power to withhold money and supplies. Only the nonannuity Chippewas of northern Minnesota and the Sioux of the plains continued to fight regularly.[33] The tribes were separated once and for all after the Santees rose up against the white man in 1862, and Congress removed them to Dakota Territory. Thus ended 150 years of bloody, intertribal confrontations.

Ax-swinging settlers who pushed into Kitchigami land after the War of 1812 eventually had a far greater impact on lake Chippewa culture than either intertribal warfare with the Sioux or participation in the fur trade. The white vanguard consisted of religious missionaries and agents of the federal government bent on Christianizing and "civilizing" the red men of the south shore through formal education and the encouragement of an agrarian economy. In their wake came white developers, who by 1854 had forced the lake bands to surrender most of their ancestral lands and confine themselves to small reservations scattered from Grand Portage to Keweenaw Bay.

La Pointe, already a trading center, became the focus for governmental work among the Chippewas in 1826, when Schoolcraft stationed Subagent George Johnston on Madeline Island. Until that time, federal agents at the Sault and at Fort Snelling had no reliable or regular source of information about affairs in the interior, since only fur traders and a few missionaries lived among the scattered and remote Lake Superior bands.[34] La Pointe became an official subagency in 1836; fifteen years later it was made a full agency. Johnston's work consisted of regulating intercourse between the races, especially the licensing of traders, promoting Chippewa acculturation, and establishing communications between Washington and the local natives. He and his successors exercised much influ-

ence over Indian-white relations on the south shore, because they
controlled the distribution of valuable Indian annuity goods and
were the local representatives of the federal government. Until later
in the century they had no police force at their command and relied
on military support from fort commanders.[35]

The BIA appointed Daniel P. Bushnell the first permanent subagent for La Pointe in November, 1836, at an annual salary of $750.
When he arrived at his Madeline Island headquarters there were no
government buildings or fixed property. His personnel consisted of
one interpreter, Jean B. St. Ivan, who was paid $300 a year. As the
subagency's activities increased, Bushnell added to his staff Jere-
miah Russell, a government farmer, three blacksmiths, and three
assistant smiths.[36] One of the remote subagent's most serious administrative headaches during these early years was the lack of a
post office at La Pointe. Reliance on the private transport of mail to
and from the Sault often meant delays of six to eight months. A
letter sent from Washington on January 25, 1840, took fifteen
months to reach Madeline Island![37] By the mid-1840's, the La Pointe
subagency was playing a major role in the affairs of the Lake
Superior country. William Whipple Warren served as Subagent
James P. Hays' interpreter. Other officials included blacksmiths and
assistant smiths stationed at La Pointe, Fond du Lac, and Sandy
Lake; federal farmers at Bad River, Fond du Lac, and Sandy Lake;
and a carpenter at Fond du Lac.[38] In 1843 the subagency issued the
first accurate census of Chippewa bands living south and west of
Lake Superior.[39]

*Indians Receiving Annuities*

| Where | Number of Indians | Half-bloods | Total |
|---|---|---|---|
| La Pointe, Band 1 | 163 | 153 | 316 |
| La Pointe, Band 2 | 169 | 65 | 234 |
| La Pointe, Band 3 | 58 | — | 58 |
| Fond du Lac, Band 1 | 146 | 80 | 226 |
| Fond du Lac, Band 2 | 116 | — | 116 |
| Fond du Lac, Band 3 | 48 | 43 | 91 |
| Montreal River | 12 | 4 | 16 |
| Ke-we-we-non | 304 | 33 | 337 |
| On ta no gan | 87 | 28 | 115 |
| Lac Vieu Desert | 202 | 11 | 213 |
| Chippewa River, Band 1 | 159 | 8 | 167 |
| Chippewa River, Band 2 | 166 | 39 | 205 |
| Turtle Portage | 68 | — | 68 |
| Trout Lake | 82 | — | 82 |

## *Indians Receiving Annuities* (continued)

| *Where* | *Number of Indians* | *Half-bloods* | *Total* |
|---|---|---|---|
| Lac Cor tier ielle Band 1 | 103 | 10 | 113 |
| Lac Cor tier ielle Band 2 | 106 | — | 106 |
| Lac Flam beau | 198 | 76 | 274 |
| Wiskonsan River | 328 | 18 | 346 |
| Lac Che teck, Band 1 | 140 | 38 | 178 |
| Lac Che teck, Band 2 | 149 | 4 | 153 |
| Pelican Lake | 134 | — | 134 |
| Crow Wing, Band 1 | 120 | 29 | 149 |
| Crow Wing, Band 2 | 147 | — | 147 |
| Crow Wing, Band 3 | 76 | — | 76 |
| Crow Wing, Band 4 | 56 | 1 | 57 |
| Gull Lake | 59 | — | 59 |
| Red Ceder Lake | 131 | — | 131 |
| Yellow Lake | 126 | 7 | 133 |
| Po ka gum o, Band 1 | 111 | 10 | 121 |
| Po ka gum o, Band 2 | 40 | 12 | 52 |
| Sandy Lake, Band 1 | 125 | 79 | 204 |
| Sandy Lake, Band 2 | 74 | — | 74 |
| Snake River | 168 | 4 | 172 |
| St. Croix Lake | 71 | 8 | 79 |
| Mille Lac, Band 1 | 90 | — | 90 |
| Mille Lac, Band 2 | 61 | — | 61 |
| Rice River | 132 | — | 132 |

*Non-Annuity Bands: Population Based on Traders' Estimates*

| | | | |
|---|---|---|---|
| Leech Lake | 1000 | — | 1000 |
| Winne pee Lake | 200 | — | 200 |
| Cass Lake | 300 | — | 300 |
| Red Lake | 315 | — | 315 |
| Rainy Lake | 325 | — | 325 |
| Vermilion Lake | 200 | — | 200 |
| Hunters Island | 500 | — | 500 |
| Grand Portage | 145 | — | 145 |

Annuity payments, in return for the Chippewa land cessions of 1837 and 1842, eventually replaced the trade goods supplied by Nor'Westers and Astorians; likewise, the Indian agent took over many of the political, social, and economic functions once performed by fur traders in Chippewa society. A breakdown of the March, 1853, Congressional appropriation for the Lake Superior and Mississippi Chippewa bands indicates the amount of annuity goods and monies involved in a typical payment.[40]

According to the terms of Article 2 of the July 29, 1837 treaty:

$9,500 for the 17th of 20 installments in money;
$19,000 for the 17th of 20 installments in goods;
$3,000 for 17th of 20 installments for three smiths' shops,
    supporting three smiths, furnishing iron and steel;
$1,000 for 17th of 20 installments for farmers, purchase of
    implements, grain or seed, to carry on agricultural pursuits;
$2,000 for 17th of 20 installments for provisions;
$500 for 17th of 20 installments for tobacco.

According to the terms of Article 4 of the October 4, 1842 treaty:

$12,500 for the 12th of 25 installments in money;
$10,500 for the 12th of 25 installments in goods;
$2,000 for the 12th of 25 installments for support of two
    smiths' shops, including pay for two smiths, iron and steel;
$1,000 for 12th of 25 installments for two farmers;
$1,200 for 12th of 25 installments for pay of two carpenters;
$2,000 for 12th of 25 installments for school support;
$2,000 for 12th of 25 installments for provisions and tobacco.

The Indian Office shipped annuity goods to Madeline Island, where the La Pointe agent and his interpreter issued them when the bands arrived in September. Each Chippewa family came forward as its name was called from the roll and was identified by the band chief. Adults and children got point blankets which they spread out on the ground to hold other items. For the man, these items included broadcloth for pants, calico or linsey-woolsey for shirts, a comb, knife, gun, and lead for bullets; for the woman, a comb, dressmaking items (material, thread, thimble, needles, scissors), and tin plates. Flour, pork, and other food staples were also issued to adults. For the children there was cloth and a variety of other necessities. Families then tied up the corners of their blankets and packed them off. Cash payments to the Chippewas often ended up in the pockets of traders, who were permitted by the BIA to settle their accounts at the annuity ground.[41]

Washington's ignorance of the needs of woodland natives sometimes led to the purchase of ridiculously inappropriate annuity goods. The BIA once shipped saddles and bridles to the Chippewas, who had no horses and no need for them along the roadless and forested south shore. A few Indians, so the story went, tried unsuccessfully to mount the saddles in their canoes! The horse trappings eventually were sent to a warehouse in Detroit. Subagent Alfred

Brunson requested in January, 1843, that no more superfine cloth or ladies dress combs be sent to his charges. Cheap pots, pans, cutlery, thin blankets, and other poor goods were also a problem. Ammunition was rarely included in the shipments to the La Pointe sub-agency, and government guns were so poorly made that they often exploded, crippling scores of Indian hunters.[42]

A serious problem at annuity time was the presence of nefarious whiskey peddlers, attracted by the large amounts of cash and government goods. When the Indians consumed intoxicants, the results were the same as they had been for two hundred years: quarrels, drunken rows, murders, and occasional depredations on white communities. Attempts to stop the hucksters were largely unsuccessful, especially at the payment grounds. Troops stationed on the island made the lawbreakers more cautious, but could not stop them. In the summer, whiskey was smuggled to Madeline Island in dry-goods boxes. At annuity time the whiskey dealers disguised themselves as Indians and entered the Chippewa camps at night with flasks in their pockets. If one were caught, the nearest court with jurisdiction was three hundred miles away. Witnesses hated traveling so far, and Indians often would not testify. Frontier juries usually acquitted the culprits anyway.[43]

The BIA did not intend to make the Chippewas dependent on annuity payments forever. The land cession treaties of 1837, 1842, and 1854 provided for a cultural transformation of Lake Superior bands through a program of technical assistance and education. Government officials hoped that civilization of the "savage" Chippewas would improve their economic and social situation, restore peace to the troubled Northwest frontier, and free the BIA of a financial burden. Changing the character and condition of the red man involved three distinct steps, according to policy makers: abandonment of his seminomadic communal life; supplying him with needed agricultural equipment, blacksmith supplies, hogs, cattle, seeds, and sawmills or gristmills; and the establishment of schools to teach reading, writing, and Christianity. Early in 1818 the House Committee on Indian Affairs confidently predicted the changes that would come about:

Put into the hands of their children the primer and the hoe, and they will naturally, in time, take hold of the plough, and, as their minds become enlightened and expand, the Bible will be their book, and they will grow up in habits of morality and industry, leave the chase to those whose minds are less cultivated, and become useful members of society.[44]

There was much work to be done by the civilizers and Christianizers. Chippewa involvement in the Iron Age fur trade, as Schoolcraft observed in 1832, had modified their mode of living, dress, and subsistence, but it had made no significant change in their traditional culture.[45]

Two outstanding Christian missionaries to the Chippewas were the Reverend Leonard H. Wheeler, whose work at Bad River was supported by the American Board of Commissioners for Foreign Missions, a Congregationalist and New School Presbyterian evangelical organization, and Catholic Bishop Frederick Baraga.

Born to a Slovenian family in 1797 near Dobrnič, Austria, Baraga was educated at the Laibach Gymnasium, the University of Vienna, where he graduated with a law degree in 1821, and at Laibach Seminary. An aggressive and very able young man, Baraga came to America at his own request under the auspices of the Leopoldine Society, an Austrian missionary foundation. He preached among the Ottawas at Arbre Croche and Grand River, Michigan, until 1835, when he was transferred to La Pointe, where the Protestants were "deluding the poor Indians of that place into *damnable errors.*" Within a few months he had baptised more than a hundred converts and, with Indian help, built a log church, a residence for himself, and a school.[46]

Father Baraga's three decades of missionary work in Kitchigami land have been chronicled so extensively that it will suffice merely to sketch the highlights here.[47] Blessed with boundless energy, he not only tended his flock at La Pointe but journeyed by canoe in summer and snowshoed in winter to Grand Portage, Fond du Lac, and L'Anse, at the head of Keweenaw Bay. "It is little wonder," wrote local historian Hamilton N. Ross, that Baraga "was accepted in the lodges of the Indians as an honored and beloved guest."[48] He spent many long months studying the Chippewa language (the universal speech of the Superior country) and translating portions of the Bible into their native tongue. Two of the most useful published works were his *Theoretical and Practical Grammar of the Otchipwe Language* (Detroit, 1850) and his *Dictionary of the Otchipwe Language* (Cincinnati, 1853). Baraga also went to Europe to recruit priests and raise funds for his expanding mission.

In 1838, Baraga sent Father Francis Pierz to Grand Portage, where the Indians' poverty, famine, suffering, and needs were obvious. During the next ten years, Pierz and Father Otto Skolla built a mission church at Grand Portage and encouraged the Indians to farm and to send their children to the new Catholic school. Adequate financial and staff support for the mission was not forthcoming, however. By the mid-1840's the local Chippewas had changed little.[49] Far more successful was the mission Baraga personally started in 1844 among the L'Anse band. He made such rapid progress that within two years thirty-three families had converted to Catholicism, lived in wooden houses, and were farming the land. The priest also ministered to the spiritual needs of the white copper miners who came to the northern peninsula of Michigan in the early 1840's.[50]

In recognition of this work among the Chippewas and white settlers, in 1853 Baraga was consecrated the first Bishop of Upper Michigan. He guided the Lake Superior Catholic missions until his death in 1868.[51]

Baraga's task, as he saw it, was the creation of a series of new missions—at Arbre Croche, Grand River, La Pointe, L'Anse—each of which he entrusted to another Catholic clergyman as soon as it was well established. Wheeler, on the other hand, concentrated entirely on the Chippewa band at Bad River.

Born on April 18, 1811, in Shrewsbury, Massachusetts, Wheeler was an ordained minister who had determined to become a missionary upon first entering the theological seminary at Andover. In the summer of 1841 he and his wife, the Reverend and Mrs. Woodbridge L. James, and Miss Abigail Spooner arrived at the La Pointe mission station of the American Board.[52] It was founded ten years earlier by Frederick Ayer, the son of a Presbyterian minister, whom Lyman Warren had convinced to give up his job as a lay teacher at the Mackinac mission school and move to La Pointe. To assist Ayer the American Board sent other serious-minded and intense young missionaries and their wives, many of them Yankee educated: William T. Boutwell, Edmund T. Ely, Sherman Hall, Granville T. Sproat, James, and Wheeler. In the mid-1830's the Methodists, also active among the lake Chippewas, ran a day school at Lac Court Oreilles. The Methodist-Episcopal Church established a permanent mission at L'Anse in 1833.[53]

The devout missionaries at first adapted better to the physical frontier than to its native inhabitants. Sherman Hall reported in 1832:

There is no more healthy climate in the world than that about Lake Superior, and from thence to the head waters of the Mississippi; and no northern climate perhaps more agreeable, especially in the vicinity of the lake. I think we are less liable to violent and sudden changes of weather

here than in N. England. On the lake we do not experience greater degrees
of heat and cold than are common to the northern parts of N.E. We make use
of nearly the same kinds and quantity of clothing here, that we used to do at
the East. Our living is necessarily simple, being principally fish, salt meat
and bread. The staple article of living is fish which is taken out of the lake.
It is of good quality and every foreigner soon becomes fond of it as an article
of living. We raise garden vegetables of almost all kinds. There are no fruits
in the country except a few wild ones.[54]

Their reactions to Chippewa culture ran the gamut from perplexity
to horror. The shouting, wild dancing, and dog feasts that accompanied the burial ceremonies for local Indians shocked Mrs. Hall
and Mrs. Sproat. For the Reverend Boutwell it was the natives'
manners:

To see them eat is enough to disgust forever even a hungry man. All get
around the kettle, or soup dish, and each uses his fingers or the whole hand
even, to the best advantage. Children, entirely naked, except a strip of cloth
two inches in width, tied in a knot before, and which served for a breechcloth, these I could endure, but to see a squaw lick a kettle cover, both in
diameter and circumference, is a little too much.[55]

Nonetheless the missionaries made up in dedication what they
lacked in frontier experience; they studied the Chippewa language,
translated parts of the New Testament, wrote a Chippewa spelling
book, taught school for Indian children, held dual-language religious services, and built a complex of missionary buildings. By the
fall of 1840, a few months before Wheeler's arrival, the La Pointe
station boasted a school enrollment of sixty-four, with a daily average attendance of eighteen. Classes were taught in English and
Chippewa, with the result that twenty-six Indians could read the
Chippewa New Testament and twenty-one could read English.
Spelling, writing, composition, English grammar, arithmetic, geography, and drawing were also part of the curriculum. Valued at
$1,295, mission property included cattle, fishing gear, farming and
mechanical tools, buildings and improvements. All this was quite an
accomplishment when one considers that the American Board appropriated only $1,000 annually to support the missionaries, their
families, and the tuition-free school.[56]

Wheeler's primary purpose at La Pointe was to preach Christianity. Yet, like so many other missionaries among the Indians, he
realized the need to "civilize" and educate the red man so that he
could attain intellectual and economic independence and be saved
from extermination by "civilized" white frontiersmen. Wheeler be-

lieved this could best be done by having the seminomadic Chippewas settle down, by educating their children in mission schools,
and by raising their whole standard of living through the introduc-
tion of scientific farming. Since Madeline Island was unsuitable for
large-scale agriculture, he selected a level spot with rich soil on the
Bad River, nine miles east of present-day Ashland. The Chippewas
had once farmed a little at this place because it was so close to a
favorite sugar bush and was just south of the extensive wild rice
fields of Kakagan sloughs. Wheeler, his family, and a number
of willing Madeline Island Chippewas moved to Bad River on
May 1, 1845—thereby forming a nucleus for the Bad River band,
as it came to be called. He named the new mission Odanah, after the
Chippewa word *odena,* meaning village. By the early 1850's it consisted of comfortable and substantial houses for the staff, a school
building that operated throughout the year, and various outbuildings.[57]

As the holder of various civil offices in the newly formed La Pointe
county, Wheeler played a leading role in the affairs of white settlers
who moved to Chequamegon Bay. He was also the first to preach in
nearby Ashland. That the burden of so many duties oppressed him
was underscored in one of his wife's letters, penned in July 1853:

He has grown old fast since we returned from the East [where they had been
for a rest two years before], and I sometimes look anxiously forward to the
future. He is obliged to attend to all the secular affairs of our station, and
has charge of the property of the [mission] board here, oversees all our own
and the Indians' farming,—giving out their seed, plowing their ground, etc.
He is doctor for both places [Odanah and La Pointe], chairman of the board
of county commissioners, besides numberless other things too small to men-
tion perhaps, but which nevertheless break in upon his time and divert his
mind from his more appropriate work.[58]

Wheeler had good reason to feel encouraged in 1853 by what his
evangelical diligence had produced. Many of the Bad River Chippewas engaged in farming, sent their children to the mission school,
attended church services, abstained from their native dances, and
greatly reduced their addiction to alcohol. Wheeler considered the
following year to be one of particular progress; a number of Indians,
including three chiefs, joined the Christians and called themselves
"Praying Indians."[59]

Missionaries like Wheeler and Baraga labored long and un-
selfishly against staggering odds. Foremost was the cultural in-
transigence of the Chippewas, who as yet had no real reason to

abandon or modify their traditional ways. Sherman Hall observed in
the late 1830's:

Few are desirous to learn any thing of the religion of the Bible. Most seem to
have the impression that the white man's religion is not made for them. His
religion, mode of life, and learning are well for him; but to them they are of
no use. They would not make them any more successful in hunting and
fishing. Their habits are best for them. They say they are a distinct race,
and that the Great Spirit designed them to be different. They live dif-
ferently, and go to a different place when they die.[60]

Inadequate funds and staff for the missionaries, personal illness,
isolation, and the sheer physical difficulty of making the rounds to
distant Indian villages and cutting enough firewood to warm their
homes through seemingly endless, subzero winter months increased
the odds against the missionaries.[61] How many Chippewas converted completely to Christianity is a moot question which even
church records cannot answer satisfactorily; like their white
neighbors, the Chippewas found it rather easy to confine their
Christianity to Sunday mornings. More measurable successes may
be seen if we focus on the acculturation work of the missionaries. On
the eve of the La Pointe treaty council in 1854, the six-hundred-
member L'Anse band was comparatively "civilized." Many dwelt in
houses, dressed like whites, attended church and school at the
Catholic mission, and farmed the land. In 1848 they had produced
three thousand bushels of potatoes and five hundred of turnips, sold
furs worth twenty-five hundred dollars and salted five hundred barrels of fish.[62] Many of the Bad River Chippewas had also adopted the
white man's ways. Likewise, the small Grand Portage band at the
mouth of the Pigeon River on the north shore was making progress
again, and was considered one of the more "civilized" of the lake
bands.[63] This, however, was the extent of Chippewa acculturation
after about two decades of serious effort by missionaries and Indian
agents. The remote villages of Lac de Flambeau, Lac Court Oreilles,
and Fond du Lac received no regular attention from the civilizers
and consequently continued the traditional way of life.

A few missionaries and BIA bureaucrats posed no real threat to
Chippewa traditionalists. It was the invasion by copper miners,
lumbermen, farmers, and townbuilders, and their subsequent demand for removal or concentration of the red man, that precipitated
the climactic treaty of 1854. Local removal pressures were common
all along the American frontier—from Wisconsin to Florida—after
the War of 1812. In 1830, Congress made Indian removal a national

policy, and by mid-century nearly a hundred thousand eastern tribesmen had been driven beyond the Mississippi to the Louisiana Purchase tract.

In late July, 1837, about a thousand Chippewas from the Mississippi and Lake Superior bands met at Fort Snelling with federal commissioner Henry Dodge, governor of Wisconsin, and concluded a treaty ceding a large tract of land in north central Wisconsin and eastern Minnesota (see map). Dodge had never seen this area, but reports convinced him that it had plenty of pine timber and copper and was suitable for agriculture. He feared bloodshed if aggressive whites were not allowed to purchase and exploit this attractive region. In return for the sale the Chippewas received $70,000 to settle traders' claims, $100,000 in cash for influential half-breeds, $35,000 in annuities each year for twenty years, and the right to hunt, fish, and gather wild rice on their cession subject to removal at the pleasure of the president.[64] Washington's price was ridiculously low—about enough to furnish "a breechcloth and a pair of leggings apiece," lamented Lyman Warren. He was especially bitter because the Chippewa River and St. Croix River bands had surrendered most of the territory, yet had to share half the meager annuities with their Mississippi cousins. That the Chippewas had been seduced "to fritter away their large domain for temporary and local ends, without making any general and permanent provision for their prosperity" disturbed Schoolcraft. What would become of them after they relinquished all their homeland for promises of money and goods?[65]

As lumberjacks felled the woodland wealth of the 1837 cession, miners invaded Kitchigami land, spurred on by a Michigan State geologist's report of vast copper deposits on the south shore. The BIA had no choice but to arrange another treaty council with the Chippewas. Robert Stuart of Detroit, a former Astorian, went to La Pointe, and on October 4, 1842, representatives of the Mississippi and Lake Superior bands sold their last hunting grounds in northern Wisconsin and in the upper peninsula of Michigan as far east as Marquette (see map). The terms of the sale were similar to those of 1837: payoffs for traders and half-bloods ($75,000 and $15,000), a twenty-five year annuity schedule (with $36,200 to be appropriated annually and divided equally between the Mississippi and Lake Superior Chippewas) and the right to remain temporarily in the ceded region.[66]

While copper mining boomed on the south shore during the 1840's and 1850's, various presidents of the United States permitted the

Lake Superior Chippewas to remain temporarily in the ceded region in view of white farmers' disinterest in its dank pinelands, harsh winters, and short growing season. Soon, however, the BIA grew dissatisfied with this interim arrangement and recommended removing the Chippewas west of the Mississippi, where they would be beyond the reach of white frontiersmen, especially whiskey sellers, and could find permanent homes and engage in farming and other "civilized" pursuits. In the summer of 1847 Commissioner of Indian Affairs William Medill sent two officials to the south shore to arrange for Chippewa resettlement. But the bands had no intention of leaving their beloved land.[67] In the face of continued recommendations that they be removed, several Chippewa headmen went to Washington in 1849 to solicit a donation of lands encompassing seven of their present villages plus their sugar orchards and rice lakes. In their view, to be removed north to Canada or west among the vicious Plains tribes was tantamount to a death sentence.[68]

Nevertheless, on February 6, 1850, President Zachary Taylor ordered the Chippewas living on ceded land to be ready for removal that summer. Many tribesmen insisted they had only signed the 1842 treaty so that whites could dig the copper out of the south shore. They had no intentions of ever leaving.[69] The enforced exodus was postponed, but to lure the lake bands westward the BIA announced that annuities under the treaty of 1842 would be paid on October 15 at Sandy Lake, Minnesota, rather than at La Pointe. For the bands which did journey to Sandy Lake for supplies there was a long wait, because Agent S. Watrous did not arrive until late November. By that time sickness had decimated the malnourished Chippewas. Winter had the lake country in its icy grip when Watrous finished distributing supplies on December 3. The bands had to abandon their canoes and backpack the goods home to their villages—resolved more than ever to resist removal to Minnesota.[70]

Wheeler and the American Board also opposed removal, fearing that all of the effort and money invested in the La Pointe and Bad River missions would be lost. They further pointed out that local white settlers and miners had no desire to uproot the Indian. A joint resolution of the Michigan legislature in January, 1853, urged that Lake Superior Chippewas who were acculturated, voting citizens of the state not be moved to Minnesota. Later that year Agent Gilbert warned that the Indians "will sooner submit to extermination than comply" with the removal order. He advised abandoning the whole program.[71]

In 1852, during Millard Fillmore's administration, a Chippewa delegation to Washington convinced him to countermand the removal order.[72] Plans could thus begin for the La Pointe council. The BIA cooperated fully; by then it was interested in buying the rich mineral lands on the north shore and knew that the bands would never sell unless they could remain on reservations near Lake Superior.[73] In August, 1854, Commissioner Manypenny directed Agents Gilbert and Herriman to arrange for the treaty meeting at La Pointe—the most important event in Chippewa history since the coming of the white man.

The year 1854 was a turning point for the Lake Superior bands. It climaxed the traumatic times of the previous forty years and foreshadowed even greater cultural changes during the next century. After the War of 1812, American Fur Company outfits had encouraged the Chippewas to overtrap the north woods from Keweenaw to Grand Portage, leaving all the bands dangerously dependent upon white traders for food, clothing, political advice, and paternal leadership. Competitive fur companies bribed them with whiskey to procure pelts and thereby intensified Sioux-Chippewa warfare over dwindling game resources. Still, as Schoolcraft noted in 1832, Chippewas participation in the fur trade only somewhat modified their mode of living. Their south shore wilderness homeland and the heart of their seminomadic traditional culture (family-centered social ties; child rearing, marriage, death, and burial customs; religious thought and practice; art; music; loose political ties; transportation; cooperative economic spirit; seasonal rovings to sugar bush, fishing grounds, wild rice fields, garden and berry patches; and attitudes toward land ownership) remained unchanged. Far more significant changes were wrought by the agents of civilization: white Indian agents, missionaries, copper miners, farmers, lumbermen, and townbuilders. These men and women waged war on Chippewa culture and seized nearly all of Kitchigami land for white exploitation. From the Chippewa perspective there was some cause for optimism, however. By 1854 the lake bands, unlike so many of their uprooted cousins to the west, had at least retained a portion of their homeland at L'Anse, Ontonagon, Bad River, Red Cliff, Lac du Flambeau, Lac Court Oreilles, Fond du Lac, and Grand Portage. Moreover, missionaries like Wheeler and Baraga had made few radical changes in Chippewa lifestyles. On the darker side, again from the Chippewa point of view, their reservations were too small to maintain a traditional hunting-fishing-gathering economy. More than ever they were dependent on the white man's largess. Their precarious economic position and confinement on reservations by 1854 also made them rather vulnerable to the BIA's program of forced acculturation. Prior to 1854 the Chippewas had enjoyed the freedom of adopting only those features of white culture which appealed to them. The luxury of selectivity was no longer theirs; when chiefs touched their pens to the La Pointe treaty the bands began a new journey down the white man's road. For nearly a century it was a road without turning, a one-way street to cultural disintegration and crushing poverty.

# 6. Life on the New Reservations, 1854-1900

It would be profitable at this point to examine the new Chippewa reservations in Wisconsin, Michigan, and Minnesota. There it was hoped they would become "civilized" and sufficiently inculcated with the white man's work ethic to earn a living by farming.

Directly east of Ashland lay the Bad River Reservation, roughly rectangular and encompassing slightly more than five townships. Dense forests enveloped most of these lands except for a fan-shaped northern stretch at the mouth of the Bad River. Known as Kakagan Sloughs, it consisted of twelve square miles of wild rice fields alive with fish and nesting waterfowl. A thick stand of sugar maple, elm, basswood, and ash carpeted the fertile river bottoms of the Bad, Marengo, Potato, and the White. The level uplands were also fertile for producing crops suitable to the climate. Bad River apparently could support a large Indian population.[1] An executive order in 1856 added sixteen sections to the one set aside for Buffalo's band, thereby creating the Red Cliff Reservation, whose red sandstone cliffs jutted into Lake Superior at the northern tip of Bayfield County. Back from its fingernail coastline the reserve was rich in soil, timber, water, and wild fruit.[2] The Lac Court Oreilles band lived in Sawyer County, southwest of Ashland, on a rolling, heavily wooded tract with many lakes. Game was scarce, but fish and a variety of fruits (strawberries, raspberries, blueberries, cranberries) abounded. The reservation's French name, meaning "Lake of Short Ears," probably refers to the many bays extending inland from the main lake. In Vilas County, to the east, a reserve of about the same size—approximately four townships—was assigned to the Lac du Flambeau band. More than 126 spring-fed lakes dotted the majestic cedar and spruce forests. The practice of spearing fish by torchlight explained the Indians' name for the area: Waus-Waug-Im-Ing, or "Lake of Torches."[3]

Five reserves lay outside Wisconsin. The treaty set apart ninety square miles at the head of Keweenaw Bay for the L'Anse and Vieux de Sert bands. The well-watered land could grow vegetables adapted to the latitude. By 1855 the tract had been surveyed and subdivided;

the Indians merely awaited the allotment of farms to each family. Likewise fit for agriculture was the township on Lake Superior assigned to the tiny Ontonagon band, but these Michigan Chippewas preferred to fish for a living. No land was cleared and no houses built.[4] Just west of Duluth, Minnesota, and south of the St. Louis River, lay the Fond du Lac Reservation, comprising five townships of rolling meadows and timberland, which, if cleared, could be cultivated. Streams and lakes were well stocked with fish and fowl. The Grand Portage Reserve, in the extreme northeast corner of Minnesota, 150 miles from Duluth, boasted one of the most beautiful shorelines on Lake Superior. However, its rugged and stony surface offered little timber or farmland of value. Doubtless the band would have to rely largely on fishing for subsistence.[5] Article XII of the La Pointe treaty encouraged the Bois Forte band to select a reservation, but by 1866 their chosen land at Vermilion Lake, some hundred miles west of Grand Portage, had not been defined, and the Indians ceded claim to it in a treaty that April. To compensate them, the United States laid out 107,509 forested and swampy acres at Nett Lake, forty miles northwest of Vermilion Lake and about the same distance from the Canadian border. The reserve, encompassing extensive wild rice fields and blueberry marshes, could best be reached in winter by dog train or on snowshoes. Executive orders established two additional tracts for the Bois Forte: 1,080 acres at Vermilion Lake in December, 1881, and one township on Grand Fork River at the mouth of Deer Creek in June, 1883. Moose, caribou, deer, and black bears still roamed in large numbers throughout the Bois Forte country.[6]

Until the 1930's the federal government's primary goal for the reservation Chippewas was "civilization" (or acculturation), meaning eradication of the most apparent features of Chippewas traditional culture and their replacement by such white cultural traits as the work ethic in reference to cultivating the soil. Once this was accomplished, "assimilation" (or social integration) and economic self-sufficiency would logically follow.

Data about Chippewa acculturation before 1854 is meager. As previously noted, many of the L'Anse, Bad River, and Grand Portage tribesmen lived in houses, dressed like whites, sent their children to school, and attended Christian church services. Some farmed. Others, in isolated villages at Red Cliff, Lac du Flambeau, Lac Court Oreilles, Fond du Lac, and west of Grand Portage, kept more of their traditional ways. Since the mid-nineteenth century

the BIA has systematically collected information about the adoption
of white cultural traits by the Lake Superior bands, thereby making
possible a more precise measurement of the rate of Chippewa "civilization." Economic figures include tribal and individual land ownership, family incomes, occupation of the head of the house, and seasonal sources of subsistence—production of maple sugar, fishing,
berry picking, wild rice gathering, hunting, and trapping. Data
about housing, transportation, and health enable us to generalize
about the standard of living. Educational facts on Indian enrollment, dropout rate, and achievement tests scores are also available.
Of less importance to federal fact-gatherers was the persistence of
Chippewa social customs (clan relations, child rearing, courtship
and marriage, village life, death and burial rites), religious thought
and practice, artistic expression, and tribal political organization.
Thus the historian cannot speak with as much authority about these
significant facets of acculturation.

To the BIA fell the task of promoting Chippewa acculturation.
Stationed first at Bayfield, Wisconsin, and after 1881 at Ashland,
the La Pointe agent supervised the affairs of lake Chippewas from
Keweenaw Bay west to Vermilion Lake until 1897. The Mackinac
Agency was then reactivated and given charge of the L'Anse and
Ontonagon bands. Notwithstanding such farflung responsibility,
Agent Isaac L. Mahan was allotted only a fifteen-hundred-dollar
annual salary during the late 1870's and an equally modest staff: a
superintendent-clerk, a storekeeper, an interpreter, a farmer, a
blacksmith, and a teacher at Red Cliff; an interpreter, a farmer, and
a blacksmith at Bad River; a farmer and a teacher at Lac Court
Oreilles; a farmer and a blacksmith at Vermilion Lake; and at
Grand Portage a teacher.[7]

Problems with whiskey peddlers and rowdyism among the young
men at Grand Portage prompted Mahan to use Indian police and
judges to assist in local government. Reservation residents elected
five policemen, including one captain, who were trained in peace-
keeping procedures, then uniformed and commissioned. Reportedly,
their new positions were a source of much pride. The reservation
court, with three elderly chiefs presiding, tried persons arrested
for misdemeanors, thefts, and other felonies. No corporal punishment could be meted out. Mahan deemed the experiment at Grand
Portage a modest success.[8]

Efforts to establish police units at other reservations brought
mixed results. During the summer of 1889, for example, the Bad

River council unanimously authorized Agent M. A. Leahy to train
an Indian force for protection against trespassers, whiskey dealers,
and other lawless elements. Two years later the band requested that
the unit be dissolved because three of the four policemen were
habitual drunkards.[9] The force was maintained at Bad River, and so
was the alcohol problem. Two particularly troublesome officers
ought to have been replaced, according to reservation farmer Roger
Patterson, but it was difficult to attract policemen of better character when the government paid them only ten dollars a month. Despite such pernicious problems, small native police units at Bad
River, Lac du Flambeau, Lac Court Oreilles, Fond du Lac, and Vermilion Lake maintained better law and order and helped the La
Pointe Agency to enforce the directives of its farmers.[10]

Economic acculturation was spurred on when it became obvious
that the new reservations, despite their rustic beauty, lacked essential resources to support in the traditional manner the growing
number of natives. By the 1890's, the L'Anse and Ontonagon residents numbered 850; 609 Chippewas were enrolled in the Bad River
band, 500 at Red Cliff, 1,214 at Lac Court Oreilles, 669 at Lac du
Flambeau, 735 at Fond du Lac, 315 at Grand Portage, and 774 at
Bois Forte.[11] The seminomadic Chippewas stayed on the reservations only in winter and supported themselves by hunting, fishing, and gathering forest products. But this livelihood was unreli-
able. During the fall of 1869, cold rains and floods destroyed the wild
rice crop; deep snows followed which killed game and kept Chippewa
hunters out of the woods. Some survivors fled to white settlements,
but many died of starvation and exposure.[12]

The rapid growth of new industries and towns on the south shore
provided employment opportunities outside the reservation. Ashland, Wisconsin, in the heart of the lake Chippewa country, was
founded about the time of the La Pointe treaty and has played an
important role in reservation affairs ever since. Flush times began
in 1877 with the Wisconsin Central's first regular rail service between Ashland and key cities on Lake Michigan. As a port where
rails and lake freighters met, it became an important shipping
center. Forty miles southeast of Ashland lay the Gogebic Iron
Range; the tapping of its fabulous ore deposits in the mid-1880's
triggered a widespread mining boom, making Ashland a chief ben-
eficiary. Trains hauled ore to its several loading docks, and ships
then took the cargo to lower lake ports to feed the hungry furnaces of

American steel mills. Brownstone quarried nearby and timber were also shipped from Ashland. By 1890, eight sawmills buzzed day and night. Four railroads served the town, whose population had climbed to 9,956. Ashland's frame houses and bustling business district lay on a plateau at the edge of the forest and curved for five miles around the south shore of the bay. Chequamegon's icy blue waters were busily astir as lake boats steamed in and out with ore and lumber barges in tow.[13]

While old men and sturdy women, with their daughters and small children, farmed patches at Bad River and Red Cliff, several of the men found jobs more to their liking (at $1.25 to $2.50 a day) in Ashland mills, sash-and-door factories, and in cooper, blacksmith, and carpentry shops. After the survey and allotment of their reservation in the mid-1870's, Bad River Indians realized additional monies from the lumber industry. Between 1886 and 1894, for example, forest products marketed along the lines of the two railroads that crossed the reservation amounted to $400,000. Indian men also worked in lumber camps driving logs down rivers and as choppers, sawyers, pilers, and loaders.[14] Red Cliff and Michigan bands worked in sawmills and also for mining companies as wood choppers and loaders. Some Red Cliff men signed on as deck hands aboard lake freighters; others operated a small fishing fleet which, with the use of gill and pound nets, brought back large enough catches to sell at nearby Bayfield.[15] The Northern Pacific and the Duluth and Winnipeg railroads passed through Fond du Lac and furnished a market for Indian timber. Another outlet was the flourishing town of Cloquet, Minnesota, just east of the reservation. Young men worked in logging camps, at sawmills, and with the railroads, while their families gathered berries, fished, and hunted.[16] Some of the Grand Portage Chippewas were packers and guides into the remote mining districts of the United States and Canada. Some at Vermilion Lake held jobs in neighboring iron mines, but the expense of transported foodstuffs—flour sold for twenty dollars per hundred pounds—devalued their real wages.[17]

Seminomadic bands also relied on annuity payments, much like the traders' provisions of an earlier era. The following figures from the 1856 Congressional appropriation indicate the level of Washington's support: (1) the last of twenty installments under the treaty of July, 1837, included $6,333.33 in money, $12,666.67 in goods, $1,333.33 for provisions, and $333.33 for tobacco; (2) in accordance with the treaty of October, 1842, the fifteenth of twenty-five payments included $8,333.33 in money, $7,000 in goods, $1,333.33 for school support, and $1,333.33 for provisions and tobacco; (3) the second of twenty installments under the treaty of September, 1854, was $19,000 in coin, goods, household furniture, cooking utensils, agricultural implements, cattle, tools, and building materials, $5,040 for six smiths and assistants, $1,320 for the support of smith shops, and $2,000 for the second of five installments in blankets, cloths, nets, guns, and ammunition for the Bois Forte.[18] When appropriations set by the treaty of 1854 expired in the mid-1870's, Congress continued supporting reservation schools, blacksmiths, and farmers. By 1899 the appropriation had declined to a total of $7,125, which included $1,200 for a physician.[19]

The obvious lack of economic opportunity and the Chippewas' seminomadic ways drove them away from the reservations. Until the BIA settled them on their reserves, there was little hope of agricultural self-sufficiency. Two years after the La Pointe treaty the BIA advocated further concentration of the scattered bands—to superintend their farming operations with such a limited staff would be impossible. In 1863, both the Commissioner of Indian Affairs and the Secretary of the Interior urged a visiting Indian delegation to consolidate on one or two reservations. The chiefs and headmen presented the idea at home, but the young men refused.[20] Pressure from Washington to concentrate the bands intensified in the early 1870's. Congress selected Bad River to receive the Chippewas from Fond du Lac, Lac Court Oreilles, and Lac du Flambeau, whose lands were considered unsuitable for agriculture and who were too remote for BIA guidance and protection. When annuities expired in 1874 these bands surely would become vagrants, squeezed by white settlers and railroaders from all sides. The La Pointe agent reported the consent of the Fond du Lac Chippewas in 1872, but on the appointed day most of the band claimed they had never agreed to relocate. When the Lac du Flambeau and Lac Court Oreilles refused to move, the consolidation program was abandoned.[21] The only option left to the BIA was to confine the Chippewas, if possible, and to encourage agriculture simultaneously on all the reservations.

At first, farming proved neither a profitable nor an appealing substitute for traditional woodland resources. Tribesmen roamed, half-starved, through the territory ceded in the 1840's and 1850's—

hunting, gathering, fishing, looking for employment, and stealing pigs, chickens, and geese from white farmers. Cultivation of the soil was "women's work" in the eyes of Chippewa males, but there were other reasons for the early lack of agricultural success on the reservations. The Indians insisted that the government first clear the heavy timber—at a cost of twenty-five to thirty dollars an acre— before they could farm. They also demanded provisions until the crops were harvested. Agents reported that the Chippewas actually favored the adoption of "civilized habits," though they needed constant encouragement, technical advice, and financial support. Unfortunately, the reserves were too widely scattered to make this possible. In addition to these drawbacks, the growing season in Kitchigami land was so short and the climate so cold that only root crops and garden vegetables thrived, particularly potatoes, turnips, beets, parsnips, and cabbages. Even if corn and wheat had time to mature, the BIA owned no mills, and transportation costs to Detroit would be more than the meal and flour were worth. Of 536,840 reservation acres in 1868, about 115 were cultivated by the Indians and 100 by government farmers. The Chippewas simply lacked the incentive to settle down during these early reservation years. Those who tried it were equally destitute. Even industrious white farmers could not make a good living in the northland.[22]

By the 1860's, as an incentive for individual family farming and self-support, the BIA began allotting the Lake Superior Chippewa reservations into eighty-acre tracts, as provided for in the Madeline Island treaty. On a national scale, allotment was also promoted by the Dawes Severalty Act of 1887. Federal allotment agents had detailed instructions about how to divide Chippewa reserves. Heads of Indian families were to select choice portions of the reserves, which encompassed improvements already made. A Chippewa woman married to a white man was considered head of the family for allotment purposes. Persons of mixed blood were required to make sworn statements, substantiated by two witnesses, that they (or their parents) were recognized members of the band on whose reservation they desired an allotment. Chippewa tracts were to be kept contiguous when possible, and each allottee shown the distinctly marked boundaries of his or her land.[23] Under provisions of the La Pointe treaty and the Dawes Act, the Indians received trust payments; allotments could be sold only with the consent of the president. Experience had taught the BIA that when fee simple

titles were given, red men frequently bartered lands away at
ridiculously low prices. By August, 1900, after more than three decades of federal allotment efforts, La Pointe Agent S. W. Campell
reported the following figures:[24]

| Reservation | Number of Allotments | Number of Acres |
|---|---|---|
| Bad River | 662 | 51,884.02 |
| Red Cliff | 205 | 14,166.01 |
| Lac du Flambeau | 458 | 36,634.32 |
| Lac Court Oreilles | 702 | 54,862.13 |
| Fond du Lac | 450 | 30,296.73 |
| Grand Portage | 304 | 24,191.31 |
| Totals | 2,781 | 212,034.52 |

Allotment was only a first step. The Chippewas were then
strongly encouraged to farm their small tracts and become self-
supporting as soon as possible. Washington had had enough of the
high cost of feeding reservation red men. Congress passed a bill in
1884 denying government provisions to able-bodied reservation Indians who refused to work. It seemed that the time had come when
the red man must farm or starve. A few years later, government
farmers—second in importance only to the agents—were brought
under closer supervision and ordered to be more forceful in encouraging and assisting Indian agriculture. Chippewas who already
farmed should be told to expand their operations; others should be
encouraged to begin, and given needed assistance. Indians ought to
have the proper tools and be taught how to use them. Agency farmers were told to provide help and advice about dozens of matters that
make for successful agriculture: plowing and seeding in the fall,
proper cultivation, harvesting and hay-making, storage of crops,
care of milk cows, oxen, and brood mares, and the maintenance
of fences, and equipment. By setting good personal examples, government farmers could show the Chippewas that self-support was
possible, and that such work need not be degrading. So that the
Commissioner of Indian Affairs could judge the effectiveness of
this more aggressive promotion of agriculture, government farmers
henceforth had to dispatch monthly reports to Washington.[25]

Agricultural statistics collected in the 1890's showed the produc-
tivity of the allotment farms (see table, opposite page).[26]

These figures alone are misleading unless compared with total

Lake Superior Chippewa Reservations in 1895 (except those in Michigan)

| Bushels of Wheat | Bushels of Oats and Barley | Bushels of Corn | Bushels of Vegetables | Tons of Hay | Pounds of Butter Made | Cords of Wood Cut | Value of Products of Indian Labor Sold | Indian-owned Horses & Mules | Indian-owned Cattle | Indian-owned Swine | Domestic Fowl |
|---|---|---|---|---|---|---|---|---|---|---|---|
| — | 200 | 100 | 2,350 | 50 | 300 | 200 | $1,200 | 7 | 15 | — | 500 |
| — | — | 200 | 13,120 | 200 | 400 | 200 | 2,000 | 93 | 72 | 18 | 450 |
| — | 50 | 200 | 10,735 | 400 | 500 | 40 | 6,200 | 24 | 85 | — | 800 |
| — | — | — | 865 | 30 | — | 200 | 2,000 | — | 15 | — | 50 |
| — | — | 400 | 1,070 | 250 | — | 700 | — | 122 | 250 | 150 | 1,000 |
| — | 50 | 50 | 4,100 | 50 | — | 75 | 3,600 | 6 | 6 | 20 | 100 |
| — | — | 200 | 735 | 25 | — | 400 | 1,000 | 40 | 9 | — | 225 |

L'Anse and Vieux de Sert Reservation in 1898

| Bushels of Wheat | Bushels of Oats and Barley | Bushels of Corn | Bushels of Vegetables | Tons of Hay | Pounds of Butter Made | Cords of Wood Cut | Value of Products of Indian Labor Sold | Indian-owned Horses & Mules | Indian-owned Cattle | Indian-owned Swine | Domestic Fowl |
|---|---|---|---|---|---|---|---|---|---|---|---|
| 25 | 175 | 3,000 | 2,100 | 250 | — | 1,000 | — | 40 | 200 | — | 500 |

reservation populations and allotments. By the turn of the century, for example:[27]

| Reservation | Estimated Population | Allotments |
|---|---|---|
| Bad River | 609 | 662 |
| Red Cliff | 500 | 205 |
| Lac Court Oreilles | 1,214 | 702 |
| Lac du Flambeau | 660 | 458 |
| Fond du Lac | 735 | 450 |
| Grand Portage | 315 | 304 |

At Bad River, families lived on only 79 of the 662 allotments, and only 754 acres of their 51,884.02 were under cultivation. At Lac Court Oreilles only 163 of 702 allotments were regularly occupied, and of 54,862.13 total acres, only 650 were farmed. Statistics were similar on other reserves. Obviously, Chippewa agriculture was still in its early stages by 1900, and provided but a minor source of food and income.

One of the biggest roadblocks to Chippewa agriculture had been the magnificent pine and hardwood forests which enveloped the reservations and, in the eyes of the BIA, prolonged the traditional woodland culture. If their land was cleared of timber, the reasoning was, then larger numbers of Chippewas could cultivate the soil. And since annuities had expired in the mid-1870's, lumbering would also generate a new source of income. Consequently, in 1882 the Interior Department granted Chippewa allottees the right to cut and sell standing timber from their eighty-acre tracts under the supervision of the BIA.[28]

Two other factors contributed to the upper Great Lakes lumber bonanza in the late nineteenth and early twentieth centuries. First, a great demand for new homes, barns, and fences was created when the white settler surged onto the prairies and plains of the Louisiana Purchase country during the Civil War era. Though fertile, the farmland was generally treeless. But forests stretching across Kitchigami land contained apparently inexhaustible stands of white pine, which was easily worked and light enough to float down on the large streams that laced the north woods. Thousands of lakes and rivers provided storage for logs and power for sawmills. Finally, the railroads opened up previously inaccessible portions of the lake country to timber companies and linked them with Great Plains farmers. Little wonder that lumbering boomed on the reservations and elsewhere along the south shore. In 1899, Wisconsin led the nation by harvesting 3.4 billion board feet of timber.[29]

The average Indian allottee lacked the business experience, equipment, and capital to log his own tract. From the beginning, the Chippewas contracted with experienced white lumbermen to dispose of their timber. Contractors set up the isolated winter logging camps, constructed the forest roads, hired dozens of high-priced lumberjacks, foremen, and cooks (the cost of running one such winter camp often exceeded $10,000), hauled in provisions and other equipment with teams of oxen and horses, and cut and banked the timber on the driving stream. All camp expenses were charged against the contracted price paid to the landowners. If the logger managed well, the patentee received his fair net return for his timber. Yet all the risks were his; the contractor escaped all costs of delivering banked logs—even those caused by accidents of weather.[30]

The BIA minimized the risks by regulating the price of native timber, insisting that only reliable and properly bonded contractors logged reservation lands, and supervising the camps so that the tribesmen were not exploited and the intercourse laws were observed. (Indian forest workers, whom contractors were required to hire when available, reportedly became expert and industrious loggers but could not be depended upon to remain regularly at their jobs. Protected from competition with cheaper white workers, inefficient native crews further increased the costs passed on to allottees.)[31] Initially the La Pointe agent only managed the cash timber profits paid to Chippewa landowners deemed incompetent. But beginning in the 1890's, because some Indians squandered their proceeds on whiskey, trinkets, and gambling, the BIA demanded that the Indians spend the money for permanent improvements on each allotment—such as construction of a house or pulling stumps in preparation for planting.[32]

Bad River Indians also played a role in regulating the local contractor, the J. S. Stearns Lumber Company. During a band council meeting in May, 1895, which Stearns attended, members selected a three-man Business Committee to investigate each month the fairness of logging camp hiring practices and prices charged at the company store. Any differences arising between the committee and Stearns were to be adjusted with the help of the agent and the government farmer.[33]

During the 1883–84 season the Chippewas, with the guidance of the BIA, signed eighty-eight contracts with white lumber companies, which felled over 48,000,000 feet of timber valued at more than $250,000. Indian logging reached a high point in 1888, when 731 contracts for cutting and banking pine timber yielded 190,206,080 board feet which sold for $4.75 to $7.00 per 1,000 feet. Between 1894 and 1922, the J. S. Stearns Lumber Company paid $6,813,373 for one and a quarter billion feet of timber taken from Bad River, and spent over a million dollars in wages for hundreds of Indian lumberjacks. The company mill at Odanah was eventually enlarged to a capacity of sixty million board feet a year. Stearns shipped thousands of carloads of lumber by rail throughout the Midwest.[34]

Large-scale logging altered the lifestyles of many Indians. By white standards, the general condition of Indian communities improved as more and more natives abandoned hunting and fishing and worked in logging camps or on allotment farms. Pine profits paid for comfortable houses and good farm machinery. Some Chippewas bought logging outfits and took timber contracts. Such prosperous tribesmen stimulated others "to live better and accumulate property," according to Agent James T. Gregory, who predicted that those adopting white work habits and other customs would never return to their traditional way of living—thanks to reservation logging. In February, 1889, Secretary of the Interior William F. Vilas reported to the United States Senate:[35]

The removal of the pine from lands belonging to Indians in severalty is no more to be deplored, if they have enjoyed fair compensation for its value, than the clearing of the forests everywhere before civilized improvement.

Chippewa cultural "progress" was great, but so was their dependence on lumber monies, which amounted to $428,221.41 during the winter of 1887–88. Gregory predicted, ominously, that if logging operations ever ceased, there would be great hardship and unrest on the reservations.[36] In 1889, the Interior Department suspended timber sales because of irregularities; the following February Congress had to authorize an emergency appropriation of $75,000 just to keep the bands alive until summer. Besides clothing, the La Pointe agent purchased with the funds:[37]

2,000 barrels of mess pork
3,343 pounds of baking powder
10,000 pounds of bacon
13,375 pounds of salt

20,060 pounds of beans
100,000 pounds of corn meal
325,000 pounds of flour

The Chippewas were also vulnerable to encroachment by un-authorized lumber crews, which stripped timber from reservations without much fear of capture and prosecution. The seriousness of this problem forced the enactment of special federal anti-trespass legislation in 1888.[38] The most notorious timber fraud, however, concerned illegally obtained Chippewa half-blood scrip.

The treaty of 1854 unwittingly unlocked a treasure in federal timberlands. The seventh clause of Article 2 provided, as was common in such agreements, that:[39]

Each head of a family or single person over twenty-one years of age at the present time of the mixed bloods, belonging to the Chippewas of Lake Superior, shall be entitled to eighty acres of land, to be selected by them under the direction of the President, and which shall be secured to them by patent in the usual form.

By the close of 1856, Agent Gilbert had issued to 312 mixed bloods land certificates which contained a clause forbidding their sale, transfer, or mortgage. This should have ended Washington's obliga-tion to the Chippewa half bloods. Instead, it was but the prelude to a lurid tale of theft and deceit. In 1863, by ruling that mixed-blood scrip applicants need not have lived among the Chippewas of Lake Superior at the time of the treaty, the commissioner of Indian affairs threw open to white scalawags the lands ceded at La Pointe. Rationalizing that since all Chippewas were related (thereby all were Chippewas of Lake Superior), organizations at La Pointe and St. Paul ferreted out mixed bloods as far away as the Red River of the North and induced them to apply for government scrip. By the mid-1860's the Interior Department had approved 564 requests. In-dian applicants subsequently executed powers of attorney to white speculators who were free to receive and locate the tracts as well as strip them of valuable pine timber. A special commission in 1871 investigated these swindles and exposed a shockingly large number of fraudulent applications made by whites posing as Chippewas, by Indians applying more than once, by deceased half bloods, and by husbands and wives each claiming headship for the same family. The commission recommended cancellation of the illegally-obtained scrip. Further investigation revealed that, except for the original Gilbert certificates and forty-five other grants, the rest were so tainted by fraud as to be of no value.[40]

During their first fifty years of reservation life, many of the more than fifty-six hundred enrolled Lake Superior Chippewas turned to new enterprises in order to make a living. Figures released by the BIA about the turn of the century reveal the extent of Chippewa economic acculturation:[41]

### Percentage of Each Band's Subsistence

| | Labor in Civilized Pursuits | Hunting, Fishing, Gathering | Government Annuities |
|---|---|---|---|
| Red Cliff | 37 | 50 | 13 |
| Bad River | 95 | 5 | — |
| Lac Court Oreilles | 50 | 50 | — |
| Lac du Flambeau | 87 | 13 | — |
| Fond du Lac | 90 | 5 | 5 |
| Grand Portage | 50 | 44 | 6 |
| Bois Forte | 34 | 66 | — |
| L'Anse and Vieux de Sert | 100 | — | — |

By 1900, the Interior Department had allotted 2,781 heads of families over 212,034.52 acres of reservation land, with the hope that they would farm and support themselves.[42] While the tracts were cleared of timber by white contractors, agricultural progress was slow—only 2,865 acres were farmed by Indians in the mid-1890's;[43] but with substantial timber profits available for making permanent improvements on individual allotments and for buying farm machinery, there was real reason for optimism about the reservation Chippewa's ability, with encouragement and technical assistance from government farmers, to support themselves by means of agriculture.

Just as intensive acculturation on the reservation changed the old Chippewa economy "from a food-gathering to a money-gathering" system, as anthropologist Robert Ritzenthaler put it, it also modified their standard of living. Thousands of woodland hunters and their families abandoned traditional seminomadic ways and lived on the tracts assigned to various bands.[44] By the late 1890's, the portable birch-bark wigwams gave way to one-room log or frame cabins. Nearly a thousand such dwellings dotted the reserves, and each housed one to three families. Tubercular red men, coughing away in smoke-filled rooms, must have doubted the virtues of reservation life. But in the eyes of the BIA, busily compiling housing statistics, this was "progress": 46 cabins occupied by Chippewas at Red Cliff, 175 at Bad River, 210 at Lac Court Oreilles, 148 at Lac du Flambeau, 85 at Fond du Lac, 65 at Grand Portage, 120 at Bois Forte and 150 at L'Anse.[45]

Once the reservation Chippewas contracted diseases like tuberculosis, their fatality rate exceeded that of neighboring whites. Agency physicians attributed the difference largely to the crowded and poorly ventilated Indian cabins, where the sick and the well breathed the same air. (During the winter of 1893–94, Dr. James H. Spencer visited an elderly Chippewa couple dying of tuberculosis. They were huddled in the same room with sixteen others. He found the "filth and stench" almost unbearable.) Lack of cleanliness likewise characterized Chippewa clothing, bedding, and food preparation—further frustrating the physician who tried to treat a patient. The Indians were often unwilling to nurse the sick. Whatever the season of the year, if a Chippewa family judged that a member would soon die, he was carried to a specially built shelter near the cabin. Here the doctors sometimes found him critically, but not always fatally, ill—cold, wet, and choking amidst smoky smudge fires. As more and more Indian families received allotments and built cabins, tuberculosis became their most serious health problem. Still, La Pointe Agency officials were hopeful about the improvement of health conditions. In 1895, the Chippewa birth rate exceeded the death rate. An increasing number of Indians sought treatment from white doctors and showed less confidence in tribal medicine men.[46]

Another way to make sure that the Lake Superior Chippewas would not remain "savage, uncivilized, uneducated" and "dependent" was the establishment of one or more government schools on all reservations by the 1890's. Each frame schoolhouse, valued at between seven and eight hundred dollars and having room for about thirty-five students, was heated by a woodburning stove. It had no indoor plumbing. Teachers' quarters were either attached to the school or located nearby.[47] Since the late 1850's the most impressive complex had been Wheeler's Odanah mission; it included a day school and a commodious boarding school with two wings, built at a cost of eight thousand dollars, of which the federal government contributed three thousand. In Bayfield, near the Red Cliff reserve, was another Chippewa boarding school.[48] Curriculum was designed to give Indian children a practical education and to prepare them for citizenship, as envisioned by the Dawes Act. Besides the usual curriculum of reading, writing, spelling, English grammar and composition, arithmetic, geography, and drawing, Commissioner Thomas J. Morgan in 1889 encouraged Indian schools across the country to teach patriotism. Civics talks, use of appropriate textbooks, flying the American flag on school grounds, singing patriotic songs, observing national holidays and the anniversary of the Dawes Act (February 8, 1887) all were encouraged in order to awaken in the pupils a "reverence for the Nation's power, gratitude for its beneficence, pride in its history, and a laudable ambition to contribute to its prosperity." Instruction in American history might include the "wrongs of their [Indians'] ancestors" and the "injustice which their race has suffered," but primarily should emphasize the duties and opportunities open to red citizens for earning a livelihood and "honorable places in life."[49]

Truancy, the foremost problem faced by Indian schools, thwarted the best-laid educational plans. Some families lived so far from the school that their children could not come every day. Others were disinterested or openly hostile to white man's education. For most Chippewa pupils, however, it was the seasonal moves of their families—to sugar bush, berry patches, fishing and hunting grounds, wild rice fields—that prevented their regular attendance.[50] One solution was the boarding school, advocated by Leonard Wheeler. It separated the children from the degrading influence of their "heathen homes." Besides the regular course of study, similar to that prescribed for state public schools, instructors at Bad River taught industrial arts to the boys, utilizing the boarding school's shop and farm, and domestic arts to the girls.[51] The boarding school, efficient but expensive, was not a practical educational solution for all native children; Congress therefore strengthened the network of day schools in 1891 by ordering every school-age child who was in good health and a member of an Indian group under the special protection of the United States government to attend school. Thereafter, day-school teachers could call on Indian police to track down truants.[52] Another inducement to parents and children was the noon lunches—"well cooked and cleanly served"—offered at several Chippewa reservation schools. Yet enrollment figures illustrated that irregular attendance remained an unsolved problem:[53]

| Reservation | 1895 School Age Children | 1895 Number Enrolled | 1892 Average Attendance |
|---|---|---|---|
| Bad River | 140 | 117 | 45 |
| Red Cliff | 170 | 155 | 104 |
| Lac du Flambeau | 147 | — | 28 |
| Lac Court Oreilles | 275 | 179 | 83 |
| Fond du Lac | 235 | 46 | 38 |
| Grand Portage | 94 | 20 | 8 |
| Vermilion Lake | 203 | 60 | 37 |

Chippewa families, via their school-age children, were doubtless subjected to intensive acculturation. When regular classroom attendance for all youngsters was enforced, families could not wander at will. New jobs, permanent homes, and children in school tied them to the reservation and drove another wedge between them and the old woodland ways.

Some facets of the complex interplay between the Chippewa and white American cultures defy analysis. We simply lack the sources to determine, for example, the rate of acculturation of each Lake Superior band, how reservation life altered the full spectrum of native social values, attitudes, and institutions by 1900, and what the Chippewas themselves wanted regarding the physical development of their reservations, housing, education, and the like. Two generalizations are strongly supported by the evidence, however. Chippewa traditional culture was rapidly disintegrating; the first forty-five years of reservation life made them a people of two worlds. Secondly, they had become, in the process, the wards of Washington. Oblivious to the integrity of Chippewa culture, Ashland Indian agents directed the acculturation program on scattered and self-contained reservations, each with its resident federal bureaucrat, police force, school, and welfare system. Tribal bonds, already loose, gave way from lack of contact among the bands.

At the turn of the century, the 850 Chippewas at Keweenaw Bay lived mainly in the towns of Baraga, on the west side, and L'Anse, on the opposite shore. All wore "citizen's dress," half held membership in Christian churches, 750 knew enough English for everyday conversation, and 500 could read. Labor in "civilized pursuits" provided all their support, according to BIA records.[54]

The Bad River band was similarly acculturated; out of a population of 645, all wore white men's clothing, 575 could read, 500 could speak English and 95 percent supported themselves in "civilized pursuits." Church membership of 455 testified to the enduring effect of Leonard Wheeler's work.[55] When his mission was at its apex in the early 1860's, eighty to a hundred Chippewas regularly attended Sunday services conducted in their native language. Consumption forced Wheeler's retirement in October, 1866. He moved to Beloit, Wisconsin, with his wife and eight of his nine children—son Leonard remained in charge of the school at Odanah. The Bad River mission was soon taken over by the Presbyterian Church. The Reverend Isaac Baird directed its work until the mid-1880's.[56] Wealthy Kate Drexel, of Philadelphia, then purchased and turned over to the Catholic Church the entire complex—several large buildings and two hundred acres of fertile farmland. Thus the Christian work of the mission continued.[57] That the Bad River band found itself in two cultural worlds during the decade of the nineties was evidenced by the presence of two factions, the "progressives" and the "non-progressives" or "vagabonds," as the La Pointe agent dubbed them. The latter opposed clearing reservation land, farming allotments, and any other "civilized industry." This conflict was also evident each Fourth of July, when Ashland tourists took a special train to Odanah to see their neighbors, in native garb, celebrate the national holiday with a traditional war dance and lacrosse game.[58]

Red Cliff residents were also highly acculturated in terms of housing, dress, and speech. Indeed, because the reserve was so small, many had moved to nearby white towns and intermarried. The principal Indian village was at Buffalo Bay, five miles north of Bayfield via a good wagon road.[59]

On the Lac du Flambeau reservation, all wore "citizen's dress" and lived in log or frame houses. However, out of 796, only 175 could read and only 250 could use English. Forty were Christian church members. The Indians' handsome timber profits and easy access to the reservation on the Wisconsin Central Railroad created an attractive target for whiskey sellers, fourteen of whom were prosecuted in 1895. The liquor traffic at Lac du Flambeau, the most serious in the entire agency, was considered a great drawback to its advancement.[60]

Whiskey was also the "curse" of lumber-rich Lac Court Oreilles reservation. According to reports it was ringed with rum shops. Four whiskey sellers were prosecuted in 1895. Generally, these 1,150 Chippewas were quite advanced in "civilization." More than half belonged to churches, 425 could read, 500 could speak English in ordinary conversation, and all dressed in white men's clothes. They lived in wooden houses clustered mainly in the villages of Lac Court Oreilles and Pahquauhwong. A good wagon road connected these settlements with the white town of Hayward.[61]

By 1895 two of the three Lake Superior bands in Minnesota had taken major steps down the white man's road. The Fond du Lac Chippewas, who numbered nearly eight hundred, occupied permanent wooden houses and wore "citizen's dress." Half could read, and three-fourths could speak English in ordinary conversation. Two villages dominated the reserve. One lay two miles from Cloquet, the other, Normantown, was ten miles from Cloquet and near Sawyer, a station on the Northern Pacific Railroad.[62]

Moderate acculturation also characterized the 313 Chippewas at Grand Portage, near the Canadian border. About one-fifth of their village claimed Christian church membership. The Bois Forte band lived on three reservations, the principal one being Nett Lake. All 378 dressed in white-style clothing, yet less than half could read or speak English, and many still lived in wigwams and earned a living by hunting, fishing, and gathering.[63]

The end seemed near for the old woodland ways of the Chippewas of Kitchigami land. An *Ashland Daily News* reporter sensed it on September 11, 1896, when a special train brought to town ten coaches filled with Indians from nearby reservations who had come to help celebrate a visit of Buffalo Bill's show. Hundreds of whites flocked to Front Street to see the Chippewas.

Ashland people will probably never again be offered the opportunity of seeing so many Indians who still retain their old customs. The old leaders are yearly passing away, the new generation taking their places are being educated with a view of making them industrious citizens of the United States, and soon the reservations in this vicinity will be converted into flourishing agricultural communities, whose residents will be indeed educated, civilized and progressive citizens of the United States.

The Chippewas of Lake Superior, already a people of two worlds, were indeed on the verge of another new era in their history.

# 7. Descent to Depression, 1900-1934

During the first thirty years of the twentieth century, Chippewa reservations continued to be the target of BIA acculturation programs involving economic development, the improvement of housing, health, and schools, and the maintenance of law and order. Many allottees seemingly abandoned their ethnic past and embraced the new way of life and work. Then, in the late 1920's, with timber monies finally exhausted, reservation farmers sold their equipment and stock. The national depression so deepened the crisis that 50 per cent of the Bad River band was destitute by the early thirties. There were no permanent jobs either on or off that reservation, and no money available to care for the sick, the old, and the indigent.[1] Just when the future of native Americans seemed bleakest, the Indian Reorganization Act of 1934 was passed. It launched a regenerative era for the Chippewas and dozens of other tribes across the country by reversing the federal policy of allotment, which for nearly a century had carved up Indian reservations and damaged native organizations and institutions. A period of cultural independence began in the 1930's, when the Lake Superior Chippewas were encouraged to revitalize tribal communal life in order to survive as a people.

BIA field officials implemented federal Indian policy. In 1910 the La Pointe Agency was staffed by a superintendent of schools (superintendents replaced agents as administrative heads after 1893), five clerks, a stenographer, an interpreter, a lumberman, three physicians, five farmers, six policemen, five teachers, and a school housekeeper.[2]

Detailed financial matters consumed most of the superintendents' time. Philip S. Everest managed two and a half million dollars in timber monies belonging to 1,200 individual Indians. Having deposited the funds in twenty-five different banks by 1913, he doled out sums for what he judged to be the legitimate needs of allottees and probated estates.[3] Likewise, when the new Consolidated Chippewa Agency took charge of the Grand Portage, Nett Lake (including Vermilion Lake), and Fond du Lac Chippewas and other Minnesota bands in 1922, the superintendent at Cass Lake reported that his duties largely involved handling Indian finances.

The BIA's paternalistic role as trust agent for Chippewa reservation lands was necessary, noted Superintendent James W. Balmer, because "The Indians are like a lot of children." They "are not very far advanced in white men's ways and do not look ahead to provide for the future."[4] Superintendents at Ashland and Cass Lake could not always deal with Indians as individuals, hence they encouraged each band to replace its chiefs with official representatives selected by a majority of the tribe at its meetings in open council on each reservation. Business Committees, as they were called, supervised the general interests of the bands and were useful to the agencies in making contracts and settling estates.[5]

Since the 1860's the foundation for the BIA's Chippewa acculturation program had been the allotment system, which broke up communal reservation lands into eight-acre family tracts to be used for timber sales and farming. By 1910 most available Indian lands were apportioned and occupied "more or less" by the allottees. Complete figures are available for the following locations that year:[6]

| Reservation | Allotments | Acreage |
| --- | --- | --- |
| Bad River | 1,021 | 80,628.50 |
| Red Cliff | 205 | 14,166.01 |
| Lac du Flambeau | 578 | 45,459.10 |
| Lac Court Oreilles | 814 | 63,835.22 |
| Grand Portage | 304 | 24,191.31 |

Indian allottees each received a trust patent. According to its terms Washington restricted sale of the land for twenty-five years—unless there was good reason for early termination of the trust period, such as the acknowledged competency of a Chippewa owner. Isolated interior bands (mainly full bloods) at Lac Court Oreilles, Lac du Flambeau, and Nett Lake did not exhibit enough "civilized" behavior to prove competency to the BIA. But by the late 1920's about five-sixths of the allottees at L'Anse, half at Bad River, four-fifths at Red Cliff, three-fifths at Fond du Lac, and one-tenth at Grand Portage had received patents in fee simple through certificates of competency.[7] Their future seemed bright. In full control of family plots and as United States citizens after July, 1924, Chippewa allottees could use their timber money to establish permanent homes, improve their farms, and work for economic self-sufficiency. Such was the hope of the federal government.

By October and November of each year, when swamps were frozen and snow-covered roads passable, contractors started cutting timber on Indian allotments. The lumberjacks skidded some logs to river banks in preparation for spring drives, others were hauled on sleds to lumber mills or railroad lines.[8] Both Indian allottees and laborers profited from the timber industry. The J. S. Stearns Lumber Company employed fifteen hundred men at Bad River in 1914. A third were Chippewas who earned from $1.15 to $4.00 per day. Indian wages that year totaled $34,799.60, and the timber output from allotments 40,000,000 feet. But the boom was over within a decade. Odanah's shrieking sawmills fell silent. During its twenty-eight years at Bad River, the Stearns company logged one and a quarter billion feet of timber and paid seven million dollars to reservation residents.[9] Elsewhere, contractors also harvested large quantities of white pine, Norway pine, spruce, hemlock, tamarack, birch, and balsam.[10]

| Reservation | Season | Timber Footage | Money Received by Chippewas |
|---|---|---|---|
| Red Cliff | 1903–04 | 7,486,530 | $ 12,168.40 |
| Lac Court Oreilles | 1903–04 | 2,827,660 | 9,499.12 |
| Fond du Lac | 1911–12 | 6,600,000 | 58,961.11 |
| Lac du Flambeau | 1912–13 | 23,049,110 | 117,764.85 |

The BIA closely regulated Chippewa lumbering operations. It controlled the price of reservation timber, permitted only reputable and properly bonded contractors to log allotments, supervised labor conditions, and managed the profits. The latter function was open to controversy.

Before 1900, the government often turned over timber profits in lump sums to La Pointe Agency Chippewas. Most of this money was spent "uselessly and foolishly and recklessly," ending up in the possession of "grafters and the saloons." When S. W. Campbell took over at Ashland shortly after the turn of the century, he inaugurated a new policy of depositing timber monies for individual Indians in interest-bearing accounts at twenty national banks. From these accounts the superintendent regularly paid monthly allowances to destitute, aged, or sick Chippewas. With no questions asked, he also disbursed up to twenty-five dollars a month to Indian depositors.

Major withdrawals were forbidden unless the allottee used the money for such permanent improvements as pulling stumps, buying cattle, or constructing a house, barn, or fences. First a Chippewa with credit at the agency submitted detailed plans for expending his funds. The proposal was investigated by the government farmer, and, if it seemed worthy, the superintendent forwarded the application to Washington. Once it had been approved by the commissioner, the agency supervised the project in order to guarantee that the money was spent properly. The new policy worked beautifully; allottees increased the number of their permanent improvements three- or fourfold. About a hundred Bad River families cleared nearly sixty acres each. Nevertheless, the superintendent was misled by some two dozen Chippewas whom he judged to be capable of handling their financial affairs without BIA guidance. Most of them wasted their money by buying farms off the reservations and reselling them "for little or nothing."[11]

Campbell listened to many tales of woe by Indians hoping to get money from him. His withholding policy also led to occasional lawsuits. In the case of Antoine G. Starr (a Bad River allottee) v. S. W. Campbell, the Supreme Court in 1907 upheld the right of the BIA to regulate the disposition of Indian timber monies by virtue of the authority given to the President over Chippewa allotments in Article III of the La Pointe treaty of 1854.[12]

In light of the Chippewa fiscal problems that Superintendent Campbell inherited, his paternalism was not unreasonable. The Chippewas, their traditional livelihood taken away, seemingly had no choice but to farm. But it could not be done if there was no money. "The trouble with these Indians," Campbell wrote,[13]

is that they have never had any experience in finance. To pay them their money would be like paying over to a child ten years old, eight or ten thousand dollars and turn him out. How long would he hold it? They do not know what to do with it, as they have never had any experience in any way, and the proper thing to do is to teach them gradually how to handle it, and how to make themselves self-supporting.

Agency forest reports also emphasized how closely the BIA watched over Chippewa timber resources. In 1930, Forest Supervisor Elmer J. Carlson filed one such detailed account for Nett Lake and Grand Portage. After a general description of the reservation country, he estimated forest resources, the percentges of predominating species of trees, and the value of timber lands exclusive of timber. Photographs of forest lands, logging and scaling operations, as well as equipment used for the prevention and fighting of forest fires highlighted the account. Most reservation fires raged during the months of May and October, when there were strong winds, low humidity, and bare trees. At Nett Lake, Carlson distributed fire-fighting equipment (Smith water pumps, shovels, axes) to each logging camp. A telephone line linked agency headquarters with a state-owned and operated fire tower overlooking the whole reservation. The greatest handicap to fire fighting was poor roads. Because there were no taxpayers at Nett Lake, and because Indian allotments were so scattered, the cost of constructing new roads was for fire fighters.

Carlson was assisted in another important duty by three government scalers, who measured the volume of logs cut. The forest supervisor could include in each annual report a "cost analysis of timber sale units," broken down by species of tree, volume scaled, amount owed to allottees, and the cost of the harvest. In 1930 the BIA scaled 16,424,640 board feet at Grand Portage and Nett Lake, valued at $52,130.35, an average of $3.17 per thousand. Administrative costs for salaries and wages (scaling, marking, supervision), material and supplies, and travel expenses totaled $7,948.56.[14]

The self-sufficient Chippewa family farm was the economic goal of the BIA and the logical result of the allotment of reservations and the federal regulation of Indian timber sales. When Native Americans were assimilated into the white world, they would cease to be a financial and psychological burden to the United States. Such had been the dream of Washington policy makers since the era of Thomas Jefferson. Though there was a certain logic to it, the dream almost always foundered on the rocky realities of frontier economics: reservations unsuited for agriculture, white seizure of Indian farm land (by means of treaty cessions, sale, leasing, or outright fraud), and nation-wide depressions which destroyed family farm profits. The story of the Lake Superior bands was no exception to this historical truism.

Nevertheless, the future of Chippewa agriculture brightened when President Woodrow Wilson took office in 1913. With their forests nearly gone, many reservations were ready to be farmed. Lumber profits could be used for permanent improvements on allotments. Good markets awaited Indian farm produce. Despite the short growing season, Superintendent Everest was enthusiastic about the possibilities for growing vegetables and all grains except corn. Moreover, there was "no better country under the sun for stock raising and dairying," which went hand in hand with farming. Everest's major challenge was the Chippewa's long-standing prejudice against farming and permanent settlement. The majority of families cultivated gardens, but only about 15 per cent engaged in extensive agriculture.[15] Many were at Bad River, which had the best soil of all the Lake Superior reserves. Here, Everest zealously and imaginatively concentrated the efforts of the La Pointe Agency.

In 1910, the Ashland *Daily Press* announced that the time had come at Bad River when the Chippewas must either "make farms out of their allotments or leave them to grow up to weeds and underbrush." Superintendent Everest, who doubtless shared this sentiment, was quite successful in encouraging reservation families to farm. By the summer of 1915, more than 100 Indians had left Odanah, cleared their allotments, and built modern and attractive homes and barns. More than two dozen families used their timber monies to buy improved farms off the reservation. Thanks to agency purchases, all these agriculturists had teams of work horses—the best to be seen in any state, according to one government inspector. Soon each farmer also owned from two to seven cows. Crops were mainly forage, since the fine reservation grazing land made dairying particularly profitable.[16]

For nine years, with Everest's encouragement and help, Bad River farmers presented an agricultural fair at Odanah to display the prizewinning fruits of their labors. The event stimulated agricultural interest among Indians and demonstrated to thousands of county visitors just what Native Americans had accomplished by means of self-help. Receipts from concessions, donations, and admission fees (35¢ for adults, 15¢ for children under twelve) were spent largely on prizes for various sporting events, games, and the best exhibits of livestock and farm produce. A program booklet from the 7th Annual Bad River Indian Fair, held September 24–26, 1919, shows that prominent Odanah and Ashland merchants supported the project by purchasing advertisements. According to the rules and regulations for exhibitors, "All articles offered for exhibit must be raised or made by the exhibitor who must be an Indian resident of Bad River Reservation." A special feature was a baby show, sponsored by the Child's Welfare Committee:

A solid gold initial ring will again be given at the coming Fair to the best type of Indian boy and girl babies under the age of 18 months, and in addition a photograph of the mother and each of the individual babies, as well as a group picture of all contestants will be given to parents of each baby entering the

BETTER BABIES SHOW

Games and athletic contests included egg, potato, three-legged and hurdle races, the pole vault, tugs of war, and a lacrosse game. There were also four parades and a lecture on an agricultural subject. First and second place prizewinners were chosen in twenty-eight categories of livestock and poultry, thirty-four of farm and garden produce, three of fresh fruit, thirty-eight of knitted and fancy work, twenty-two of cooking and sixteen of beadwork. In 1921 the plowing and planting of the St. Mary's School grounds at Odanah, previously leased for the fairs, put an end to these colorful and competitive gatherings.[17]

Of basic assistance to the development of Indian farms was the annual farm institute at Bad River sponsored by the University of Wisconsin's Agricultural Extension Service. The first session at Odanah in March, 1918, demonstrated tests for soil acidity. Over the years, women learned about household economy, domestic science and canning and preserving. Root cellars were a most useful project started by the institutes. In 1932, when the Stearns Lumber Company abandoned its sawmill at Odanah, Indians used bricks from the engine room to build three communal cellars for winter storage. They worked so well for Indian potatoes, cabbages, onions, rutabagas, beets, carrots, pumpkins, squash, and canned goods, that a dozen more were built the next year.[18]

There remained serious handicaps to economic self-sufficiency at Bad River. Because of stumpage and dense undergrowth, clearing the land was difficult and expensive. Allottees paid $60 an acre in 1916 to hire stumps grubbed with dynamite and levers. Until the 1920's there were few roads that could handle teams and wagons. By the mid-twenties, however, eighteen miles of state trunk highway system opened up large areas of unimproved farm land. A new post road soon linked Ashland with the northwest portion of the reservation and provided rural free mail delivery to Chippewa allottees living outside of Odanah.[19]

With the building of wagon roads and the clearing of reservation land, the future of farming seemed even brighter at Bad River.

Unfortunately for Chippewa economic security, agricultural success at Bad River was not matched on other lake band reservations.

At L'Anse in Michigan the soil was fertile, especially in the hardwood sections, but few allottees were interested in raising crops or livestock. By the early 1920's only about six hundred out of fifteen thousand acres were cleared and cultivated. These farmer Indians were well equipped with teams and machinery and seed furnished by the BIA. For the rest of the band the allotments were practically worthless once the timber had been stripped. In addition to the high cost of clearing the land, much hard work and money had to be invested to build homes, farms, outbuildings, and fences. All this before any profits could be realized. The abundance of day labor jobs at decent wages in nearby mines and lumber camps further explained why most L'Anse men shunned farming. It should be pointed out, however, that Indian families raised about as much garden produce as their white neighbors. Few white farmers prospered in the Keweenaw region, either.[20]

In Wisconsin, the Indian farmer faced similar difficulties. Much of Red Cliff was suitable for agriculture, yet allottees did not have convenient access to their land until the mid-1920's because there was no state and county trunk highway system through the reservation. To clear an acre of this stump-and-brush land in 1927 cost between forty and sixty-five dollars, thus the percentage of reservation farmers was understandably low. Most men had jobs as day laborers in the lumber and fishing industries. (Red Cliff Chippewas were known as good fishermen and expert sailors.) So lacking was the reservation in economic opportunity that about 30 per cent of the band lived and worked in nearby Bayfield.[21]

Lands of the Lac du Flambeau reservation were too poor to farm. By the 1920's cut-over allotments were covered with decayed logs, stumps, brush, and a dense growth of young trees, so that the cost of clearing an acre was greater than its value. Even if readied for farming, the light, sandy soil would not support the kind of intensive agriculture found at Bad River. The BIA also had to deal with the lack of farm machinery at Lac du Flambeau and with the scarcity of labor because most able-bodied men found work off the reservation. To encourage Indians to cultivate at least part of their land, Superintendent James W. Balmer sent government farmers from home to home demonstrating the best ways to plant, cultivate, and harvest. Agricultural Indian fairs similar to those at Odanah gave the successful farmers a chance to exhibit their products. An Indian Farmers' Institute in May, 1922, offered helpful sessions on: "How Best to Clear Cut-over Land at Lac du Flambeau", "How Can We

Best Build up Sandy Soils", "What to do to Reclaim Marsh Lands", "Some Good Ways of Growing Potatoes", and "How to Take Care of a Dairy Cow." Despite encouragement, the Chippewas had cleared only 520 acres by 1922. Their "efforts were crude, crops small, and not very remunerative."

What this beautiful, lake-spangled reservation lacked in agricultural potential it made up for in its attractiveness to city people and resort owners, who flocked in increasing numbers to the north woods in the twenties. As owners of this outdoor playground, the Chippewas discovered they could make more money faster by providing the free-spending tourists with guides, helpers, caretakers, bead, birch, and buckskin handiwork, fish from well-stocked lakes, firewood, and other supplies than they could by farming. Several non-farmer Indians also worked for good wages in northern Wisconsin mills and camps.[22]

At Lac Court Oreilles, where few Indians lived on their allotments, farms were equally small and poorly managed. With the encouragement of Farm Institutes and agency personnel, some Chippewas developed an interest in vegetable growing. As at Lac du Flambeau, the tourist industry and work off the reservation probably provided most of the band's income.[23]

The expense of clearing logged-off allotments, the unsuitability of reservation land for farming, and the lure of employment in nearby mills also plagued Indian agriculture in northeast Minnesota. By 1932 about 95 per cent of Fond du Lac Indian families had gardens and raised various kinds of root crops. Only 5 per cent farmed extensively, a figure unchanged since 1910, despite vigorous efforts by government farmers.

The Grand Portage story was downright grim. The land was rough and rocky and worth no more than five dollars an acre, and the climate was cold. Moreover, by the early 1930's the three hundred band members had only three acres per person of the original tract set aside in 1854. About 40 per cent of the families had gardens, but most of them made their living by fishing, trapping, hunting, and working as unskilled laborers.

Although the Nett Lake Chippewas owned approximately fifty acres of land per capita, most of it was swampy. On the eve of the New Deal only 1 per cent of the allottees lived on their land and farmed extensively. No more than 15 per cent had gardens. What sustained the band was hunting, fishing, gathering berries, harvesting wild rice, the manufacture of maple sugar, guiding white hunters, and the sale of curios.[24]

The Great Depression delivered a stunning blow to fledgling Chippewa agriculturalists and day laborers. At Bad River many farmers had sold their stock and equipment. By March, 1932, only eight or ten families even tried to make a living by cultivating the soil. Jobs disappeared for Indian loggers, millers, and other workers off the reservation. As the unemployed drifted back to Odanah, the number of destitute bandsmen rose to 50 per cent (about 450 persons). The situation was the same at Lac du Flambeau, where only 45 out of 220 families supported themselves—at odd jobs, guiding, caretaking, cutting firewood, and putting up ice. Because of the greater abundance of fish, game, and other traditional woodland resources at Fond du Lac, Grand Portage, and Nett Lake, these bands relied much less on government rations when the Depression hit. Before the widespread economic collapse, about 25 per cent of Lake Superior bandsmen lived and worked off the reservations.

In the 1930's, unemployed Chippewas drifted back because living was cheaper on the reservation, and most families were eligible for federal aid. Nonwards, who held patents in fee simple for their allotments, got some assistance from the state and local authorities, and sometimes they also moved in with relatives or friends.[25] BIA plans for Chippewa self-sufficiency through agriculture had been halted, at least for the time being. The most pressing problem for the Chippewas and for the BIA bureaucrats at that time was Indian survival—through the distribution of provisions, creation of new jobs, and priming the pump for still another economic development program in Kitchigami land.

Poverty among the Lake Superior bands during the early decades of the twentieth century brought a general deterioration of living conditions, and eventually a health crisis. A La Pointe Agency physician noted in July, 1903, the comparatively low incidence of tuberculosis among Indian children enrolled in boarding schools compared with those who lived at home and attended day schools. It was generally agreed among BIA bureaucrats that Chippewa housing was neither clean nor sanitary, despite government promotion of good hygiene.[26] The village of Odanah, where 75 per cent of the Bad River band lived in 1913, became a rather vile case in point. Sidewalks had rotted out, open outhouses stank under the summer sun, and low places in backyards filled up with stagnant water, rubbish, and refuse. Each spring the north bank of the Bad River overflowed and spread raw sewage from open privies throughout the town. Indian meals consisted almost entirely of meat and bread. Agency doctors who tried to put patients on diets or arrange for family nursing care in Odanah's filthy one-room homes had little success.[27]

Shabby living conditions brought an onslaught of communicable diseases such as smallpox, tuberculosis, and venereal infection. Although BIA mortality and morbidity statistics (so necessary for efficient health service planning) are lacking, reports of superintendents and reservation physicians suggest that quarantines and vaccinations greatly reduced the number of smallpox epidemics after the turn of the century. Tuberculosis, however, raged unchecked on all the Lake Superior reservations. Considered the most widespread human disease, it infected one out of sixty United States citizens in 1903 and about one in twenty Chippewas, especially those between the ages of fifteen and thirty-five.[28] A physician who examined 898 Bad River residents in 1915 discovered tuberculosis among 130. As late as 1932, 15 per cent of Minnesota's Indians were thought to have contracted tuberculosis. This figure included about 10 per cent of the Chippewas at Grand Portage, over 4 per cent at Fond du Lac, and 30 per cent at Nett Lake.[29]

When Chippewa "immorality" was added to uncleanliness and poor diet, venereal disease spread swiftly among family members. Shortly after the turn of the century, hereditary syphilis killed nearly one-fifth of all Chippewa children before they reached the age of six months. A report that "immorality runs rampant at Odanah" seemed to be confirmed when a Wassermann test given to a random sample of sixty males and females in 1915 showed that 35 per cent had syphilis. Gonorrhea was almost universal among the band. Superintendent Everest attributed the high incidence of venereal infection to the presence of so-called Indian "riffraff" from other reserves, lured to Bad River by its timber wealth and labor opportunities. At Lac du Flambeau in 1926 the school doctor estimated that probably 5 per cent of the boys and 10 per cent of the girls were infected with venereal disease.[30]

That the seriously sick rarely recovered is not surprising when it is noted how the BIA battled communicable diseases with inadequate facilities and understaffed, underpaid, and substandard health care personnel. Intemperate, roving native bands—seemingly irresponsible in their refusal to be vaccinated, isolated, or doctored— also contributed to the dismal state of Indian health.[31]

The Indian Service struggled to improve reservation living conditions and medical services. A young Ashland doctor encouraged
good care of infants by means of the "Better Baby Contests" at the
agricultural fairs. Twenty-two children competed in 1916. Their
parents attended lectures on bathing, feeding, and general child
care and received BIA medical booklets. At Lac du Flambeau that
same year, the superintendent and a field matron launched a door-
to-door campaign to improve home hygiene and to promote proper
infant feeding and cleanliness. A decade later the BIA was still
doing what it could "short of force" to improve living conditions. By
that time reservation school children received periodic medical examinations and all were vaccinated for smallpox.[32]

In Michigan, county officials supplemented BIA medical services
for the L'Anse reservation, which had neither a hospital nor a resident physician. (In 1922, the contract doctor lived in nearby
Pequaming and the seriously ill had to be sent to the hospital at
Hancock.) The area Tuberculosis Society's county nurse examined
the band and sent those suffering from the disease to local
sanatoriums at county expense. The Michigan State Sanatorium,
servicing the entire state, also accepted Indian patients in the early
stages of infection, provided room was available.[33] Besides the contract physicians for Grand Portage and Nett Lake, the Chippewas of
Minnesota in 1932 also had access to the Fond du Lac hospital at
Cloquet, a rather old two-story frame building badly in need of
paint. With a capacity for twenty patients, a recently remodeled
operating room, dining room, kitchen, hallways, and bathrooms, it
was adequate, clean, and sanitary. Head nurse Clara Smith administered the hospital with the assistance of a registered nurse and
a practical nurse. Contract surgeon Dr. Roy Raiter, with help from
his physician brother, furnished "efficient and capable" medical services at Cloquet. That year they performed more than two hundred
major operations for Chippewas from all over northern Minnesota.[34]

Poverty and poor living conditions also intensified the problem
with alcohol in Kitchigami land. "With the pitiful lack of work and
recreation existing on the [Lac du Flambeau] reservation," noted
Special Agent B. G. Courtright in 1933, "can it be wondered that the
Indians turn to drink and its attending evils, come home and get
into trouble?"[35] From Grand Portage to Keweenaw Bay, whiskey
had been one of the most serious drawbacks to Indian advancement—
in the judgment of the BIA—since the turn of the century. In
1902, debauched and drunken Grand Portage Chippewas could be
found day and night sprawled in the bush outside Grand Marais,

where many of them lived; it was the same story at L'Anse and
Lac du Flambeau.[36] Superintendent Everest estimated that 90 per
cent of the Bad River Chippewas used liquor to some extent in
1914. And they had no trouble getting it. Nearby Ashland claimed
fifty-three saloons, with train connections to and from the reservation three times daily. "The liquor curse is the black page in
the history of this tribe," he wrote. "I have already concluded that
the so-called 'Indian Problem' is secondary on this reservation and
that the 'whiskey problem' takes its place in all its discouraging and
degenerating influences." Even after the commencement of national
prohibition in 1919, the percentage of Indian addicts remained very
high at Bad River. Odanah residents with enough money either
manufactured their own moonshine whiskey or bought drinks from
neighboring whites. Some even imbibed large enough quantities of
lemon extract and other patent medicines to become dependent upon
them.[37]

The whiskey traffic was difficult to halt. In defiance of twenty-
four-hour patrols by the Bad River Indian police, for example, liquor
was smuggled onto the reservation by white lumberjacks, shipped to
Odanah in grocery boxes, hidden under women's clothing, strapped
under automobiles, and thrown from passing trains. Hucksters convicted of selling alcohol to Indians merely paid their fines and went
back to hawking "hooch."[38] To eliminate saloon sales in Ashland,
Agent Campbell convened a group of fifty local brewers, members of
the Protestant and Catholic clergy, lawyers, and businessmen. Discussion led to the formation of a Committee of Nine, with Campbell
as chairman, which was to meet with saloon-keepers and bring sufficient moral suasion to bear so that they would pledge not to sell to
Indians. Campbell started similar community action groups in other
northern Wisconsin towns. The Ashland *Daily Press* perhaps spoke
for many area whites when it editorialized:[39]

> The Indian is simply an overgrown child. Selling liquor to him, is very
> much like selling to a child. . . . What the public objects to, is selling liquor
> to a partly drunken Indian, or white man for that matter, and sending him
> out into the streets in a beastly state of intoxication, and also, of allowing
> Indian women to congregate in the back part of saloons and selling them
> liquor until they are drunk.

The BIA reports suggest that the whiskey traffic was curbed somewhat. In 1910, Indian police arrested seventy-three persons for in-
troducing alcohol onto the reservations of the La Pointe Agency, five

for selling liquor to Indians, and fifty for drunkenness; they also seized thirty-one and a half quarts of whiskey and twenty and a half quarts of alcohol. More often, the attempts to prosecute Indian and white offenders brought only frustration. Many Lac Court Oreilles Chippewas considered the tavern keepers their friends and refused to testify against them in court. This is "'saloon country'—saloons and their supporters nominate and elect local officials," lamented Superintendent William A. Light in 1913. Those who denied whiskey to the Indian were considered his enemies![40]

Likewise, if a Bad River Chippewa were arrested and convicted of trafficking in alcoholic beverages, his social standing did not diminish. "Indians are calloused to punishment and are willing to run any risk," wrote a frustrated federal inspector. "So—conscience, conscientiousness, shame and degradation play no part as deterrents." State and municipal authorities often ignored those statutes which prohibited the sale of liquor to Indians; they preferred to let Washington handle the situation. Even after prohibition, when county and state authorities became more cooperative, there were never enough special federal liquor officers to gather evidence against the multitude of offenders. In 1933, one such person was responsible for patrolling both Wisconsin and Minnesota.[41]

Although the improvement of living conditions and the economic development of reservations consumed much of the time and resources of the BIA, it did not neglect the Chippewa children during the first three decades of the twentieth century. An ambitious educational program provided schooling and preparation for citizenship.

Reservation children went to three types of schools. Government or mission day schools held classes at Nett Lake, Grand Portage, Lac Court Oreilles, Lac du Flambeau, Red Cliff, Bad River, and L'Anse. In 1922, thirty-six children from the L'Anse band attended the Indian day school conducted by the Catholic Sisters, Order of St. Agnes. Located on the beautiful west shore of Keweenaw Bay, two and a half miles from Baraga, its stone buildings were erected about 1846 under the direction of Father Baraga himself. A Catholic Indian boarding school, part of the complex, enrolled forty-six students.[42] Boarding schools—the second kind of educational institution for Chippewa children—also operated at Bad River, Bayfield, and at Lac du Flambeau. Visiting Teacher Dorothy Dean filed a detailed report on Lac du Flambeau in 1931. The school plant consisted of a boys' dormitory, combined dining hall and kitchen and girls' dormitory, classroom building, two warehouses, barn, blacksmith shop, root cellar, garage, stationary room and two apartments. Principal Teacher Claude W. Webb ($1,680 per annum) and teachers Alice V. LaBelle, Anna J. Webb, and Nellie A. Wenberg ($1,560 per annum each) provided instruction. During the late 1920's the average daily attendance of Indian pupils was about thirty-four.[43] Chippewa families who lived on allotments far from government or mission day schools were encouraged to send their children to public schools. In July, 1902, the BIA signed a typical "articles of agreement" with the directors of Public School District No. 1, Ashland County, Wisconsin, who promised:[44]

1. To admit to the public school maintained at public expense in school district named, during the fiscal year ending June 30, 1903, six (6) Indian pupils, which Indian pupils shall be entitled to all the privileges of white pupils attending said school.

2. To instruct such Indian pupils in classes with the white children (except as provided hereinafter) in the Common English branches, giving to each of said Indian pupils the same care and attention in matter and methods of instruction as is given to the white pupils in said classes and school.

3. To maintain a separate primary class in case five or more Indian pupils enter the school at one time, all of whom are ignorant of the English language, in which instruction shall be given at least forty minutes of each day with special reference to teaching them to converse in English. The Indian pupils to be advanced to classes containing white children as soon as their knowledge of English makes their instruction with white children practicable.

4. To protect the pupils included in this contract from ridicule, insult, and other improper conduct at the hands of fellow pupils and to encourage them in every reasonable manner to attend school exercises punctually, regularly, and to perform their duties with the same degree of interest and industry as their fellow pupils, the children of white citizens.

On this basis, large numbers of Chippewa children from L'Anse, Bad River, Red Cliff, Lac du Flambeau, Fond du Lac, and Grand Portage attended state-maintained district schools (on or off the reservation) or city schools. By the 1920's this arrangement included more than half the eligible youngsters at Red Cliff and L'Anse, three-fifths of those at Lac du Flambeau, and all at Fond du Lac.[45]

Government and mission schools emphasized industrial education as well as the standard academic training previously discussed—reading, writing, spelling, English grammar and composition, arithmetic, geography, and drawing. Superintendent C. H. Gensler noted that at Lac du Flambeau industrial studies consisted of "such work as any young man or woman will have to do as soon as he or she leaves school." For girls, "domestic science" included cooking, sewing, laundry work, and housekeeping. Boys engaged in gardening, farming, general dairying, and learning the rudiments of carpentry and other trades.[46]

Despite a variety of institutions and their emphasis on a practical curriculum, serious educational problems plagued teachers, children, and their parents. As late as 1910 attendance was irregular because of seasonal rovings to hunting and fishing grounds, rice and berry fields, and the family sugar bush.[47]

During the Depression many children were sent to boarding schools because impoverished Chippewa communities could not support neighborhood public schools. The situation at Odanah probably was typical. The board claimed that the yearly operating cost for the fifty-five enrolled children was about $5,000. An assessed property evaluation of $197,000 in 1930 should have yielded some $7,500—more than enough to meet expenses; instead, only about 34 per cent (or $2,500) could be collected. Of the forty students with Indian blood, only four had parents who paid taxes; only six, who had more than one quarter Indian blood, were eligible for BIA tuition payments. With the collapsed national economy, "Pauperized home conditions and attendant malnutrition" faced many Chippewa young people living with their parents. Conditions at Lac du Flambeau were especially grim; of the fifty-five families from the old village and the town of Lac du Flambeau who sent children to the Lac du Flambeau Boarding School, only seventeen were self-supporting. The general economic situation was as follows:

|  | Old Village | Town | Total |
|---|---|---|---|
| Total homes sending children to boarding school | 13 | 42 | 55 |
| Total children in home | 50 | 182 | 232 |
| Number of parents with steady work |  |  |  |
| Men | 1 | 2 | 3 |
| Women | 1 | 9 | 10 |
| Number with certificates of competency | 3 | 4 | 7 |
| Number with allotments | 4 | 3 | 7 |
| Number with gardens | 7 | 14 | 21 |
| Families with pony | 4 | 3 | 7 |
| Families with other stock (1 cow; 3 families have chickens) | 0 | 4 | 4 |
| Families with cars | 7 | 15 | 22 |
| Families with adequate home necessities for children through the year | 4 | 13 | 17 |

After five weeks on the reservation, Visiting Teacher Dean concluded that the most serious threat to education and the reason why
these Chippewa children should be kept in boarding school was their
appalling moral situation at home. Day school students would not
only suffer from "hunger and other forms of privation," but "would
return each evening to homes of vice and immorality, where the law
is ignored or evaded." Figures on broken homes were most distressing:[48]

|                                                                | Old Village | Town | Total |
|----------------------------------------------------------------|-------------|------|-------|
| Total homes in which both parents now living                   | 6           | 14   | 20    |
| Total number of broken homes (all causes)                      | 7           | 28   | 35    |
| Homes where children's own father not present                  | 7           | 21   | 28    |
| Homes where children's own mother not present                  | 1           | 18   | 19    |
| Homes where one or the other parent is unmar- ried to present step-parent in home | 6 | 9 | 15 |
| Homes where some other immoral situations (aside from drinking and its immediate consequences) are present | 9 | 3 | 12 |

Thus did the heavy hand of poverty blight the home environment
and impair the education of Chippewa young people. Sadly, special
Agent B. G. Courtright reported in 1933:[49]

And such is life in Lac du Flambeau. Family fights, broken homes, disorderly conduct, children drifting for themselves.
  Walk down the little "main street" of the village any evening after dark.
You will meet girls in their teens with men much older. They disappear into
dark places.
  There is the "Club Seven," located on deeded land. During the dance
young Indian girls are taken out by not only the mixed-bloods but white
men as well. Some of the younger girls are given drinks and they are picked
up later anywhere on the street or side-roads and taken "home."
  I asked some of the parents if they knew about this. Yes, they knew about
it. The apathy on the part of the parents is appalling. Some times the sons
and daughters involved are illegitimate, which, I suppose, some times accounts for this indifference.

  To what extent the schools caused Lake Superior Chippewa children to abandon their ethnic past can only be judged in conjunction
with the overall "progress" of acculturation. As early as 1910 Agent
Campbell observed that the bands lived very much like their white
neighbors "of the same class." Traditional Indian customs, "primi-
tive" dances, wigwams, medicine men, powerful chiefs, and influen-

tial head speakers were fast disappearing—along with the Chippewa people. Racial amalgamation, the result mainly of Indian women marrying white men, became so common that only one-eighth of the enrolled population was full blooded, and 50 per cent had less than half Chippewa blood.[50]

Superintendent Everest proudly reported in the summer of 1930 that the L'Anse Chippewas were "so far advanced in the way of industry, self-help, modern living methods and civilization generally, that they do not engage to any extent in the old tribal customs and pastimes." Nearly all the original reservation allotments had been sold, and approximately 40 per cent had left the reservation in search of employment. Of those who remained, 80 percent were "turned-loose, non-ward, voting citizens and taxpayers." In times of national crises, such as World War I, the band responded by subscribing to several thousand dollars' worth of war bonds, donating generously to the Red Cross, and sending 705 young men to fight in France.[51]

At Bad River it had become quite common for white men to marry Indian women, especially those with large bank accounts from timber sales. Of the forty Chippewa children enrolled at the Odanah district school in 1931, only six had more than one-quarter Indian blood. Practically all band members adopted the white man's living habits and sent their children to school. At the railroad station at Birch, ten miles east of Odanah, several resident Indian allottees petitioned for a school and the Sanborn Township Board built them one in the early 1920's, without federal funds. About that time, 615 out of 1,083 Bad River Chippewas were Wisconsin state citizens. Eight hundred spoke English, and 520 could read and write English. Approximately 80 per cent of the band belonged to one of the three Christian churches on the reserve. During World War I, it subscribed $437,000 in trust funds for Liberty Loan securities. Sixty men served in the army and navy, about 40 per cent voluntarily.[52] Few differences were discernible between white neighbors and the "progressive and industrious" Red Cliff mixed bloods, whether they lived on the reservation, on nearby Madeline Island, or at Bayfield. The latter were voting, taxpaying citizens.[53]

By the mid-1920's the BIA pronounced Chippewa culture "extinct" at Lac du Flambeau, although many older residents spoke no English and "are practically pagans and practice various superstitious rites and ceremonies." About 75 per cent of the children finished the eighth grade. In addition to the "civilizing" influence of the

schools and the Presbyterian and Catholic missions, north woods
tourists introduced the Lac du Flambeau Chippewas to luxury consumer goods such as the automobile. Several Indians invested in
Fords and abandoned their farms and gardens to ride around or
smuggle whiskey onto the reservation.[54] At the head of Lake
Superior, most of the Fond du Lac and Grand Portage Chippewas
were mixed bloods as well as full-fledged taxpayers and Minnesota
citizens by the 1920's. The scattered and remote Bois Forte were still
the least acculturated.[55]

Despite BIA-perceived progress in acculturation, the general condition of the Chippewas as well as other tribes throughout the
United States was desperate. In the spring of 1926 informal conferences between representatives of the Department of the Interior and
the Institute for Government Research, a private agency, convinced
participants that it would be useful if an impartial group of
specialists comprehensively surveyed the economic and social condition of the American Indians. Satisfied that the institute itself was
especially well qualified and that the results of such a survey would
make a "constructive contribution in this difficult field of government administration," Secretary of the Interior Hubert Work formally requested that it undertake the task.

Director W. P. Willoughby accepted the challenge in October,
1926, after enough private pledges had been made to assure that
expenses for this special project could be met. Under the immediate
direction of the institute's own Lewis Meriam, the nine-member
staff included an Indian adviser and specialists in the legal aspects
of Indian problems, economic conditions, Indian migrants to urban
centers, Indian health, family life, education, and agriculture. Their
field work, which lasted seven months and took one or more staff
members to ninety-five different locations, included informal conferences with superintendents, Indians, traders, and missionaries.
Specialists also examined government records, health facilities,
schools, native homes, observed overall economic conditions, and
visited off-reservation communities to which Indians had migrated.[56]

Completed early in 1928, the Meriam Report, as it came to be
called, revealed the extreme poverty and maladjustment of a large
majority of American Indians. The survey team spent little time
with the Lake Superior Chippewas, but its national analysis of native social and economic conditions underscored the fact that the
Chippewa's plight in the early twentieth century was not unique.

It has been noted, for example, that the personnel of the Consolidated Chippewa and La Pointe Agencies were poorly paid and the agencies were understaffed, and that detailed business matters consumed most of the superintendents' time. Institute specialists reached similar conclusions about the Indian Service:[57]

Limited appropriations have often necessitated the employment of persons not possessed of the qualifications requisite for the efficient performance of the duties of their positions, but the employees generally are as good as could be expected for the salaries paid. Frequently the number of positions is too small for the work to be done. The survey staff estimates roughly that it would take almost twice the present appropriations for the Indian Service if each of its major activities were brought abreast of the better if not the best practice of other organizations doing like work for the general population.

As an economic panacea, Uncle Sam's reservation allotment policy proved as unsuccessful nationally as it had among the Chippewas.[58]

When the government adopted the policy of individual ownership of the land on the reservations, the expectation was that the Indians would become farmers. Part of the plan was to instruct and aid them in agriculture, but this vital part was not pressed with vigor and intelligence. It almost seems as if the government assumed that some magic in individual ownership of property would in itself prove an educational civilizing factor, but unfortunately this policy has for the most part operated in the opposite direction. Individual ownership has in many instances permitted Indians to sell their allotments and to live for a time on the unearned income resulting from the sale. . . . Many Indians were not ready to make effective use of their individual allotments. Some of the allotments were of such a character that they could not be effectively used by anyone in small units.

In the eyes of the institute, BIA management of Indian property was still necessary, as in the case of Chippewa timber resources and lumber profits. The typical Indian,[59]

has not yet advanced to the point where he has the knowledge of money and values, and of business methods that will permit him to control his own property without aid, advice, and some restrictions; nor is he ready to work consistently and regularly at more or less routine labor.

The Meriam Report's conclusions about the economic condition of the Indian tribes bore a striking similarity to the sad state of the Chippewas by the late 1920's.[60]

The income of the typical Indian family is low and the earned income extremely low. . . . Much of his activity is expended in lines which produce a relatively small return either in goods or money. He generally ekes out an existence through unearned income from leases of his land, the sale of land, per capita payments from tribal funds, or in exceptional cases through rations given him by the government. The number of Indians who are supporting themselves through their own efforts, according to what a white man would regard as the minimum standard of health and decency, is extremely small. What little they secure from their own efforts or from other sources is rarely effectively used.

The main occupations of the men are some outdoor work, mostly of an agricultural nature, but the number of real farmers is comparatively small. A considerable proportion engage more or less casually in unskilled labor. By many Indians several different kinds of activity are followed spasmodically, a little agriculture, a little fishing, hunting, trapping, wood cutting, or gathering of native products, occasional labor and hauling, and a great deal of just idling....

In justice to the Indians it should be said that many of them are living on lands from which a trained and experienced white man could scarcely wrest a reasonable living. In some instances the land originally set apart for the Indians was of little value for agricultural operations other than grazing....

The remoteness of their homes often prevents them from easily securing opportunities for wage earning, nor do they have many contacts with persons dwelling in urban communities where they might find employment.

Low incomes, which led to a low standard of living and poor health on Chippewa reservations, adversely affected the lives of other tribesmen throughout the United States. Both tuberculosis and trachoma were prevalent, the result of the Indians' poor diet—lacking in milk, fruit, and vegetables—as well as overcrowded and unsanitary housing. Suffering and discontent were equally widespread.[61]

Some people assert that the Indians prefer to live as they do; that they are happier in their idleness and irresponsibility. The question may be raised whether these persons do not mistake for happiness and contentment an almost oriental fatalism and resignation. The survey staff found altogether too much evidence of real suffering and discontent to subscribe to the belief that the Indians are reasonably satisfied with their condition. The amount of serious illness and poverty is too great to permit of real contentment. The Indian is like the white man in his affection for his children and he feels keenly the sickness and the loss of his offspring.

Because of insufficient funding, the BIA's delivery of health services nationally was judged inadequate—doctors, nurses, and dentists were too few; hospitals and sanatoriums were understaffed, badly designed and equipped, and poorly managed; programs in public health and preventative medicine were weak; and vital statistics for federal health planning and control were inadequate.[62]

Nor were the Chippewa's experiences with formal education very different from other Indians. The boarding school children received inadequate care, the teaching in government schools was substandard and their curriculum inflexible when compared with "progressive white communities," and there were insufficient funds to provide job placement services for boys and girls graduating from BIA schools.[63]

The institute's survey specialists concluded that,

Both the government and the missionaries have often failed to study, understand, and take a sympathetic attitude toward Indian ways, Indian ethics, and Indian religion. The exceptional government worker and the exceptional missionary have demonstrated what can be done by building on what is sound and good in the Indian's own life.

By 1928 the results of the century-long assault on the culture of the Chippewas and other Indian people were extreme poverty on the reservations and a general maladjustment "to the economic and social system of the dominant white civilization."[64]

The monumental Meriam Report was but a facet of what Randolph C. Downes called the "crusade for Indian reform" between 1922 and 1934. Evidence accumulated after World War I showed that individual allotment of land was a mistake; severalty had broken up their holdings and alienated 139 million acres of land owned by Indian tribes in 1887. The disastrous Dawes Act, wrote New Deal Commissioner of Indian Affairs John Collier in 1935, "disrupted tribal bonds, has destroyed old incentives to action, and has created a race of petty landlords who in generous Indian manner have shared their constantly shrinking income with the ever-increasing number of their landless relatives and friends." With reforms so desperately needed, several organizations championed the cause of landless, poverty-stricken Native Americans and lobbied to improve the administration of federal Indian policy. The most prominent pressure group was the seventeen-hundred-member American Indian Defense Association, founded in 1923 and led by zealous Executive Secretary John Collier. His activities, together with those of muckraking journalists who exposed the outrageous treatment of Indians on several reservations, sparked the Institute for Government Research in its thorough study of the BIA and provided impetus for the alteration of federal Indian policy, which culminated in the passage of the Wheeler-Howard Act in 1934.[65]

More than just the welfare of the Native Americans motivated Collier during the decade-long campaign for Indian reform. His knowledge of Pueblo and other Indian cultures convinced him that their community life and cooperative experience—a creative balance between communalism and individualism—offered a valuable alternative for a sophisticated but economically depressed and joyless white world, fragmented by industrialization and so materialistic that it had lost appreciation for the beauties of nature, human companionship, and a close relationship with God. Roosevelt's appointment of Collier brought a new spirit and an exciting philosophy of cultural pluralism to the Indian Service. Secretary of the Interior Harold Ickes claimed that the colorful new commissioner was "the best equipped man who ever held this office."[66]

Collier accelerated the reforms begun during the pre–New Deal phase of the crusade. In January, 1934, he issued two executive orders to preserve Indian heritage by limiting missionary interference with tribal religious life and education. Henceforth all Native Americans would enjoy "the fullest constitutional liberty, in all matters affecting religion, conscience and culture." Determined to build his program on a strong legal foundation, the commissioner also drafted and secured the passage of the Indian Reorganization (Wheeler-Howard) Act in June, 1934.[67]

The Indian Reorganization Act launched a regenerative era across the country by reversing the allotment, Americanization, and assimilation policies. Congress recognized—at long last—that the Indian was not a "rugged individualist," that he functioned best as an integrated member of a group. The IRA prohibited further allotments and sale of Indian land except to tribes and encouraged consolidation and development of native land holdings. It authorized a $10 million revolving loan fund for those tribes which organized and incorporated in order to create community responsibility and new incentives for collective action. The act applied only to tribes which accepted it at a special election. A series of 263 such referendums were held. Sixty-two per cent of all adult Indians participated, and 172 bands and tribes, including the Chippewas of Lake Superior, voted in favor of the IRA.[68]

| Reservation | Population | Voting Population | Yes | No | Election Date |
|---|---|---|---|---|---|
| Grand Portage | 377 | 179 | 75 | 4 | October 27, 1934 |
| Nett Lake | 627 | 317 | 159 | 7 | October 27, 1934 |

| Reservation | Population | Voting Population | Yes | No | Election Date |
|---|---|---|---|---|---|
| Fond du Lac | 1,298 | 725 | 167 | 28 | November 17, 1934 |
| Bad River | 1,211 | 697 | 296 | 47 | November 17, 1934 |
| Red Cliff | 506 | 360 | 122 | 7 | December 7, 1934 |
| Lac Court Oreilles | 1,559 | 871 | 205 | 175 | December 15, 1934 |
| Lac du Flambeau | 853 | 492 | 162 | 57 | June 15, 1935 |
| L'Anse and Ontonagon | — | 558 | 413 | 8 | June 15, 1935 |

When Willoughby presented his completed report to Secretary of the Interior Work early in 1928, it was with the hope:[69]

that it is a sound policy of national economy to make generous expenditures in the next few decades with the object of winding up the national administration of Indian affairs. The people of the United States have the opportunity, if they will, to write the closing chapters of the history of the relationship of the national government and the Indians. The early chapters contain little of which the country may be proud. It would be something of a national atonement to the Indians if the closing chapters should disclose the national government supplying the Indians with an Indian Service which would be a model for all governments concerned with the development and advancement of a retarded race.

Six years later, with John Collier at the helm of a BIA determined to promote cultural pluralism and to preserve Indian cultures, the Lake Superior Chippewa bands had good reason to be optimistic about their survival as a people.

# 8. Freedom Amidst Poverty, 1934-1964

The Chippewas were greatly affected by the two major thrusts of the 1934 Indian Reorganization Act. Administratively, the Lake Superior bands were encouraged to take much greater responsibility for their own affairs by initiating the establishment of reservation policies and programs and carrying them out. In part, this meant learning to function successfully within the greater white community. A second objective of the Indian New Deal was cultural independence. Although Commissioner Collier wished to preserve and encourage tribal communal life, as previously noted, he advocated a much more flexible and pragmatic policy than mere contra-acculturation. We have tried to energize the individual Indian and the group," he reported to the House Appropriations Subcommittee in March, 1944,

and to equip individual and group with knowledge and skills to enable them to go into the white world successfully if they want to or to hold their own and make their way where they are if they want to. That is the meaning of the Indian Reorganization Act and of all other major things we have been working at.... In brief, we have quit thinking about assimilation and segregation as opposite poles and as matters of "all or nothing." They are oversimplifications of thinking which do not connect themselves with the dynamic realities.[1]

Two of the most important programs inaugurated by the BIA to achieve these goals provided for limited Indian self-government and for tribal organizations to be chartered as federal corporations.

Approved by a majority of the band in May, 1936, the Bad River Constitution and Bylaws closely resembled those adopted by other Chippewa communities. The preamble underscored the hope that home rule would promote the Indian's welfare through education, by insuring domestic tranquility, by conserving and developing natural resources, and by forming business and other organizations. Membership was limited to those presently on the tribal rolls or born to members. Ordinances passed by the Tribal Council would determine future memberships. Qualified voters (band members aged twenty-one or over and in continuous residence on the reservation for six months prior to the election) selected for two-year terms each of the seven members of the Tribal Council. As the governing body of the band it was empowered to negotiate with federal, state, and local governments, to employ counsel, manage the economic affairs and enterprises of the band (such as land sales and leases, the inheritance of property, and hunting and fishing on tribal and restricted lands), to levy taxes, to safeguard and promote the peace, safety, morals, and general welfare of the band, to enact and enforce ordinances, and to foster Chippewa culture.

Most influential actions of the Tribal Council, it should be noted, were subject to review by the secretary of the interior. The bylaws of the Bad River Band described the duties of its officers—a tribal chairman, vice-chairman, secretary, treasurer—whom the councilmen elected from their membership.[2]

One interesting variation from the Bad River model involved the Fond du Lac, Grand Portage, and Bois Forte bands, which had been under the jurisdiction of the Consolidated Chippewa Agency since 1922. Together with Chippewa groups at White Earth, Leech Lake, and Mille Lac they organized in the 1930's the Minnesota Chippewa Tribe—a federal scheme in which a Tribal Executive Committee made up of two delegates from each group exercised central governing powers over interband matters; local jurisdiction was maintained by each reservation.[3]

The rights, privileges, and immunities of the new Bad River Corporation likewise paralleled those chartered by other Lake Superior Chippewa bands. Designed to promote reservation economic development and independence, they included the power to: purchase, manage, and dispose of property; borrow money from the Indian Credit Fund or other sources; engage in business as well as other economic activities; and enter into contracts. Heretofore, the BIA and the Secretary of the Interior had performed many of these functions.[4]

The Bad River Tribal Council exercised all corporate powers. During the Depression much of its energy was devoted to the investment of loan funds in what it hoped would be productive enterprises. Minutes from a typical council meeting (at Odanah on February 8, 1938) read as follows:

*Subjects*
Bills ordered paid: Ashland Print. Co., 8.75

Mrs. William Denomie appointed to serve for one year as the Bad River representative of the Educational Loan Committee, said representative to assist with school applications, educational loans, etc.

Council approved application of Mrs. Katherine M. Mattson for a Rehabilitation loan for moving her home to another site, said loan being for labor only.

Because estimates and plans were not available, Council postponed consideration of applications for new homes to be constructed from Rehabilitation funds until the next meeting.

Council approved application of George Ackley for Rehabilitation loan for labor only for moving his house further back on his property.

Council approved applications of the following for repairs to dwellings or for handicraft material loans: Kate Armstrong, George Bender (home repairs), Margaret Mannypenny, Marie Livingston, Mary Houle, Mrs. Joe Craig, Mrs. Frank G. Smart, Lillian White, Mary Twobirds, Mary Shaw, Agnes Scott, Mrs. Fred Soulier (handicraft material loan).

Council approved the application of George Parker for a Rehabilitation loan for labor only for repairing the buildings on his farm.[5]

Tribal councils on other Chippewa reservations also had to contend with the complexities of a credit program: the acquisition of new funds, appointment of loan committees, application reviews, and foreclosure proceedings.

Setting up Chippewa bands as business organizations with limited self-government, as authorized by the IRA, created considerable factionalism and discord on some reservations during the New Deal years. By 1941 the Keweenaw Bay Tribal Council, for example, no longer functioned efficiently because of a built-in factionalism. Of twelve representatives, six were elected from the L'Anse district on the east shore, and six from the Baraga side of the bay. The latter accused the chairman of ignoring a Baraga petition which protested a corporate project promoted by the L'Anse faction.[6] Dissension was so serious at Lac Court Oreilles that the group was unable to adopt a constitution. In August, 1940, BIA Superintendent J. C. Cavill reported that a disaffected faction—mainly older, uneducated, and non-progressive residents—wished to return to a time when chiefs and headmen handled reservation affairs and were treated with more deference by the BIA. The band's rejection of a tribal constitution, it insisted, proved that the majority opposed the Indian New Deal—including all federal expenditures which offered employment for band members. The dissidents accused the Business Committee, which had since taken over the financial affairs of the tribe, of being a bunch of BIA lackeys who used this subterfuge to force the IRA on the Lac Court Oreilles band. In a letter to Commissioner Collier, Cavill claimed that the old system of reservation chiefs and headmen was corrupt and inefficient; agitators from outside had misrepresented the IRA just before the referendum on the constitution, thus assuring its failure; the Business Committee was democratically elected each year and did a fine job under the leadership of intelligent and well-educated young Indians. Rather than discriminate against the reservation, as was also charged, the BIA had made a special effort to see that the band received an equal share of federal relief and rehabilitation funds. The superintendent had "leaned over backwards" several times to answer the complaints of the dissidents. Since they refused to listen to reason, he was determined to continue cooperation with the progressive faction, which represented the majority, in order to meet the pressing economic needs of the band.[7]

Without question, factional discord at Lac Court Oreilles, Keweenaw, and perhaps elsewhere loomed as a serious threat to Chippewa self-government and cultural independence—one that needed BIA attention. Nevertheless, Cavill was correct in insisting that his office's primary task was to provide the poverty-stricken bands with jobs, relief, loans, and education.

When Harry Hopkins informed Franklin D. Roosevelt that emergency measures must be taken for the country to survive the winter of 1933–34, the President authorized the establishment of the Civil Works Administration—a federal job program which paid minimum wages to the four million men and women quickly mobilized by Hopkins.[8] In the Lake Superior country much of the work force was Chippewas. Between late November, 1933 and the following May, 363 Indians were employed at various times at the Bad River, Red Cliff, and Lac du Flambeau reservations and at the federal building in Ashland. They repaired and remodeled homes and schools, did road work, installed wells and pumps, and made clothing and bedding for old and indigent tribesmen. The CWA furnished the materials (worth $8,933.99) and paid wages and salaries totaling $32,480.40, most of which went to the Chippewas. BIA Superintendent L. E. Baumgarten reported on May 3:

The C.W.A. was not only a great benefit to the local housing conditions etc., but I do not know how we would have gotten through the winter without it.

The Indians in this jurisdiction, due to the C.W.A., fared much better the past winter than for quite a few years past.[9]

Although it was very popular nationally for the same reasons, FDR disbanded the agency for fear it might create a permanent welfare group. By the time Baumgarten typed his report, four million federal employees had been summarily fired.[10]

By the late 1930's the BIA's Rehabilitation Division, under the direction of Xavier Vigeant, had partially replaced the CWA in Uncle Sam's attack on the twin problems of relief and reservation development. The President allotted these emergency funds to the BIA with the understanding that loans and grants would be limited to:

1) ... individuals for the contruction and repair of houses, barns, outbuildings, and root cellars; for the development of wells and springs for domestic water; and for the clearing and improvement of lands for gardens and small farms.

2) ... work projects in order to furnish outright work relief. Work projects may consist of the construction and repair of community buildings connected with the Indians' agricultural pursuits, the development of wells and springs for domestic water for community use, and the clearing and improvement of garden and farm lands for community use. Work projects may also include the manufacture of furniture and other hand-craft products, and the manufacture and processing of such articles as clothing and food, provided the products of such enterprises are for community, school, or relief consumption.

3) ... groups or associations of Indians for the establishment of small self-help projects of a self-liquidating or partially self-liquidating nature, such as small mills, grist mills, canneries, clothing factories, furniture shops, and arts and crafts projects.[11]

Unfortunately, there was not much money available. In 1938 Fond du Lac received $3,600, Grand Portage $1,800, and Nett Lake $3,000.[12] The 1941 figures for Wisconsin and Michigan were not much better: Keweenaw Bay, $5,107.81; Bad River, $6,632.94; Red Cliff, $6,055.00; Lac du Flambeau, $3,634.93; Lac Court Oreilles, $5,509.71; Mole Lake, $654.50.[13]

The Indian Division of the newly formed Civilian Conservation Corps played a more important role in creating jobs for the Chippewas and conserving, as well as developing, reservation resources. In April, 1933, CCC officials extended the agency's activities to Native Americans. Thousands of them were destitute, and the return to the reservations of jobless urban Indians compounded the problem. Because of the unique circumstances of the Chippewas and other tribes, the Indian Division differed significantly from the regular CCC. The BIA administered its projects, usually in consultation with tribal councils. Local agencies selected the male Indian enrollees, who had to be physically fit, and rotated their employment so that funds (each worker received a cash allowance of up to forty-two dollars a month) would benefit a maximum number of families. Few CCC–ID camps were established, because many of the enrollees were married, worked on their own reservations, and lived at home.[14]

In the 1930's Chippewa CCC crews undertook the following projects, which may be divided into two categories:[15]

| Physical Improvement | Development of Natural Resources |
|---|---|
| bridge maintenance and construction | fish hatchery |
| fire tower maintenance | lake development |
| water supply systems | seeding wild rice lakes |
| trail maintenance and construction | forest planting |
| minor road maintenance and graveling | forest stand improvement |
| hazard reduction | white pine blister rust control |
| telephone installation | fire fighting |
| ditch drainage | fire prevention |
| dam construction and maintenance | firebreak construction and maintenance |
| garage, cabin, warehouse, CCC–ID camp building construction | public camp ground and picnic ground development |
| razing undesirable structures | stream development |
| restoration of historic structures | wildlife preservation |
| signs, markers, monuments— construction and maintenance | map making and miscellaneous surveys |

In more personal terms, employment data from four reservations suggests how many Chippewa families must have benefited from opportunities afforded by the CCC–ID:[16]

| Reservation | Average Number of Men Employed per Month in 1937 | Average Number of Families Benefited | Total Money Spent on Indian Labor up to March 31, 1937 |
|---|---|---|---|
| Bad River | 43 | 40 | $ 82,211 |
| Lac Court Oreilles | 44 | 40 | $105,000 |
| Lac du Flambeau | 83 | 75 | $178,324 |
| Keweenaw Bay | 35 | 30 | $ 43,350 |

Unless one delves into the voluminous records of the CCC–ID, it is difficult to judge how complex the operating problems must have been for each improvement and development project. Historian Calvin Gower discovered, for example, that the construction of six miles of telephone lines at Nett Lake

necessitated one sitting with the city council and conferences with two county boards, the state highway department, and six individual landowners. Because so much land on the reservation was allotted and easements had to be obtained before work could be done, Nett Lake officials had corresponded with allottees and heirs in twenty-eight states and three countries (in addition to driving one automobile into the ground) by the end of the CCC's first two years.[17]

Obviously the CCC–ID proved extremely valuable during its nine years of existence. It was one of the first federal programs to give the poverty-stricken Chippewas a financial boost, and, rather than forcing them to do things the white man's way, it adjusted to reservation life styles and encouraged Indian self-rule.[18] Another of Commissioner Collier's goals—cultural independence—was fostered by the agency. For those who wished to remain on the reservations, physical resources were conserved and added to. At the same time, other Indians acquired skills and valuable work experience that would aid them in off-reservation employment once the Depression was over.

A final federal agency which provided major relief and rehabilitation work for the Lake Superior Chippewas was the Works Progress Administration. By the close of 1937, for example, it sponsored projects valued at $297,906 at Bad River, $139,403 at Red Cliff, $157,181 at Lac du Flambeau and $236,688 at Lac Court Oreilles.[19]

Chippewa self-development was closely tied to a fuller utilization of reservation resources—both people and land—by means of collective action. The CWA, CCC–ID, and WPA furnished much needed relief and rehabilitation projects, but this massive federal aid would not last indefinitely. To become self-sustaining the Chippewas would have to have seed money to finance promising individual and tribal economic enterprises. Happily, the Indian Reorganization Act created just such a credit system—a ten million dollar revolving loan fund—based on the principles of a credit union. Loans extended at Bad River and Red Cliff will serve as cases in point.

In 1938, BIA Credit Agent Shirley McKinsey and her assistant, D. D. Mani, reported that 86.7 percent of the income at Bad River came from government sources, 2 per cent from off-reservation wages and only 11.3 per cent from Indian-owned local businesses. It was hoped that capital investments would increase the latter category. McKin-

sey and Mani recommended several individual and group enterprises which could return a sufficient profit and thus were worthy of
consideration. Fishing and farming offered the best opportunities
for individuals; a three-year fishing loan of $270, for example, would
be self-liquidating and at the same time yield a sufficient return to
support an average family:[20]

| *Expense* | | *Income* | |
| --- | --- | --- | --- |
| 1 boat | 65.00 | 5 T Herring | 150.00 |
| 1 outboard | | Lake Trout | 150.00 |
| motor | 60.00 | Misc. fish | 100.00 |
| 10 gill nets | 80.00 | Guiding and | |
| gas, oil, | | rentals | 50.00 |
| repairs | 25.00 | | $450.00 |
| labor | 40.00 | Repayment on | |
| | $270.00 | loan | 90.00 |
| | | Net to Producer | $360.00 |

Similar loan plans were submitted for dairy, bean, and poultry
farms. Between 1938 and 1945, Bad River Chippewas borrowed individually from the corporation's credit account to the amount of
$17,466.23 for the purchase of seed, feed, machinery, livestock,
boats, fishing gear, and other items. To establish a tribal muskrat
enterprise, $4,500 was advanced to build a muskrat skinning and
drying shed, to hire game wardens, and to buy a fur baler, two boats,
an outboard motor, 1,000 steel-wire fur stretchers, and several
dozen traps. By 1945, all but $1,950 had been repaid from fur pro-
fits.[21]

The Bad River Tribal Council was convinced by 1941 that the loan
program was generally beneficial to the band. Long years of hard
work and sacrifice lay ahead before they could become self-
supporting. Still, the leaders were optimistic, perhaps because the
economic status of several borrowers had already improved so dra-
matically. BIA Junior Credit Agent Wood was particularly pleased
by the progress of Miss Mandy Manypenny:

Here is an individual truly worthy of commendable citation, for not only
has she achieved a degree of success in her dairy enterprise but rarely does
one find a young lady who is willing to make the sacrifices that must go
hand-in-hand with every small farming enterprise that is started with limited capital and resources. The success of Miss Manypenny's enterprise can
logically be attributed in part to her well-established farming background.
Her parents had been farmers for a good number of years. Although it
cannot be said that they achieved any measurable degree of success in their
farming endeavors, they did provide well for the daily needs of their small

family. They farmed an eighty acre allotment which is the same land now being operated by their enterprising daughter, Mandy. The allotment belonged to Mandy's mother.

Undoubtedly, there were several factors that played an equally important role in creating a desire on the part of Miss Manypenny to start out on the goal toward a large scale dairy enterprise. In the first place, she was the type of girl that wanted to "pay her own way." Secondly, she was probably impressed by the income she was deriving from her own few cows. Third, she unquestionably enjoyed farming and felt confident that she could successfully manage a dairy enterprise. Fourth, she had the assurance of her parents that they would cooperate and aid her in carrying out the project.

At the time Mandy Manypenny made her application for a loan in December 1938, she was 26 years of age. Her father, Charles, was 65 and her mother, Maggie, was 64. Her sister, Margaret, who was also residing at home was 22. Although the Manypennys were in modest circumstances at the time Mandy secured her loan in January of 1939, they had a nice home and kept their place looking attractive. . . .

The family income was rather limited at the time Man[d]y secured her loan. The chief sustaining sources of income were from Mr. Manypenny's WPA wages and sales of dairy products, particularly milk and cream. Mandy had three cows and three yearling heifers and her sister also had three cows. An appreciable amount of income was realized for the family budget from these cows which comprised the entire dairy herd on the Manypenny farm. In addition to these cows and heifers, the only other livestock on the farm was a yearling bull owned by Mandy and a 24 year old mare which was owned by her father. They had some farm machinery and equipment which were in fair condition.

Mandy borrowed $358.85 from the Bad River Corporation with which she purchased a horse to team with her father's horse, four cows, a sow, and seed. The seed was a relatively big item, for Miss Manypenny knew that the success of her enterprise depended to a great extent on the amount of feed which she could raise instead of purchase for her stock. She had the courage to plan an extensive use of the cultivable land for grains and forage. The eighty acre farm contained 35¼ acres suitable for farming and the balance, or 44¾ acres, was cut-over timber land suitable for pasture purposes.

The loan provided that Mandy would have full use of the land, buildings, father's horse, and farm equipment. Further provisions were that Mandy would be permitted to live at home and that in exchange for the use of the land, buildings, and equipment she was to furnish the dairy products for home use. Her sister and father agreed to help her with the farm work. . . .

Mandy has traveled a considerable distance up hill during the two and one-half years that her enterprise has been in operation. At the time she submitted her loan application during the closing days of 1938, she reported her cash income for that year as $190 (Cream and milk, $165; poultry, $25). For the year from June 1, 1940 to June 1, 1941, she reported her cash income as $540 (Cream and milk, $448; sale of cattle, $65; soil conservation, $13; bean sales, $14). Accordingly, during the period so far in which she has had the loan, she has increased her cash income nearly three-fold. . . .

On May 27, 1941 Mandy submitted a new loan application for the refinance of her old loan and to enable her to purchase a new horse to replace her father's old horse which had died the preceding month. At this time Mandy's assets (disregarding interest in land and buildings) consisted of 10 cows, 4 heifers, 3 bulls, 4 calves, 1 horse, and 18 chickens. These assets were valued at $1064. Her liabilities consisted of the balance remaining on her old loan, a sum of $156.34, and a veterinary bill of $10.00, making her total liabilities $166.34. This gave her a present net worth of $897.66 as compared to $337.50 two and one half years ago. It is interesting to note that during this same period her net worth increased slightly more than two and one-half times. This increase in net worth is accounted for largely by increase in cattle. . . .

Several factors have been brought out in the preceding discussion which have contributed to the fine showing which Miss Manypenny has made. However, in summing up, it should be stated that a good farming background and a helpful family are deserving factors, but like good tools—they are only as efficient as the workman who uses them. The scale of worth must be tipped in favor of Miss Manypenny herself. Her good business judgment, sense of proper economy, and industry should be overwhelmingly stressed in analyzing Miss Manypenny's commendable advancement in her dairy enterprise. . . .[22]

Across Chequamegon Bay at Red Cliff, several Chippewas individually borrowed from the corporation's credit fund to the amount of $12,182.95 during the decade following 1937. Most loans were for seed, livestock, boats, nets, and other items needed to farm and fish. Despite five foreclosures by 1941, which caused the corporation serious financial loss, the Red Cliff Tribal Council agreed that, overall, the program greatly improved the economic condition of the band. In the judgment of Tribal Chairman Mike J. Gordon, the remarks of one councilman, himself a borrower, characterized the feelings of most loan recipients: "My loan has helped me a lot. Before I received the loan, I just got a living. If I ever do get my loan paid for, I will have some stock that I can call my own. I'm glad I got the loan."[23]

The New Deal's education program for the Chippewas and other tribes was firmly rooted in Collier's desire to "energize" individual Indians as well as groups so that they would be prepared for life both on and off the reservation. During the 1930's, BIA school teachers studied Indian values and the possibilities of cross-cultural education. Because the daily reinforcement of home and community values was so important in this type of Indian education, some boarding schools were closed and the number of local schools increased. The program of study at both was modified to include aspects of Indian culture as well as standard vocational training. The Johnson-O'Malley Act, passed in April, 1934, likewise had far-reaching curricular repercussions. It authorized the BIA to contract on a statewide basis for single, annual Indian tuition payments rather than negotiating agreements with hundreds of local public schools, which had been the case since the 1890's. Unhappily, federal-state contracting created the serious new problem of how to convince state administrators that Johnson–O'Malley funds should be used to develop special programs for the growing number of Indian children in public schools—53 per cent in 1930—not simply added to general operating budgets. For thirty years no solution could be found. Public school education remained largely inappropriate to the unique needs of Native Americans.[24]

For older Indians with inferior backgrounds in formal education, the CCC–ID and WPA provided vocational training in job skills (such as carpentry, truck driving, radio operation, surveying) as well as in academic subjects. As part of the rehabilitation program of the CCC–ID's Minneapolis District, for example, WPA instructors taught pupils enough reading, writing, and arithmetic to get them certified as eighth-grade graduates. To the north at Nett Lake camp, eight public school staff members conducted classes during the mid-1930's in beginning English, general science, and other basic subjects.[25]

In order to grasp the grass roots significance of the innovative New Deal programs in education, reservation development, relief, and self-government, one must take a closer look at some of the Lake Superior Chippewa reservations during the decade following the enactment of the Indian Reorganization Act.

Allotment and fifty-five years of logging exacted a harsh toll at Keweenaw Bay. Of the 52,370 acres (heavily timbered with valuable hardwoods) originally set aside for the band, their descendants retained only 11,597.34 cut-over acres by 1937.[26]

Government relief agencies such as CCC–ID and WPA provided only 32.8 per cent of the band's income in 1937. Nearly 50 per cent was derived from private employment in the area where the wage-minded Chippewas were considered "efficient and reliable." The average income for 226 families (851 individuals) was $608.98— roughly equivalent to that of other economically depressed farm units in the north country. Actually, these earnings were far better for reservation residents; their costs of living were minimal, with little or no rents to pay and cheap fuel available as well as fish and game. To boost profits even higher, more dairy farms needed to be established. Out of 274 such Indian enterprises, 77 yielded yearly incomes of $1,500 to $5,999 and only 28 produced less than $600.[27]

Thanks to the medical care provided by the Baraga County Health Department and the contract physician, Dr. F. F. Marshall, general health at Keweenaw Bay showed marked improvement by 1942. All known cases of tuberculosis were hospitalized and venereal disease was practically nonexistent. Because the BIA facility at Hayward was too far away, adult emergency cases went to St. Joseph's Hospital in Hancock—a costly service involving serious transportation problems. Happily for the children, the Couzens Fund made possible special hospital care at St. Luke's in Marquette. Moreover, at six months of age, nearly 100 per cent of Indian infants were innoculated by county health officials against smallpox and diphtheria; all youngsters in school, regardless of race, got medical examinations which included Mantoux tests for tuberculosis.[28]

Improved housing and transportation facilities also contributed to more healthful conditions on Keweenaw Bay. Except for recurrent overcrowding (1.4 families per dwelling), Indian homes at Baraga, L'Anse, and Zeba were clean and neat inside—a "credit to any community" according to one BIA report. Twenty-six families used electricity and many more planned to wire their homes; meanwhile kerosene provided light. For winter fuel they burned wood, occasionally supplemented with coal. The reservation was crossed by two major commercial arteries during the New Deal era: the Duluth, South Shore, and Atlantic Railroad and a paved highway, U.S. 41. Graveled county roads and backwoods logging trails also intertwined the area. Fifty-six cars and trucks furnished the major means of travel for Chippewa families. When desired, bus service and rail service were available at Baraga and L'Anse. Goods trucked in from Marquette and Houghton via U.S. 41 kept stores in both towns well supplied.[29] For seriously ill Indians, the same highway of course gave access to St. Joseph's and St. Luke's hospitals.

Continued acculturation of the L'Anse band was to be expected in light of its economic integration with south shore industries, the breakdown of physical isolation, and Collier's encouragement of cultural independence. Living much as their white neighbors, the Chippewas eventually intermarried and became "church-going, kind, sympathetic, energetic, intelligent, and constructive" parts of each community. The Methodist congregation at Zeba and the Catholic Mission at Assinins exerted a particularly strong moral and religious influence on family life. Church groups also sponsored most of the reservation social gatherings.[30]

A hundred miles west, on Lake Superior's blustery south shore, the Bad River band courageously battled the elements as well as a depressed economy in order to sustain itself during the New Deal years. Sixty-five per cent of the 875 members clustered in and around the unincorporated village of Odanah. Still situated on the reservation's northern lowlands and inundated for three or four days each spring by the backwashed waters of the Bad River, Odanah consisted of the following public buildings in 1938: two general stores, a post office (in conjunction with a small shop), a pool hall, an auto repair shop, two licensed taverns, a Catholic church, a Methodist church, a parochial school, a public school, a community hall, and a general office building and warehouse owned by the Great Lakes Indian Agency, headquartered at Ashland. Of the 128,132.29 reservation acres once allotted to Bad River Chippewas, more than 50,000 had been alienated.[31]

Ever since Leonard H. Wheeler's experiments in the 1840's, white agriculturists had insisted that the region could be productive under proper management. Over the years, dairying had certainly proved a profitable way to market clover, grass, and other farm products. Root and berry crops also flourished. But Indians who wished to farm faced high costs of clearing and draining cut-over timberland in addition to stocking and equipping their farms. By the close of the 1930's, only 37 of 235 Bad River families farmed the land, and few of these enterprises were profitable. With less than 400 reservation acres under cultivation, their total return was $3,680—3.8 per cent of the band's $97,745.86 yearly income. In striking contrast to Mandy Manypenny's efficient operation, a typical farm consisted of sixty acres, half of which were put into crops. About ten acres were used for pasturing the family cow, a couple of horses, and a few dozen chickens. The farm house was frame or log-frame construction, the leaky barn and shed badly needed paint and repair, while the equipment was in such poor shape it needed to be replaced. An additional 10 per cent of the reservation's self-generated income came from wages, the sale of arts and crafts, and furs. What kept the band alive in 1938 was Washington's contribution of 86.7 per cent to the Bad River income:

|  | Amount | Per cent |
|---|---|---|
| WPA | $46,659.27 | 47.73 |
| CCC-ID | 8,064.50 | 8.27 |
| Pensions | 8,386.05 | 8.57 |
| Direct Relief | 5,602.19 | 5.73 |
| Roads, Indian | 16,046.35 | 16.50 |
|  | $84,758.36 | 86.70 |

The band's yearly gain from all sources averaged a dismal $413.64

per family. Real income was somewhat higher, since the band lived practically rent and tax free and could gather fuel, wild rice, wild fruit, and game. Also, more than half the families gardened. In an attempt to look "on the bright side," the BIA calculated that an annual income as meager as $282.56 could have sustained at the subsistence level an average-sized family at Bad River.[32]

Though most Bad River youngsters attended public and parochial schools, there is no evidence that special cross-cultural programs— as envisioned by the architects of the Indian New Deal—were developed for their unique needs. Each year during the late Thirties and early Forties, grammar school education was provided for about two hundred Chippewa children by Odanah Rural School and Odanah State Graded. Catholic Sisters still operated the latter, formerly called St. Mary's. Both institutions had Indian tuition contracts, as did Ashland High School, which registered between ten and seventeen reservation Indians. On its daily run to Ashland High, the BIA bus transported an equal number of teenagers to the parochial high schools—DePadua and St. Agnes. Non-reservation boarding schools and special institutions took twenty more pupils from Bad River. Still another twenty-six were not eligible for enrollment anywhere because of serious illness, full-time employment, marriage, or enlistment in the armed forces. The BIA, and doubtless the Catholic church, took great pride in the program at Odanah State Graded—"the best . . . in any small town in this part of Wisconsin." Leonard H. Wheeler, the father of missionary education at Bad River and one of the founders of Odanah, also would have been pleased by its modern building, lunch rooms, library, gymnasium, and particularly the practical instruction in shop work and home economics. A fine arts and music program, as well as a kindergarten, rounded out the curriculum. The persistence of the truancy problem over the past century would have disturbed the old missionary but probably would not have surprised him. The necessity of off-reservation employment for adults still forced children to follow along and miss school. Sickness, racism on the part of white teachers and pupils, and the reluctance of county officials to enforce attendance likewise contributed to the significant numbers of Indian youth who stayed out of school without permission.[33]

Besides encouraging education and reservation development, the most important services the Bad River Chippewas received from Wisconsin and BIA officials were health education and medical care. A state nurse fostered better understanding between the more than one thousand Odanah residents and the local clinic which offered free treatment. She also conducted follow-up calls in the community once the doctor had made a clinical diagnosis. During home visits she detected "prenatals" and encouraged them to get professional care during the remainder of their pregnancy and to have their children delivered at the Hayward Indian Hospital. The nurse was alerted when an Indian Service doctor, who periodically examined and immunized all school children, detected physical defects or communicable diseases.

During the late 1930's and early 1940's, contract physician Dr. John W. Prentice of Ashland examined dozens of patients and dispensed drugs two mornings a week at the newly constructed Odanah clinic. Physicians also innoculated nine hundred persons against typhoid following the serious spring floods in 1938 and 1941. The lowness of the land surrounding Odanah produced other health hazards: poor drainage permitted the breeding of large numbers of disease-carrying insects, and the damp air was certainly unhealthy for a people prone to tuberculosis and other pulmonary afflictions. Poor diets, partly due to their limited incomes, further undermined the Indians' ability to resist infection. The incidence of tuberculosis at Bad River was still much higher than among whites, but there had been a significant reduction in cases of venereal disease.[34]

Preventing the spread of communicable diseases at Bad River was especially difficult because of overcrowded housing—1.62 families per home—which prevented the isolation of a patient suffering, for example, from tuberculosis in its active and infectious stage. Nor could privies "meet any standards of sanitation." The average home, built at the turn of the century, was by 1938 a dilapidated four- or five-room frame structure worth $325. Another indication of the level of poverty to which the Chippewas had fallen was the sparseness of household goods—$77.16 worth per home. Of the 235 Bad River families, only 72 had sewing machines and only 58 had radios. When BIA Credit Agent McKinsey discovered pianos in 22 homes she regarded them rather sadly as "silent testifiers of better days." As was the case at Keweenaw, kerosene lamps provided lighting for most homes. Wood was burned for winter warmth.

When a Chippewa had an errand to run, his primary source of transportation was the automobile. Band members owned thirty-five vehicles and willingly taxied their friends around for the cost of the gasoline; otherwise they rode one of the two bus lines which serviced Odanah: the Ashland Bus Company and Greyhound. Railroad connections could be made in Ashland. Odanah's access to the outside world was greatly enhanced in the late thirties when the state highway department laid cement pavement for U.S. 2, which ran east-west through the reservation. The BIA and WPA also built a primary road south from the town to the reservation line.[35]

Completed in 1937 with BIA rehabilitation monies and WPA labor, the community hall became the social center of Odanah and was used five mornings a week by the WPA Nursery Project, four evenings for WPA or CCC–ID recreation, and periodically for dances. Besides the other obvious opportunities for individual or small group recreation—fishing, hunting, card games, movies, listening to the radio, picnics—several civic organizations thrived in the town. The local public school sponsored a PTA as well as two scout troops. Twenty-four boys and thirty girls joined the Odanah 4-H clubs organized by state farm and home extension agents. There was also a community band, a fair board, and the ever-present athletic teams.[36]

To an outsider visiting Odanah, Chippewa traditional practices seemed minimal: two or three summer powwows, a few adherents to the native religion, an occasional death ceremonial. Of the 875 members of the Bad River band, only 74 were full bloods.[37]

Circumstances similar to those at Bad River existed across Chequamegon Bay at Red Cliff, where reservation land once embraced 14,092 heavily timbered acres. By 1937, 5,236 of these had been alienated and the remainder clear-cut and burned. Tribal rolls listed 618 members that year. Nine per cent of their earnings came from fishing, farming, berrying, and the sale of such forest products as young white birch and aspen. Outside labor yielded another 13 per cent. The band depended upon the government for 78 per cent of its income.[38] Unlike their cousins at Keweenaw and Bad River, the majority of Red Cliff children (138 out of 167) enrolled in parochial schools—the St. Francis Mission in the village of Red Cliff, where the population was concentrated, and the Holy Family Mission, a two-year high school in Bayfield. Twenty-one Chippewa teenagers attended Bayfield High School.[39] The general health of band members living on the reservation and in Bayfield was good. Only two known cases of tuberculosis existed in 1942. The rate of venereal disease was no higher than among whites. Three BIA field inspectors made favorable reports about contract physician Dr. M. J. Robertson of Bayfield, who treated Indian patients during regular office hours and at his weekly clinic in the basement of the Red Cliff community building. Children received the usual school examinations and immunizations for smallpox and diphtheria.[40]

The checkerboard land situation to the southeast at Lac du Flambeau was even more enervating for the Chippewas. By the time the IRA reversed the allotment policy, permanent damage had been done. Whites had taken possession of valuable reservation acreage and dotted the shores of most lakes with resorts. The Indians retained only 31,933 acres of the original 73,600. These were cut-over, swampy lands, juxtaposed to white tracts and so subdivided among heirs and tangled in "red tape" that they were worthless. There was "no escape from the influence of past events," remarked anthropologist A. Irving Hallowell.[41]

Although nearly 200 enrolled members had moved to towns and cities by 1946, 776 remained on their picturesque reservation. Most lived in and around the village of Lac du Flambeau; like Odanah, it included a local post office, school, churches, stores, and garages. Frequently referred to as New Village, it was also the center for the band's booming summer tourist industry. Other concentrations of Chippewas could be found three miles away in Old Village, where 100 lived at Sand Lake and near the Chicago and Northwestern Railroad station.[42]

The economic, educational, and health situations at Lac du Flambeau conformed to patterns described previously. Off-reservation work plus local hunting, fishing, trapping, caretaking, handicrafts, and the harvesting of wild rice and berries produced only 23 per cent of the band's income. New Deal agencies and the BIA furnished the rest.[43] During the 1942–43 academic year, 295 youngsters attended the Lac du Flambeau federal day school, public, and boarding schools, while five post-highs took classes at BIA vocational institutions or at the University of Wisconsin. School children were examined and immunized each fall by Indian Service physicians. The same doctors reported that the number of Chippewa adults suffering from tuberculosis or venereal disease was quite small.[44]

Because of Hallowell's field work at Lac du Flambeau in 1946, we have additional data about Chippewa acculturation and do not have to rely so extensively on BIA reports. Several indices he used suggested that major modifications had occurred in the band's traditional practices. By the end of World War II, English was the accepted language. Only the aged were bilingual. All reservation families lived year-round in frame houses. The wearing of moccasins—an important cultural characteristic—was abandoned along with the centuries-old system of hunting territories. Finally, only a few older and conservative families at Old Village carried on the Midéwiwin; most Indians attended Protestant or Catholic churches.[45]

Despite this seemingly high level of acculturation, Hallowell used psychological tests to prove that the Lac du Flambeau Indians, only one quarter of whom were full bloods, were still Chippewas in terms of personality.[46]

The Ojibwa were food gatherers, hunters and fishermen; they had no agriculture or settled villages in the aboriginal period. From the standpoint of behavior one of the significant features of their culture was the absence of any institutionalized development which brought organized social sanctions to bear upon the individual. They were chiefless, courtless, jailess. Their society has been called "atomistic." The type of personality structure that we find was highly introverted. It functioned in terms of internalized controls; the individual felt the full brunt of responsibility for his own acts. Sickness and misfortune were thought to be the penalty for wrongdoing and experiences of this sort provided the occasion for deep feelings of guilt. Ego support, especially in the men, was closely linked with a belief in the necessity for supernaturally derived assistance. This was the basis of psychological security and dreams were the prime medium of human contacts with supernatural beings. On the other hand, psychological security was never absolute since besides sickness and misfortune, even the strongest man might be menaced by sorcery. Therefore, it was necessary to be extremely cautious in interpersonal relations lest aggression be aroused and covert hostility released. So a surface amiability and emotional restraint, tinged with latent suspicion and anxiety, were characteristic. With so little real give and take on an open and genuinely friendly basis, a high degree of projection colored interpersonal relations. . . .

What has happened to this characteristic configuration of Ojibwa personality . . . ? The most striking fact is the continuity of the same basic psychological pattern through these stages of acculturation. There is a persistent core of generic traits which can be identified as Ojibwa. Thus even the highly acculturated Indians at Flambeau are still Ojibwa in a psychological sense whatever their clothes, their houses, or their occupations, whether they speak English or not, and regardless of race mixture. While culturally speaking they appear like "whites" in many respects, there is no evidence at all of a fundamental psychological transformation. On the other hand, the fact of psychological continuity must not be taken to imply that no modifications in the psychological structure of the Ojibwa have taken place. The nature of these modifications will direct attention to what is perhaps the most important conclusion that can be drawn from our data. . . .

I cannot, of course, go into an extended analysis here of all the various factors that may account for the breakdown of the old personality structure of the Ojibwa under the pressures of acculturation at Flambeau. But I can say that one of the most crucial factors involved seems to be the lack of any positive substitute for that aspect of the aboriginal value system that had its core in religious belief. As I have pointed out . . . there was once an intimate connection between the content of Ojibwa beliefs, the source of their psychological security and the optimum functioning of inner controls in their psychic economy. While this inner control is still present at Flambeau it has been modified in a regressive direction so that it easily breaks down. In actual behavior, evidence of this is to be seen in the tremendous incidence of drunkenness and juvenile delinquency on the reservation and the fact that externally applied controls seem quite ineffective. The behavior of many Indians is also symptomatic of the terrific inner struggle which many individuals are experiencing in reaction to the present paucity of their inner resources. An apathy is created which they cannot overcome. . . .

What seems to have happened is that the acculturation process at Flambeau has reached a level which presents a situation in which we find the personality structure of the Ojibwa in the process of breaking down, rather than undergoing reintegration in any new or positive form. It is also at this level of acculturation that, along with the disappearance of language, old economic pursuits and customs, the native system of belief and values exhibits the most striking disintegration. Consequently there is little or nothing of genuine integrative value that the old culture can offer the individual.

Although no such elaborate psychological profile exists for the seventeen hundred Lac Court Oreilles Chippewas, three centuries of white contact obviously eroded much of their woodland culture. Anthropologist Robert E. Ritzenthaler estimated that 80 per cent of the band, mainly the middle-aged and the children, followed the white man's ways by the early 1940's—dwelling in permanent log or frame structures and wearing white man's dress, except when entertaining summer tourists. The traditional social system had collapsed to the extent that clans were functionless. The Catholic church dominated the religious life of the band. Mainly it was the old people who clung to their Indian religion, spoke only Chippewa, and wore moccasins.[47]

For the acculturated Lac Court Oreilles band, life during the New Deal era was much like that on the other Lake Superior reservations. Two-fifths of its woodlands had been alienated as a result of the allotment system, yet hunting, fishing, trapping, and gathering still furnished food for the family table. Whatever meager amounts of cash circulated among the Chippewas came from seasonal occupations (guiding, lumbering, harvesting the crops of white farmers) and federal relief projects. Of the 337 children enrolled for the 1942–43 academic year, 206 attended classes in the public schools of Sawyer County, which received $11,024.29 in tuition payments. Others went to the mission day school or non-reservation boarding schools.[48] The health picture also looked the same as at Lac du Flambeau, Red Cliff, and Bad River. No serious problems with tuberculosis or venereal disease were reported, clinics were conducted regularly in towns and villages, and yearly school examinations and immunizations were carried out.[49]

At the head of Lake Superior and upriver from Duluth was the Fond du Lac reservation, with a population of 681 in the mid-1930's. Visible signs of acculturation included permanent homes with wooden floors, modern-style dress, and the ability of nearly 500 Indians to read and write English. Also apparent was the Depression's enervating grip on the economy. The estimated average family income dropped to $310, most of which came from wages totaling $155,400. Only about $6,000 in cash income was generated by Chippewas engaged in farming, selling forest products, manufacturing arts and crafts articles, and other forms of self-employment.[50]

The four-hundred-member Grand Portage band found itself in similar financial straits. The average income of only $233 in 1935, obtained largely by hiring themselves out to whites, convinced a BIA analyst that, as soon as the market improved, commercial fishing by Indian cooperatives would be the best economic activity. The hilly, rocky, and sandy reservation soil was certainly unfit for farming, and the Indians showed no interest in making a living in any other way than fishing, their traditional enterprise. Moreover, they were as good at it as their Scandinavian neighbors.[51]

When not fishing, the Grand Portage Chippewas concentrated in two coastal communities about thirty miles apart—Grand Marais and Grand Portage. All lived in permanent homes with wooden floors, most wore white-style clothes, and about half could read and write English. Indian youngsters attended schools and received medical care there.[52]

The Nett Lake (Bois Forte) reservation offered no exceptions to trends noted elsewhere: of its 410 enrolled members in 1935, all had abandoned the wigwam as well as traditional dress; about half could read and write English; and most of their $86,200 annual income was derived from wage work rather than self-employment.[53]

The New Deal's ability to stop the alienation of Chippewa land showed itself most clearly with the so-called Lost Bands. As roaming hunters and fishermen the St. Croix were left out of the La Pointe treaty of 1854, which established reservation homes for the Lake Superior Chippewas. As a consequence, they eked out a living as squatters for the next eighty years, deep in the forests of northern Wisconsin just west of Lac Court Oreilles. BIA negotiators promised the Sakaogon a reservation of twelve square miles of land when they signed a treaty in 1855, but the United States Senate's refusal to ratify it also left them landless. Not until the enactment of the IRA in 1934 did the BIA finally take some action on their behalf. The Lost Bands finally obtained legal rights to the unwanted woodlands they had occupied for centuries. In 1939 the Sakaogon Chippewas, having adopted a constitution, took possession of 1,680 acres (to be called the Mole Lake Reservation) purchased for them on one side of Rice Lake in north-central Wisconsin—the smallest reservation in the state. For the St. Croix, the federal government bought scattered parcels of available land (1,750 acres) in five communities where these Indians were then living (in Burnett and Polk counties). The band organized as the St. Croix Chippewas of Wisconsin in 1942.[54]

Despite the acquisition of their own land, the overall condition of the Lost Bands during the New Deal years paralleled that of Chippewas elsewhere. At Mole Lake the average income for twenty-three families was $450.59 in 1939, 74 per cent of which came from government sources such as WPA and CCC–ID. Men lacked the skills for jobs off the reservation, and, to make matters worse, local agriculture seemingly had no future even with a farm credit program. Eighty per cent of the reservation remained uncleared, with the soil depleted and quack grass thriving.

By 1936, the gross income of Forest County, within which the reservation lay, ranked sixty-eighth among seventy-one Wisconsin counties; only 14 per cent was farm acreage, which yielded an average family income of $750, compared to a state figure of $1,733.89. Even though fuel, taxes, and housing drained off little Indian income, cash was still so scarce that only current household expenses for food and clothing could be met. No opportunity existed to accumulate capital for future improvements. The ninety-three reservation residents crowded into twenty houses and averaged almost three persons per room. Nevertheless, their health was generally good. Tuberculosis and venereal disease rates were low, although trachoma became fairly common. A contract doctor at nearby Crandon, Wisconsin, saw Indian patients during regular office hours and visited the reservation in emergency cases. The twenty-five youngsters who attended Mole Lake State Graded School were examined and immunized yearly. The community at Mole Lake included, in addition to the school, a post office and store. Six Indian-owned automobiles provided local transportation. Longer journeys required a drive north on State Highway 55 to Crandon, where daily train connections could be made on the Chicago and Northwestern or the Soo Line.[55]

What data we have about the St. Croix Chippewas prior to 1945 indicates that they numbered between four and five hundred and subsisted rather miserably on scattered reservations at Danbury,

Webster, and Hertel in Burnett County and at Luck and Balsam Lake in Polk County. Their lands were sandy, unproductive, and covered with glacial debris. As was the case at Sakaogon, local whites had already demonstrated the impracticality of extensive farming. The St. Croix had to make a precarious living by means of gardening and sporadic wage work. Most of their children attended tuition contract public schools by 1942-43. As a result of this education and other acculturating forces, very little traditional culture remained. Young people understood but did not speak the Chippewa language and the mixed bloods, who were hardly distinguishable from whites, made up the majority of the band. In fact, one government investigator suggested that the BIA simply consider the St. Croix as whites—indigent, poor whites, that is.[56]

America's involvement in World War II deeply affected the Chippewas of Lake Superior and the entire Indian New Deal. The Michigan Chippewas began by announcing their own war on the Axis powers: "We are standing once more shoulder to shoulder with our white brothers as we did with George Washington at Valley Forge and in every war for liberty."[57] Eventually, more than 24,000 young American Indians joined the United States armed forces. Of the approximately 300 able-bodied men at the Bad River reservation in Wisconsin, for example, 116—over 18 per cent of the population— enlisted in the American army, navy or marines by June, 1943. Seventy-five per cent volunteered, and many held responsible positions as noncommissioned officers on fighting fronts around the globe. John Basner, Lloyd Neveaux, and Allerd Corbine saw action in North Africa; James Arbuckle, one of four brothers in uniform, served in Australia and New Guinea; Ernest Harnden was with the navy's Seabees; former tribal chairman William Denomie was stationed with the U.S. Maritime Service in England, Ireland, and North Africa.[58] In the armed forces they were separated from family and tribe, brought into close association with groups from all sections of American society, forced to speak English, treated as individual soldiers rather than as faceless members of an Indian band—the personal impact of World War II on Chippewa servicemen must have been enormous.[59]

Wartime employment broadened the perspectives of approximately 40,000 American Indians who moved to urban areas to work in factories, shipyards, aircraft plants, and railroad yards. As of June, 1943, this included 129 men from Odanah. Chippewa welders, outfitters, and shipwrights helped to build cargo and escort vessels at the busy Walter Butler shipyards in Superior, Wisconsin. Tribesmen from Lac du Flambeau, with experience gained from CCC–ID projects, qualified for army and navy wartime construction jobs in Newfoundland, Canada, and Alaska.[60]

For those who remained on the reservation, the war was a part of everyday life. Women at Lac du Flambeau spent hundreds of hours in Red Cross knitting and sewing projects, and they financed a monthly newsletter for their servicemen. Chippewas throughout the Great Lakes region contributed to the national war effort by increasing food production beyond tribal needs. In 1942, they marketed 58,000 pounds of meat, fish, and fowl, 56,000 eggs, 5,000 pounds of butterfat, 4,000 pounds of cereals, 69,000 pounds of vegetables, and 750 bushels of potatoes. At the same time, these profits, together with the earnings of off-reservation servicemen and civilians, improved the quality of reservation life. Chippewa relief cases declined by 50 per cent.[61]

The nation's preoccupation with the war nevertheless forced changes in domestic priorities which blunted the thrust of the Indian New Deal. Symbolic of the setback was the BIA's exile to Chicago in 1942, "to relieve congestion in war-time Washington." Thirty-two railroad cars transported over a million pounds of file cases and office equipment to the bureau's new quarters on the tenth and twenty-fourth floors of the Merchandise Mart.[62]

Indian administration was further crippled by the loss of many staff members to the military services and by Congress's slashing of Collier's appropriations, which led to the physical deterioration of reservation facilities such as schools, hospitals, agency buildings, vehicles, roads, and telephone networks.[63] Shortly after the attack on Pearl Harbor, the CCC also fell victim to the national reallocation of resources for defense purposes. "The ending of the CCC," the Indian commissioner lamented in June, 1942, "was a heavy, heavy blow to Indian Service, to the Indians, and to social policy in the United States. It is just that: a heavy and undeserved blow." Of its contribution to the lives of the Lake Superior Chippewas, as well as other tribes throughout the United States, Collier had written just two years before: "Indian CCC ... is bone of the bone and flesh of the flesh of the Indians' new achievement. There is no part of Indian country, there are few functions of Indian life, where it has not made an indispensable contribution. Truly, Indian CCC has been a creative force."[64] An unwitting but eloquent epitaph. Still another victim of the manpower, budget, and attitudinal shifts during the war was the educational program for Native Americans. That BIA school curriculum and the whole federal policy pendulum should start a swing away from the encouragement of cultural independence and reservation self-determination was suggested by O. K. Armstrong's emotional article, "Set the American Indians Free!" which appeared in the August, 1945, *Reader's Digest*. His call for breaking tribal ties and a rapid assimilation of Indian peoples (especially veterans) into the mainstream sounded like an echo from the disastrous allotment era. Instead, it foreshadowed the tragic termination plans of the postwar years.[65]

During the twenty years after World War II, the BIA Education Division shifted its goals and curriculum. No longer emphasized were cross-cultural education and vocational training for rural living. In response to the expansion of employment opportunities in metropolitan areas and the pressures to terminate federal services to the tribes, there emerged new assimilation programs to educate increasing numbers of Native Americans for city life. In the 1950's federal funding for tribal children in public schools was augmented by impacted area legislation (Public Laws 81–815 and 81–874) which replaced the Johnson-O'Malley Act as the primary source of educational support for Indian pupils. Indian students were encouraged to pursue post-high school classwork in either college or vocational school. These postwar programs did not meet the needs of the Chippewas and most other tribes because they disregarded two key concepts of Collier's New Deal: the importance of the Indian's cultural heritage in any public or federal school curriculum, and the Indian's desire for self-determination—in this case, inclusion in educational decision making.[66]

Bureaucrats encouraged other programs designed to integrate the Indian population into the national economy. Beginning in the Eisenhower era, a sales campaign launched by the BIA Relocation Bureau prompted thousands of tribesmen to forsake the security of reservation life and, with government financial assistance, migrate to certain large urban areas—Chicago, Denver, Oakland, Los Angeles, for example—where a higher standard of living and permanent employment supposedly awaited.[67] The following chapter in this volume details the serious maladjustments among those Chippewas who left tribal lands and relocated in these new, asphalt environments without the benefits of a realistic orientation procedure, proper job training, or adequate federal financial assistance. For those who resisted voluntary resettlement propaganda, the BIA continued its century-old efforts to develop the full economic potential of reservation lands.

Under close BIA supervision, Chippewa woodland resources were still modest in value and only partially developed. By the mid-1950's timber sales became so snarled in the red tape of heirship that before stumpage could be sold the Forest Branch of the Great Lakes Agency had to check ownership, obtain signatures, and answer questions from such interested parties as county welfare agencies, attorneys, and tribal councils.[68] The following sales figures suggest that, despite these efforts, only Grand Portage and Nett Lake derived an income of more than $6,000 from the lumbering of Indian lands:[69]

| Reservation | Volume in 1,000 Board Feet | Average Stumpage Rate per Thousand | Value |
|---|---|---|---|
| | | 1958 | |
| Fond du Lac | 561 | $ 2.36 | $1,214 |
| Grand Portage | 805 | 10.81 | 6,787 |
| Nett Lake | 904 | 8.26 | 6,230 |
| | | 1959 | |
| Keweenaw Bay | 410 | 1.88 | 770 |
| Bad River | 726 | 4.19 | 3,044 |
| Court Oreilles | 593 | 6.29 | 2,720 |
| Flambeau | 312 | 9.91 | 587 |
| Red Cliff | 563 | 7.00 | 3,899 |
| Mole Lake | 252 | 4.35 | 1,095 |
| St. Croix | 100 | 3.40 | 95 |

These logging operations also generated jobs for Indian lumberjacks. Because of their remoteness, Nett Lake and Grand Portage tribesmen still profited from wildlife resources—fish, fur bearing animals, game birds, and big game. The sale of fishing and hunting permits in 1958 produced incomes of $53,358 at Grand Portage and $68,890 at Nett Lake.[70] Generally, however, recreation was an untapped land resource of the Lake Superior Chippewas. As late as 1960, Bad River, Red Cliff, and Lac Court Oreilles reservations, to name but three, had virtually no Indian-owned recreational facilities, even though they contained dozens of miles of accessible streams and thousands of acres of sparkling lakes and ponds for fishing and hunting.[71]

The federal government's revolving loan fund still encouraged tribal councils to finance promising individual as well as cooperative reservation enterprises. Between July 1, 1957 and June 30, 1958, for example, Bad River extended the following credit:[72]

| Loan for | Number | Amount |
|---|---|---|
| seed | 13 | $    288.30 |
| feed | 3 | 267.00 |
| other nonrecoverable items | 37 | 1,635.33 |
| machinery | 23 | 2,702.41 |
| livestock | 24 | 6,772.00 |
| permanent improvements | 1 | 5,500.00 |
| boats | 2 | 315.00 |
| refinancing | 15 | 6,200.00 |
| other recoverable items | 19 | 369.42 |
| | | $24,050.23 |

With industrial development a major target for tribal funds, special promotional committees were instituted at Bad River, Fond du Lac, Grand Portage, and Nett Lake by 1961. Red Cliff earmarked $3,000 for this purpose; Lac du Flambeau set aside and spent $40,000, and Lac Court Oreilles $65,000. The Shelton Basket Company at Reserve, established with a $35,000 Lac Court Oreilles loan, soon employed thirty-eight Chippewas. Indian workers at other industrial plants on or near reservations in 1962 included:[73]

| Company and Location | Nearest Reservation | Product | Indian Employees | Total Employees |
|---|---|---|---|---|
| Lost Tribes Industries Balsam Lake, Wisconsin | St. Croix | YoYo String & Accessories | 18 | 18 |
| Indianhead Moccasin Co. Webster, Wisconsin | St. Croix | Moccasins, Jackets and Beaded Articles | 12 | 12 |
| Chapplesky Lumber Co. Milltown, Wisconsin | St. Croix | Sawmill, Planer Mill and Lumber Products | 6 | 15 |

| Company and Location | Nearest Reservation | Product | Indian Employees | Total Employees |
|---|---|---|---|---|
| Shelton Box Company Hayward, Wisconsin | Court Oreilles | Ammunition Boxes | 60 | 70 |
| Rainier Company Ashland, Wisconsin | Bad River | Screw Machine Parts | 44 | 60 |
| Simpson Electric Co. Mercer, Wisconsin | Flambeau | Small Electric Parts, Testing Meters, etc. | 170 | 250 |

Simpson Electric Company of Chicago brought industrial employment north to Lac du Flambeau as early as March, 1946, when it established a branch assembly plant on the reservation. Founder and chairman of the board Ray R. Simpson first noticed the finger dexterity of Chippewa craftsmen while he vacationed in Wisconsin and thought that it could be used in manufacturing his firm's voltmeters, which demanded patience and the delicate handling of tiny wires coiled around armatures. Once hired, Chippewa personnel learned these new skills just as fast as white workers at Simpson's Chicago factory, their work was of the highest quality, and they seemed less discontent with the monotony of benchwork, experiencing only a 5 per cent annual turnover compared with Chicago's 75 per cent. By the early 1950's, the company pronounced the Indian labor force a success and planned to expand its Lac du Flambeau plant. Employees, the majority of whom were women, earned at that time an average of fifty dollars for a fifty-two-hour week. Not since the lumber boom had there been such an infusion of cash. Everywhere physical change was evident: houses painted and improved with oil-burning space heaters and electrical wiring, more Indian automobiles, workers' families better dressed, new, white-owned shops opening for business, a supermarket, hardware, and clothing stores. Thanks to a payroll savings plan at Simpson Electric, Indians had money in the bank for the first time in years. The wage-hour system modified other behavior patterns as well, for the plant supervisor insisted that his workers report promptly at 8:00 A.M., six days a week. Absenteeism because of deer season, fishing trips, or weekend alcoholic binges were not tolerated.[74]

West of Lac du Flambeau, at the Lac Court Oreilles reservation, life for the Indian residents was more typical of the Chippewa experience at Keweenaw Bay, Mole Lake, Bad River, Red Cliff, Fond du Lac, Grand Portage, and Nett Lake: no regular and substantial cash income from industrial employment, no economic expansion reminiscent of the logging boom, no upgrading of living conditions, no bank accounts. Anthropologist Bernard James dwelt among the people of New Post, a Lac Court Oreilles town, between October, 1951, and November, 1952. His findings open an important door through which we can view conditions in a postwar Chippewa community—its poverty, its social patterns, the beliefs and habits of individual villagers, the disintegration of its cultural heritage.[75]

At the time of James's visit, New Post was a small village of about forty homes on the shore of Lake Chippewa, a man-made reservoir known locally as "the flowage." Dense stands of jackpine and swamp evergreens surrounding the community created a beautiful, though somewhat secretive, setting. Actually, the town was rather isolated, with only one telephone and no rail or bus connections, Chippewas relied exclusively on their ten operable automobiles for speedy transportation outside the village—shopping trips to Couderay and Radisson, visits with distant friends, and drinking sprees at nearby resorts. Tribal rolls listed 261 residents in 1951, most of whom were either children or late middle-aged persons. Because of the scarcity of job opportunities in the vicinity, many young adults had moved away.

The New Post economy was particularly depressed in winter, when tourists had left and many families depended on relief checks. About twenty-five Chippewa women beaded belt strips for a white commercial outlet in Hayward. The pay was poor (twenty-five cents a strip), but this seasonal work added about eighteen hundred dollars to the village income. During the 1951–52 season, three thousand dollars in winter wages was collected by thirteen villagers employed on logging crews near New Post. Indian allottees earned only fifteen hundred dollars because heirship claims had become complex and confused over the years. Even the BIA's records were jumbled. To log an allotment, 51 per cent of the ownership must give its consent. Imagine the legal paperwork involved in opening one of these eighty-acre tracts which had sixty-four heirs!

Summer was the prosperous season at New Post. Tourists hired about ten Indian guides on a regular basis at an average wage of eight to ten dollars a day, which added thirty-five hundred dollars to the town's income. Fighting white pine blister rust for the Wisconsin Conservation Department provided seasonal work in the woods for another half dozen Chippewas whose earnings amounted to

twenty-eight hundred dollars in 1952. Still others secured summertime jobs off the reservation as itinerant laborers—picking cherries,
beans, rutabagas, potatoes, and cranberries on white men's land.

Sizable contributions to New Post's economy on a more year-
round basis were made by young men and women lured to the cities
by better employment opportunities and the BIA's relocation program, a salaried school bus driver, an Indian-owned resort (mainly a
summer enterprise), and those who were on pensions and relief.

One of the most disturbing features of the local economy was the
Indians' unwillingness to exploit their reservation's natural resources. Although fine gardens could be grown, only one old man
cultivated the soil in the summer of 1952. Nearby lakes abounded
with fish, yet residents rarely supplemented their diets with such
food. Traditional economic activities which also declined in importance included the gathering of wild rice and fruit, manufacturing
maple syrup, hunting, and trapping.

During Bernard James's twelve-month study of the early 1950's,
New Post thus derived its cash income as follows:

| | |
|---|---:|
| Relief, pensions, and special aid | $16,968 |
| Blister rust control crews | 2,800 |
| Guiding | 3,500 |
| Bead work | 1,800 |
| Logging (wages and sales) | 3,000 |
| Cherry picking | 500 |
| Bean picking | 1,500 |
| Rutabaga and potato picking | 900 |
| Cranberry picking | 150 |
| Gathering (greens, syrup, rice) | 340 |
| Trapping | 250 |
| Odd jobs at local resorts | 500 |
| Wages paid by Indian-owned resort | 300 |
| City work | 1,000 |
| Salaried position (bus driver) | 1,800 |
| | $35,308 |

James calculated that the per capita income amounted to $171, or
$1,008 per household.

The most conspicuous sign of poverty at New Post was the Indians' living conditions. There were thirty-nine dwellings, ranging
from run-down tarpaper shacks to frame structures nestled among
the pines. About them James wrote:

The village has a certain charm. But its homes are humble dwellings and the poverty of the owners is obvious. There is a stark contrast between the beauty of the lakes and forests of the area and the wretchedness of many of the hovels in which the people live. Outsiders usually notice the disparity and tourists who see it sometimes make tactless comments to the people about it.

A typical two-room home—what James described as a run-down frame—measured twenty-five by thirty feet. The dingy exterior was matched within by sagging cardboard-like wall coverings and flickering kerosene lamps. The lack of indoor plumbing necessitated the use of a privy, most likely unpainted, crudely constructed, and a bit tipsy. A woodburning stove generated heat and cooking smells which combined with a general mustiness and the other smells of a crowded household to produce a pungent odor. The family diet was heavily carbohydrate (potatoes, macaroni, and bread covered with greasy gravy), monotonous, and lacking in fresh fruits and vegetables. The absence of electricity and such appliances as washing and sewing machines was another index to the low living standard. It also explained the practical and drab hand-me-down dress of Chippewa villagers, especially the adults, who wore good clothes only for special dances and church services. Teenage styles, dictated as always by high schoolers, included blue jeans with cotton shirts or blouses.

Poor living conditions led to ill health as inevitably as night followed day. Besides their dietary deficiencies, New Post Chippewas neglected personal hygiene and generally dwelt in untidy houses. Indeed, 60 per cent of the dwellings were extremely dirty—"littered with filth and household debris." The tragic results could be seen everywhere: tooth decay, dental infections, and, according to statewide statistics, a high incidence of pregnancy and birth complications, infant mortality, pneumonia, and tuberculosis. The people of New Post received free medical care at the Hayward Indian Hospital, a two-story building with twenty-one beds and a full time staff of doctors and nurses. But transportation to the hospital was troublesome, and a wariness had developed between health personnel and village natives. The latter accused staff members of insensitivity. On the other hand, one former hospital employee insisted that reservation residents made unreasonable demands on Hayward, such as the care of destitute old people each month after their pension checks ran out.

White institutions which reached directly into New Post enjoyed no better relations with the Indians. By 1952, the small Catholic

mission in the center of the village, once a considerable influence on
Chippewa religious beliefs, economic practices, and social life, had
lost most of its congregation. There was no resident priest, and less
than 25 per cent of the Indians over age ten attended mass regularly. Even these people apparently accepted the mission for pragmatic rather than religious reasons, since their behavior was indis-
tinguishable from that of other villagers.

The local school, another evangelistic arm of white society, was
equally impotent despite its modern physical plant, professional
teaching staff, and an enrollment of fifty-nine Chippewa children.
Truancy took its toll, as it had for over a century, and though informed of the educational consequences, parents refused to support
the school by disciplining their children. Instruction was also
vitiated by what teachers called the psychological withdrawal of
village young people (beginning in the fourth and fifth grades) and
their growing indifference to school.

A third outside institution of influence was the BIA, with field
offices at Reserve, Wisconsin. Reminiscent of the situation at Hayward, Chippewas and white staffers reached an impasse by 1952:
bureaucrats often regarded the Lac Court Oreilles as "lazy and un-
appreciative," and the Indians, in turn, condemned the officials as
"medling, confused and often corrupt." At the heart of the trouble
lay the fact that the reservation system had destroyed the power of
the chiefs and headmen without replacing it with the sort of Indian
self-determination envisioned by New Dealers. The band, by reject-
ing corporate status under the IRA, settled instead for the partial
political autonomy of a Tribal Business Committee. The BIA's jurisdiction on the reservation was understandably confused, and the
Chippewas were frustrated because they lacked the political and
economic clout to throw off the stifling paternalism.

Despite the ineffectiveness of such white institutions, most villagers already had broken their cultural ties with the past. To mea-
sure the relative acculturation of thirty-five New Post households,
James used three criteria. At one end of his scale of cultural borrow-
ing, a purely "Indian" family must conform to three of the following
practices:
1.   Chippewa language used frequently in the home.
2.   Chippewa technical usages and/or beliefs still function
     rather strongly in the household.
3.   The marriage of the head of the household is Indian custom
     and/or common law.

Conversely, "non-Indian" or "white" families would be characterized by:

1.   English used more or less exclusively in the household.
2.   Household is electrically wired and has electric appliances.
3.   Marriage of head of the household is either Catholic or civil.

Four families conformed to all three of the Indian criteria, and three households to two standards. Thus, only one-fifth of the family units maintained a strong contact with their heritage. Fifteen homes conformed to mixed criteria ("Indian" and "white"), nine families to two "non-Indian" criteria, and four households conformed to all three "white" standards. From these findings James concluded that only a "tattered patchwork" of Chippewa culture remained at New Post.

Acculturation did not lead automatically to integration. Herein lay the human tragedy. To cite but one example of discrimination and its effects: at the New Post school, psychological withdrawal began when Indian children reached the ages of nine or ten, doubtless because of their awareness of a subordinate social position. By the time they entered high school, Chippewa teenagers, fully cognizant of their second-class citizenship, openly condemned formal schooling and saw themselves and their families as the long-suffering victims of white exploitation.

In summary it can be said that for New Post the reservation years had brought a destruction of the traditional economic and political structure—the Indians' very culture. As late as 1952 the void created by these losses had yet to be filled. Villagers were poverty stricken, politically impotent, physically and socially segregated, though acculturated. At best, their future was uncertain, like that of the rest of the Lac Court Oreilles band and of all the Lake Superior Chippewas.

Late in 1964, in answer to a request from Washington, the Minnesota Agency at Bemidji and Ashland's Great Lakes Consolidated Agency submitted comprehensive ten-year development programs for Chippewa reservations in Michigan, Wisconsin, and Minnesota. Besides providing data on the existing situation (reservation descriptions, population statistics, economic conditions, housing, health, welfare and social services, educational activities, tribal government, acculturation), each reservation report set high-priority activity goals for the next decade, recommended how each should be achieved, and estimated the costs. In hopes of tapping funds from the new Economic Opportunity Act, community development proposals were also built into the ten-year plans.

Of particular interest, the detailed Lac Court Oreilles report gauged some of the changes that had taken place since James's visit twelve years before. The reservation population, concentrated in the towns of New Post and Reserve, had stabilized at about 850. Their unemployment rate remained at a disturbingly high level—31 per cent in 1964. Only 24 adults out of the entire work force of 293 held year-round jobs. An additional 65 were employed seasonally. There was some harvesting of wild rice and forest products, yet the development of the reservation's natural resources continued to be hampered because thousands of allotted acres were so snarled in complicated heirship that they were "useless as to management or sale."

The only exceptions to these legal entanglements were lands owned by the tribe. With a BIA credit fund loan of $100,000 in 1949, the band established the Lac Court Oreilles Cranberry Enterprise, which employed a manager and Indian labor to tend the marsh and harvest the berry crop. Sound business practices and modern machinery generated sufficient profits to retire all but $30,000 of the original loan. Tourism also contributed significantly to the area economy, but only in the summertime. To improve full-time Chippewa employment opportunities, BIA staffers encouraged relocation. Between July, 1962, and June, 1964, thirty-seven Indians moved to Los Angeles, Denver, Minneapolis, Chicago, Milwaukee, and Cleveland. Another popular federal program provided training at accredited vocational schools in areas with good employment prospects, offering cosmetology, general clerical, and stenographic skills for the women and welding, automobile mechanics, carpentry, and other trades for the men. Sixty band members enrolled in these classes between 1958 and 1964.

Housing at Lac Court Oreilles was still physically deplorable and unsanitary, the standard of living well below that of off-reservation areas which themselves had been declared economically depressed. Although vital statistics did not appear in the 1964 health report, it was clear that medical services had improved. Under contract with the United States Public Health Service, doctors from Hayward held clinics on the reservation one afternoon a week. Public Health also underwrote the expenses of Indian visits to Hayward for hospitalization and dental care. The BIA, the State of Wisconsin, and Sawyer County officials still administered programs of old-age assistance, aid to dependent children, disability aid, foster homes, Indian relief, and surplus commodity distribution. Whether or not the Lac Court

Oreilles were assisted better in 1964 than in 1952 is impossible to determine from this data.

The 1964 education report, also, was too cryptic for purposes of comparison. It was clear that the band still refused to adopt a constitution or to incorporate under the terms of the IRA. The five-man Tribal Business Committee, with an office at Reserve, remained the recognized governing body. Socially, the Chippewas had built stronger relationships with neighboring whites, based largely on the substantial Indian contribution to the area's tourist economy. Ironically, despite a high-powered publicity campaign that pictured the whole region as "Indian Country," whites still referred to Lac Court Oreilles as "the reservation"—"a pocket set aside which should not be considered in the overall picture that the area wishes to portray." North woods segregation remained a reality for many acculturated Indians, much as it had been during James's sojourn in the fifties.[76]

BIA ten-year development reports revealed conditions on other Chippewa reservations strikingly similar to those at Lac Court Oreilles. Economically, each was hard-pressed despite the influx of tourist dollars and the availability of some woods work. The average yearly income at Bad River, for example, ranged between $1,500 and $2,000, compared with a statewide figure of $3,821 for rural farm families. Outside industries and businesses generated large numbers of reservation jobs only at L'Anse and at Lac du Flambeau (seventy-eight Indians worked for Simpson Electric in 1964). Tribal enterprises, like the cranberry company at Lac Court Oreilles, provided limited employment at L'Anse and Red Cliff. Women from Red Cliff, unable to travel long distances to find work, converted their community hall into a factory site and produced a variety of garment items for a contract broker. Red Cliff and L'Anse also invested tribal dollars in modern tent and trailer campsites for tourists. To further alleviate reservation unemployment, the BIA pushed relocation and adult vocational programs. Just as at Lac Court Oreilles, Chippewa living conditions were poor according to Public Housing Administration standards, being crowded, badly in need of repairs, with inadequate water and sewerage facilities.

The one "bright spot" was Lac du Flambeau, thanks to a sizable award from the United States Court of Claims (for damages in connection with swampland litigation), a grant from the Public Health Service, and donated Indian labor, which made possible a $400,000 modern water and sewage system. Managed by a tribally appointed utility committee, it served 110 homes in 1964 and was self-supporting.

Public Health also had responsibility for providing medical programs on each reservation. This was done on a contractual basis with local doctors, dentists, and hospitals. Unfortunately, the 1964 BIA reports conspicuously lacked Indian health statistics. Educational data was also vague, except for the Fond du Lac reservation, which, one suspects, was similar to public school situations elsewhere. Because youngsters from Fond du Lac comprised only 3 per cent of the student bodies, teachers, administrators, and school boards offered no special programs for Indians who were "culturally different, often intellectually starved and usually economically deprived." White insensitivity led first to the isolation of Chippewa children and then to their "dropping out" of school. Ninety per cent never finished high school. The overall local "dropout" rate was 20 per cent.

A far more pleasing picture to contemplate was the extent of adult Indian social integration with white neighbors. At Keweenaw Bay, Bad River, Red Cliff, Lac du Flambeau, Fond du Lac, and perhaps elsewhere, Chippewas increasingly got involved in local township government and off-reservation community organizations and activities. Interracial marriages were common. Where it existed, social segregation apparently was due more to the physical separation of the reservation and the extreme poverty of some residents than to racial and cultural factors.[77]

The state of the Lake Superior Chippewa reservations in 1964 also underscored the fact that shamefully little progress had occurred since the Meriam Report of the late twenties. Many Chippewas remained maladjusted "to the economic and social system of the dominant white civilization." Suffering and discontent persisted. The typical Indian family's income was still painfully low, its diet unbalanced, its home overcrowded and unsanitary. Education for assimilation ignored Indian ways and was neglectful of "what can be done by building on what is sound and good in the Indian's own life."

As of 1964, John Collier's dreams for the American Indian were unfulfilled. Obviously, the Chippewa bands were not prosperous, self-sufficient, independent communities. New Deal programs of the thirties (IRA, CWA, rehabilitation grants, CCC–ID, revolving loan funds, WPA, cross-cultural education) helped Native Americans to survive the Depression and to take the first meaningful steps toward self-determination. World War II blunted this thrust and then gave birth to a postwar world which, in the BIA's judgment, demanded new programs for the integration of fast-growing Indian populations into the expanding economies of metropolitan areas. The reservations looked like economic dead ends. The new (old?) bywords were removal and assimilation. Yet most Chippewas remained on their ancestral lands in towns like New Post—unemployed, ill-housed, undereducated, politically enfeebled, patronized by innumerable federal functionaries. The IRA had helped the bands to establish the political and economic mechanisms for self-development. Since 1945 they had not been motivated to exploit fully their human and material resources because of inadequate federal funding, the suffocation of BIA paternalism, misdirected education, and the sheer enervation of poverty. If Collier's goals were still to be pursued, an important beacon through the dark despair was the modest success of tribal enterprises in 1964. That even the BIA recognized the importance of giving the Chippewas increased responsibility and opportunity to solve their own problems could be seen in the ten-year goals which accompanied their reservation reports.

To be attained by 1975, BIA goals for the Lake Superior Chippewas needed tribal acceptance as well as considerable federal, state, and local funding. Crucial to economic development was the establishment of tribal employment committees on each reservation. They must canvas their areas for job opportunities, set up a placement program, and motivate Indians to work. Another help would be child day-care centers. Most reservation reports also included detailed plans for building a summer youth camp at an estimated cost of $98,000—seemingly a sound idea for developing both human and physical resources. Located near a lake, this commercial venture would include an administration building, dining hall, administrator's cottage, five guest houses, boat dock, playing field, nature trails, corrals and stables, and a water and sewage system. Whether tribally managed or leased to an outside firm, each installation must be staffed by local Chippewas, because association with them—learning tribal traditions and woodland skills—would have an irresistible appeal to white youths from the city. To improve reservation living conditions the BIA recommended setting up tribal planning commissions. They would undertake a housing survey to determine specific needs, make formal grant proposals to Washington agencies, draw up necessary housing codes, ordinances, and plans, and train tribal housing commissioners. Finally, Chippewas were encouraged to get more involved with the public schools—and vice versa. Liaison personnel, for example, were essential to mutual understanding and the design of special programs for Indian youngsters. So were BIA-sponsored workshops for Chippewa parents and the teachers of their children. Other needs included adult education classes and summer study skills workshops for high schoolers who planned to go on to college or vocational institutes.[78]

If tribal and governmental leaders accepted these or similar programs, there was good reason to believe that the next decade would see the Chippewas finally solving such persistent problems as high unemployment, substandard housing, and inadequate schooling.

This dirt-floored shack on the Lac du Flambeau Reservation housed nine Chippewas in the early 1930's. *Courtesy National Archives.*

At Nett Lake Camp, Minnesota, three Chippewa enrollees in the CCC-Indian Division Camp, Lac du Flambeau, Wisconsin, 1933. *Courtesy National Archives.*

Lac du Flambeau CCC-Indian Division Camp, Lac du Flambeau, Wisconsin, 1933. *Courtesy National Archives.*

Reconstructed Grand Portage stockade, built entirely by the CCC-Indian Division. *Courtesy National Archives.*

The Great Hall, Grand Portage National Monument. *Collection of the author.*

Radisson Inn on Grand Portage Reservation nears completion during the summer of 1975. *Collection of the author.*

Tribal marina, Grand Portage Reservation. *Collection of the author.*

Grand Portage Elementary School. *Collection of the author.*

Grand Portage Trading Post. *Collection of the author.*

Lac du Flambeau tribal fish hatchery. *Collection of the author.*

Lac du Flambeau tribal campground and marina. *Collection of the author.*

Lac du Flambeau Reservation Community Center. *Collection of the author.*

Red Cliff Reservation Arts and Crafts Center. *Collection of the author.*

Red Cliff tribal campground and marina. *Collection of the author.*

# 9. Progress Through Self-Determination, 1964-1975

During the past decade, the Lake Superior Chippewas and others concerned with their welfare wrestled with a variety of reservation difficulties—economic underdevelopment, poor living conditions, inadequate medical care, low educational achievement—which have persisted for over a century. What makes the contemporary scene unique and exciting is the federal government's encouragement of tribal officials to plan and administer their own programs to solve these stubborn problems. In January, 1975, Congress passed the Indian Self-Determination and Education Assistance Act, which openly confessed that

prolonged Federal domination of Indian service programs has served to retard rather than enhance the progress of Indian people and their communities by depriving Indians of the full opportunity to develop leadership skills crucial to the realization of self-government, and has denied to the Indian people an effective voice in the planning and implementation of programs for the benefit of Indians which are responsive to the true needs of Indian communities; . . .

Certainly this was the case with the Chippewas of Lake Superior. To assure "maximum Indian participation in the direction of educational as well as other Federal services to Indian communities" in the future, the secretaries of the Interior Department and of Health, Education, and Welfare (HEW) were directed, upon the request of any Indian tribe, to enter into contracts to design, carry out, and evaluate programs and services previously provided by the federal government.[1] Thus the catalyst of self-determination, combined with the rapid flow of federal funds onto reservations, has generated a great deal of activity and more Indian optimism than at any time since the heyday of the fur trade.

A look at the economic scene in the seventies reveals that only a few traditional sources of Indian income remain important. Wages paid by white employers provide some necessities for reservations like Fond du Lac, Red Cliff, Bad River, Lac du Flambeau, and

Keeweenaw Bay, which are located near towns or cities. In 1974, for example, 39 per cent of Keweenaw Bay adults worked for local industries, retail stores hired another 5 per cent, and 12 per cent held positions with state, federal, or local governments.[2] Lac du Flambeau is the only reservation with large amounts of timber worth harvesting which are not encumbered by the red tape of heirship. In 1973, Indian and non-Indian loggers cut 7,273,000 board feet—a stumpage value of $82,427.[3] Hunting, fishing, and trapping, on the other hand, continue to be important means of supplementing Indian diets throughout Kitchigami land. Also significant is the sale of wild rice. The average per capita income for Minnesota Indians from ricing was $88 in 1974. Peter DeFault of Fond du Lac, a former chairman of the Minnesota Chippewa Tribe, asserts that this sort of woods work ideally suits the Indian; he seems happier—more filled with an Indian spirit—than at any other time of the year. During these two weeks DeFault's neighbors "work their fingers to the bone to fill their canoes," delight over the cash paid them at the end of each day, hurry off to celebrate, and arrive early the next morning to resume the harvest.[4] Partly responsible for this zeal during the ricing season is the Indian's spiritual relationship with the *manomin*. Ernie Landgren of Nett Lake notes: "There's a feeling you get out there that's hard to get other places. You're close to Mother Nature, seeing things grow and harvesting the results of the water and sun and winds. . . . We sort of touch our roots when we're among the rice plants."[5]

Farming—another means of gathering nature's bounty and encouraged for many decades by the BIA—has ceased to have any economic importance for the Lake Superior Chippewas. The fate of Mandy Manypenny's Bad River farm is probably typical. After the death of her father, in 1943, and the termination of wartime federal assistance, she and her sister found it increasingly difficult to feed their dairy. Operations ended in 1948 when worn out equipment was no longer usable. Since then, field and pasture have grown up to brush. Miss Manypenny lives alone in the old farm house since the death of her sister in 1969.[6] After so many years of physical effort and the expenditure of so much precious timber money to clear this allotment and dozens of others so that Bad River residents could become economically self-sufficient, it is distressing to report that in 1975 not a single Indian farmed commercially on the reservation.

The limited economic opportunities for these Chippewa wage earners, fishermen, and ricers in Michigan and Wisconsin are emphasized by high unemployment rates and the low earning power of those with jobs. The following figures are for April, 1975:[7]

| | Indian Population on or Adjacent to the Reservation | Potential Labor Force (16 years or older) | Percentage of Potential Labor Force Unemployed | Of Those Employed, Percentage Earning $5,000 a Year or More |
|---|---|---|---|---|
| Keweenaw Bay | 915 | 453 | 28 | 72 |
| Bad River | 741 | 195 | 24 | 26 |
| Red Cliff | 742 | 204 | 20 | 17 |
| Lac du Flambeau | 1,016 | 305 | 31 | 62 |
| Lac Court Oreilles | 1,628 | 605 | 70 | 27 |
| Mole Lake | 148 | 54 | 41 | 41 |
| St. Croix | 419 | 149 | 38 | 31 |

A far more promising economic trend on the Lake Superior reservations is being initiated by Indian leaders. Early in 1975 those in Wisconsin and Michigan informed the Great Lakes Agency at Ashland that they would soon apply for planning grants in order to assume control of all government programs and services by October, 1976.[8] What the tribal councils hope to build by means of such self-determination is a full-fledged reservation economy, with more jobs close to home (as an alternative to urban migration), more education and training for employment, higher incomes, the retention of tribal lands, and a more productive development of abundant natural resources.[9] To provide the variety of economic and industrial assistance programs necessary to achieve self-sufficiency and a higher standard of living, Chippewa entrepreneurs must look to federal and state agencies. The BIA, for example, will train Indians for employment and supply land-use planning assistance as well as loans and capital grants to establish profitable tribal businesses employing Indians. Since 1970, the Economic Development Administration (EDA) of the Department of Commerce has furnished 100 per cent funding for public works on certain reservations. It also awards planning and technical grants and subsidizes interest on private business loans. Likewise committed to reservation economic development, the state of Minnesota now makes available revolving loans and staff assistance to its Indian citizens.[10]

From Keweenaw Bay to Grand Portage, tribal councils have recently launched several promising projects; many more enterprises,
conceived with the help of detailed economic development studies,
are in the planning stages. Tribal Chairman Frederick Dakota and
other councilmen of the Keweenaw Bay Indian Community operate
the Ojibway Indian Trailer Park, located beside U.S. Highway 41
north of the village of Baraga, and a mini-market carrying a complete line of groceries. They also oversee a herd of buffalo (twenty-
seven head in 1974) which someday might be a significant source of
food. A tribally operated construction company, whose employees
studied at the Indian Technical Assistance Center, Denver,
Colorado, during 1973 and 1974—at a cost of $210,800—has already
built a few new reservation houses and remodeled some older ones.
To assist the council in planning for the band's economic well-being
in the years ahead, comprehensive development programs have
been prepared by the Michigan Inter-Tribal Council and a private
consulting firm, based on sound statistical data on Indian lands,
housing, education, employment, recreation, community services,
and the attitudes of tribal members. The key recommendation of
these studies was the establishment of Indian-owned retail stores
and commercial services that would generate personal incomes as
well as revenues for the tribe. A full-service campground, a park
store, a marina, resort motel services, automotive and boat repair
shops, and a convention center were among the specific tourist-
oriented businesses suggested for the future. Economic development
specialists also encouraged the Keweenaw Bay Chippewas to support programs that would attract outside industry to the reservation
and foster such agricultural pursuits as cattle raising, dairying, and
general farming.[11]

Working within the guidelines of overall economic development
programs, Chippewa leaders at Red Cliff and Lac du Flambeau have
generated promising tribal enterprises. The Red Cliff Arts and
Crafts Center, campground, and marina complex (built with an
$800,000 EDA grant) opened to the public in the summer of 1975.
These and other reservation visitor services are being coordinated so
as to complement the new Apostle Islands National Lakeshore Park.
Plans call for the National Park Service to acquire twenty of the
twenty-two islands of this picturesque archipelago plus ten miles of
mainland shoreline by 1985, hoping to attract an estimated 750,000
to 1,000,000 new travelers annually to the Bayfield-Red Cliff area.

Some 80 to 90 per cent of these visitors are expected to spend the night outside the park boundaries. The impact on the local economy should be momentous. Tribal developers expect that cooperation between Red Cliff and the National Park Service will provide "the utmost in recreational and historical features, and the preservation of natural beauty and personal accommodations for the American public." With the anticipation of tourism becoming a year-round source of revenue, long-range reservation plans call for an Indian-owned motel, restaurant, and repair facility for boats, snowmobiles, and all types of small engines.[12] "Self-determination is strong here," observes Vice-chairman Henry Buffalo, because Red Cliff Indians are "the only ones who know what their needs are." The tribal council, he emphasizes, is behind all development projects: the marina, the campground, and the arts and crafts center.[13]

Southeast of Chequamegon Bay, Chippewa leaders at Lac du Flambeau are also investing development dollars in tourist-oriented tribal enterprises. On June 7 and 8, 1975, dedication and ribbon cutting ceremonies were held for Wa-Swa-Gon Park and the Tribal Fish Hatchery. The former consists of a new and modern campground designed to accommodate all types of campers. Adjacent to it is a marina providing sport fishermen with boat and motor rentals, bait, and a variety of accessories, and easy access to a chain of ten spring-fed lakes. For better stocking of these and other reservation waters the Tribal Fish Hatchery on Pokegama Lake, built in 1935, was extensively renovated. This facility annually supplies thirty million walleye fry. Other recent tribal projects include a new community center, a wood-products school, the purchase of alienated lands within the reservation's boundaries, and renovation of the Indian Bowl—an amphitheater located in the heart of the community where on Tuesday and Thursday evenings during the summer months Chippewas in traditional attire hold powwows to entertain tourists. Eventually the band plans to develop a winter sports facility as well as its own motel-hotel-restaurant complex and cooperative grocery store.[14]

Although on a smaller scale, certain other Indian businesses in Wisconsin and Minnesota also underscore the importance of local initiative and control in reservation development. Bad River, with the aid of an EDA grant, is experimenting with a fish hatchery in hopes of selling game fish fingerlings as well as restocking the reservation. Construction of an industrial park is likewise under consideration by the tribal council.[15] With $56,000 in EDA funds, the

Lac Court Oreilles will modernize the equipment used at its tribally owned cranberry marsh, first built in 1949 with $100,000 from the BIA's revolving loan fund. Tribal leaders recognize the income potential of tourism, too, but plans for campground development and other such facilities for the passing public must wait, says Councilman Pete Larson, until the "recapture" of the Chippewa Flowage—sixty-five hundred acres of lakeside reservation property leased to the Northern States Power Company between 1921 and 1971 for the production of hydroelectric power. Since the expiration of this agreement, control of the area continues to be debated in the courts and is a regional *cause célèbre*.[16] West of Lac Court Oreilles reservation, the St. Croix band owns and operates the Black Dirt Corporation, which contracts for heavy equipment construction, excavation, and site leveling.[17] Economic development at Nett Lake in Minnesota remains minimal, though the tribe cooperatively harvests woodland products such as wild rice and timber.[18] A water level control system to improve the Fond du Lac wild rice harvest is part of a tribal plan for a $250,000 recreational complex at Big Lake.[19]

The most ambitious development project on Lake Superior is the hundred-unit Radisson Inn, a $5 million investment launched recently by the 308-member Grand Portage band with help from the EDA. Under the control of a Radisson management firm and backed by a nonprofit Grand Portage Development Corporation, the inn is designed to serve the needs of the nearly 70,000 annual visitors to the Grand Portage National Monument, an impressive reconstruction of the once great North West Company fur depot. Moreover, the Reservation Business Committee's Fisheries Commission operates a new tribal marina and promotes sports and commercial fishing enterprises.[20] Other services to attract winter visitors, such as cross-country skiing and snowmobile routes, are under consideration. For young Ron Sherer, director of the local Community Action Program ("the arm of the Reservation Business Committee at Grand Portage that tries to get things done"), there is no question about self-determination being the byword these days. Grand Portage economic development programs, he asserts, show that Indians "can constructively manage money on their own reservation," with the result that enrolled members are moving back to Grand Portage from distant cities. The BIA has pretty much been left out of these plans. From start to finish the new tourist complex was an Indian project—and they are proud of it. Sherer describes the Reservation

Business Committee as an aggressive group which knows what the problems are and is doing what it can to solve them.[21] More cautiously optimistic about present and future plans is James Hull, a member of the Grand Portage Development Corporation, former manager of the cooperative Grand Portage Trading Post, and a fifth generation grandson of Jean Baptiste Cadotte:[22]

Although these are all giant steps when compared to past stagnation, it must be noted that each and all of the programs are the product of federal funding and can only continue to function as long as this funding is renewed.... What we need is free enterprise....

Our proposed EDA tourist complex is a first step in that direction. Hopefully, this development will be only the first of several which will ultimately cause the phaseout of public subsidies and the establishment of a sound, permanent, self-sustaining community.

Stimulating as these tribal undertakings may be, Chippewa reservation developers at Grand Portage, Red Cliff, Lac du Flambeau, Keweenaw Bay, and elsewhere, bent on self-determination, still face monumental problems in addition to the high unemployment rates and low earning power already noted. These include the necessity of consolidating checkerboard Indian land holdings—part of the evil legacy of allotment—the remoteness of some reservations from major markets, an unskilled and often small labor force, lack of trained and experienced business leaders and administrators, and insufficient capital. Above all, the noticeable waning, in certain areas, of the Chippewas' traditionally cooperative spirit must be stopped. Hence the 1973 Red Cliff "Over-all Economic Development Plan" begins with the following admonition:[23]

It is well to understand that economic development is a slow and sometimes discouraging process. Individual self interests and attitudes must give way to constructive interests and attitudes from which the entire community can benefit. Individual gain at the community's expense must be forgotten or at least drastically reduced before a better way of life for each person can be achieved. Positive thinking should replace negative "nothing can be done" thinking or the next generation cannot remain with their people and their culture.

Your object, therefore, becomes your challenge.

Another selection from the same document explains why tribal leaders have assigned a high priority to housing improvements: "The general attitude of the people [of Red Cliff] is 'Why should I care about the condition of the rest of the reservation when I can't even live in a decent dwelling?' "[24]

Just a decade ago, Chippewa homes were shockingly substandard. Shabbily constructed and overcrowded, they lacked adequate water supply and waste disposal systems, insulation, and central heating. Regarding the living conditions of its Native American citizens, the Minnesota Indian Affairs Commission reported in 1967: "Most of the buildings are old. Ten percent are considered to be 'tar-paper' shacks with unfinished interiors and exteriors. They are small and usually in poor physical condition. Five percent are considered log houses and are in extremely poor condition."[25] Indian housing in Wisconsin and Michigan was no better. Perhaps the saddest sight was the village of Odanah, founded more than a century before by the Reverend Leonard Wheeler as a model agrarian community. Twenty-four of its 116 residences stood vacant; the rest were rapidly deteriorating because of the continued flooding of the Bad River and the neglect of local inhabitants who had been warned for fifteen years of their imminent removal to a new location. Such homes, one investigator remarked, "offer shelter, but little of the dignities or comforts of modern life."[26]

Since the mid-sixties, federal housing programs have produced more healthful and comfortable living conditions at Bad River and elsewhere in Kitchigami land. The Home Improvement Program (HIP), financed through the BIA, made funds available to low-income reservation families, primarily for home repair and restoration. Monies for transitional trailer homes, down payments for buying a house, and for constructing new dwellings have also come from HIP. The Housing Assistance Administration of the Department of Housing and Urban Development (HUD) finances public housing projects providing rental houses as well as houses for Indian ownership. Moreover, in line with the government's encouragement of Indian self-determination and responsibility, HUD requires that each reservation, in order to qualify for such support, appoint a local housing authority to plan, construct, and manage its project. As a means of further upgrading old and new Chippewa homes, the Public Health Service-Indian Division installed sanitary and water systems in many Indian communities.[27] By 1975, federal funds had built for the Keweenaw Bay Indian Community over forty low-rent housing units.[28] At what is now called Old Odanah, only about two dozen families remain, mainly old people who do not wish to leave or younger couples unable to afford new housing. Most others moved to

New Odanah, an attractive modern village of pastel ranch-style homes located on high ground a few miles to the northeast and away from the ruinous flood waters of the Bad River.[29] At Red Cliff, Lac du Flambeau, Lac Court Oreilles, Mole Lake, and St. Croix at least 50 per cent of the homes meet government standards, though some overcrowding persists. Housing and sanitation have greatly improved at Fond du Lac, Nett Lake, and Grand Portage. That much remains to be done is revealed by a recent Minnesota Chippewa Tribe survey at Grand Portage, where forty-five out of seventy-five homes are still substandard.[30]

Besides HUD regulations, Indian dissatisfaction with the first new homes built at Bad River, Lac Court Oreilles, and St. Croix stimulated the involvement of tribal leaders in reservation housing programs. At New Odanah, Chippewas initially had little to say regarding either home design or construction—they were simply told to take them or leave them, recalls Councilman Sam Livingston. The upshot was shoddy workmanship, the use of green lumber, inadequate floor space, and fire hazards throughout each home. Livingston frankly admits that Bad River should have supervised this project a lot better. St. Croix historian Lolita Taylor records a similar story for her band: new homes "railroaded through by low-rent housing contractors, pretty much without approval by the prospective tenants."[31] Still other examples of insufficient advice from the Indians were the first federally financed homes at Lac Court Oreilles, which, despite the long winter months for which the north woods are famous, were built without basements or garages. These, together with other unhappy experiences, prompted reservation housing authorities to insist on better materials, better workmanship, and house plans more suitable to Indian needs.[32]

A case in point is the Mole Lake community. Having profited from mistakes made on other reservations, it first fought with HUD to get approval for high-quality homes, then insisted that only a first-rate contractor handle construction. In 1975 each of these new structures was valued at $22,000.[33] Lac Court Oreilles leaders went even further. They entered a legal partnership with a good housing developer, thereby avoiding bidded contracts altogether. And at least one councilman, Pete Larson, envisions the day when the tribe will take whole contracts itself.[34]

Notwithstanding the activities of reservation housing authorities, problems persist. The drying up of federal funding of public housing since 1971, by far the most serious, means that innovative Indian leaders with plans in hand for new housing units and community centers must be patient and wait. Meanwhile, the demand for better Chippewa housing expands at an ever-increasing rate as a result of exciting new job opportunities which lure urban tribesmen back to the reservations. One particularly distressing result of this pressure is the re-occupation of some substandard dwellings, abandoned in the late sixties by families who moved into the modern public housing. In this manner the problem of poor living conditions is perpetuated. And what of the future? At Keweenaw Bay, professional consultants projected in May, 1974, that the reservation's 728 residents would number 1,000 by 1980 and would require an additional sixty-five to seventy-eight housing units. How, one wonders, can the tribe possibly meet such a challenge when 30 percent of its existing dwellings are judged as either dilapidated or in need of major repairs?[35] A final widespread difficulty involves the procedure by which Indian residents in publicly funded housing, who are expected to become the ultimate owners, must amortize their debts. The Turnkey III program requires that low-income families be good credit risks, maintain their structures, and make monthly payments, limited to 25 per cent of their income, to the local housing authority. Indian housing authorities, to whom the builders originally turned over the keys of ownership, are expected to oversee the upkeep and repay construction costs within forty years. Trouble comes in attempting to collect regular monthly payments from fellow tribesmen whose work has become seasonal or who are unemployed.[36] Some observers argue that the crux of this rent problem really lies with the notion of repayment. For example, the Keweenaw Bay analysts concluded: "Because of the low-income character of the Indian population, housing programs must involve grant type assistance. Conventional mortgage and home improvement loans are less than realistic. . . ." Across the lake at Grand Portage, tribal leaders and residents alike resisted the whole public housing program because they disliked long-time indebtedness. They much preferred HIP grants for renovative purposes.[37]

Lingering housing problems aside, many Chippewas have enjoyed improved living conditions and the better health that goes with them. Just as with reservation economic expansion and housing developments, tribal leaders have played an important role in improving health services. On each reservation the Community Health Representative now forms the key link between the Indian people and the bewildering variety of medical services underwritten for them by the Public Health Service-Indian Division. (This organization does not furnish direct care for the Lake Superior Chippewas by means of its own hospitals and physicians; it contracts with local doctors and hospitals to provide medical care for the Indians.) Community Health Representatives, or CHRs, as they are called, often have special health training and work with the county nurses, whose salaries are also partially paid for by the Public Health Service. They organize special programs, such as child and maternal health classes, to bring up-to-date health education to reservation residents. The CHR also coordinates the transportation of patients to distant hospitals and doctors' offices.[38]

In an effort to do away with such lengthy, debilitating travel and to more closely monitor Indian health care, several tribes have established reservation health clinics. The most ambitious of these has been operating at the Keweenaw Bay Community Building since 1973, through a contract with the Public Health Service-Indian Division. Staffed by a full-time registered nurse, a family health worker, and a physician who visits the clinic twice a week, this pilot comprehensive health care center might later be duplicated at other reservations in Michigan, Wisconsin, and Minnesota. What makes it unique is the emphasis on providing prompt medical care to Chippewa residents before their cases become acute, thereby reducing the total costs of the Keweenaw Bay health delivery system as well as saving lives. To achieve this goal, tribal members are provided "preventative, curative and rehabilitative services; education about health and disease; assistance in such ancillary services as transportation, home care, agency referrals and assistance in chronic disease management."[39]

Tribal leaders and the Public Health Service confirm that living conditions and the delivery of federal health services significantly improved during the past few years, thanks in part to the work of Chippewa CHRs and tribally administered health contracts. Yet Indian leadership can only do so much. Although there was a reduction in the incidence of such reported infectious diseases as gastroenteritis after the Public Health Service-Indian Division ran modern water and sanitary lines into Indian villages and HUD financed better housing, little progress has been made in combating the undisputed number one health problem on every reservation—alcoholism. In Minnesota, where excessive Indian drinking reached

"epidemic proportions" in 1974, data furnished by the Alcohol and
Drug Authority demonstrated that Native Americans as a group
had the highest proportion of alcohol-related problems:[40]

|  | Reservation Indians | Blacks | Minnesota General Population |
|---|---|---|---|
| Trouble in the family because of drinking | 67% | 18% | 14% |
| Trouble with the law because of drinking | 50% | 11% | 10% |
| Trouble on the job or missed work because of drinking | 44% | 8% | 3% |

The seriousness of alcoholism for Chippewa tribes is not difficult
to discern. Sam Livingston of Bad River summed it up succinctly:
"There can really be no self-determination until alcoholism is
licked."[41] Alcohol has become a problem for all Indians, whether or
not they drink. What is being done to fight the disease? So far, the
emphasis has been on funding local detoxification centers (sometimes called drug dependency centers) and hiring outreach workers.
The largest rehabilitation facility is Halfway House, located on the
third floor of the Keweenaw Bay community building. Financed by
the Western Upper Peninsula Comprehensive Health Department,
it employs a house manager and an alcoholism counselor and serves
all of Michigan's Indian communities.[42]

Obviously, Chippewa alcoholism will not be cured by "detox"
centers and outreach workers; the reasons for excessive drinking are
too complex and run too deep. That heavy drinking must, in part at
least, be a temporary escape from what looks like an unpromising
future is suggested by the relatively large numbers of Minnesota
Indians who eventually commit suicide. In 1971, young men between the ages of fifteen and forty-five years of age committed
suicide at a rate three to four times that of the state's white population.[43] Certainly Livingston is correct about the future of the Chippewas, and one can only hope that new jobs created on the reservations in the mid-1970's will offer enough opportunities for earning
a decent living and thereby dispel the feelings of desperation and
futility.

Another key to improved mental health in the years ahead will be
how young reservation people view themselves. And how they, in
turn, are viewed by others. Recent educational progress at Grand

Portage and elsewhere gives cause for optimism—not only about academic achievement and the personal satisfaction it will bring to Chippewa boys and girls, but also about the power of self-determination unleashed.

In 1961, Dave and Andrea Peterson, having just graduated from college, took their first teaching jobs at Grand Portage Elementary School. She had responsibility for grades one through three, he for grades four to six. The county superintendent of schools at Grand Marais, forty miles away, admitted he really did not care how they handled their classes, because "everybody knows Indian kids can't learn." Indeed, he did not even know what instructional materials had been used in past years or where they were stored. Nothing in their formal education had prepared the Petersons for this shock. Upon arriving at the reservation they wisely followed their instincts and visited with Indian families in order to find out just what they wanted their children to learn at the old log school. Thereby the Petersons won the confidence and cooperation of Indian adults, who claimed they had always been interested in the schooling of their youngsters, but no one had ever listened to them. By encouraging boys and girls to stop and chat at their home (located next to the school) anytime after classes, Dave and Andrea likewise won the friendship of Chippewa young people. The key to the academic successes achieved at Grand Portage School was community involvement—teachers and parents working together to improve the children's basic skills and to incorporate Indian culture into the school curriculum. The children's scores on standardized achievement tests rapidly rose from the thirty-fourth to the eightieth percentile. Attendance improved. The dropout rate plummeted. Currently, when Grand Portage graduates go on to junior and then senior high school at Grand Marais, they "know who they are and feel positively about themselves and have good skill development." Their parents, proud as they can be about the school and the prizes it and the Petersons have won, continue to serve the teachers as resource persons, classroom aides, and custodians of the physical plant.[44]

One other part of the Petersons' story ought to be told. As dedicated educators, Dave and Andrea feel obliged to share their findings with others. In 1967 Dave co-authored with Virgil Wurr and Dean Crawford, *Minnesota Chippewa Indians: A Handbook for Teachers.* Two years later, at the request of the Duluth Indian Action Council, Dave developed an Indian culture kit for upper

elementary schools. A major emphasis in both publications is that
Indian people will learn if teachers will listen and be less doc-
trinaire. The call of Peterson, Wurr, and Crawford for cultural independence is reminiscent of the writings of John Collier three decades earlier:[45]

> The teacher would do well to abandon the puritan ethic that suggests that
> everyone must subject himself to arbitrary authority and feel great shame
> and experience public embarrassment if his personal behavior deviates
> from that of the dominant influences of society. We suspect that any disad-
> vantaged child quickly picks up the silent message from a teacher who is
> actually dedicated to forcing a change in his whole way of life.
> As mentioned earlier, the goal here is to familiarize the Indian pupil with
> major aspects of the majority culture and to equip him with the skills
> needed to function there when he wished to do so. We want to help him
> become multi-faceted, not narrower; to add to his repertoire of responses
> and improve his perception of appropriate settings for different kinds of
> behavior. This does not require his commitment to a single way of life as the
> only "right" way for him.

Useful as such distilled wisdom might be for teachers, the most
exciting educational news at Grand Portage in the last decade is
still the fact that the Chippewa community, with the help of the
Petersons, has designed a curriculum for its children which includes
Indian culture, has helped to teach it in the classroom, and has
encouraged its children to learn what was being taught. And the
community has fought against consolidation pressures from
Washington, D.C., and Bemidji, Minnesota, which would have
closed the log school, and has proudly watched its young people
achieve academic success in higher grades. Chippewa adults are
also supportive of the reservation Head Start and Adult Education Programs.[46] Certainly, therefore, none can deny that self-
determination in the realm of education at Grand Portage has
worked—and without the Indians' abandoning their ethnic identity.

Since 1969 the federal government has encouraged throughout
the country the same sort of local Indian involvement in education
that the Petersons pioneered on Lake Superior's north shore. That
year the Senate Special Subcommittee on Indian Education published a study entitled *Indian Education: A National Tragedy—A
National Challenge*. The Kennedy Report, as it came to be called
(Senator Edward Kennedy chaired the group during the final
months of research and writing), was the culmination of two years of
extensive research, including field investigations in various parts of

the country, hearings in Washington, and the employment of professional consultants to analyze organizational failures within the BIA's education program. Once gathered, the data left no doubt in the minds of committee members that the federal government's policy of "coercive assimilation" had had "disastrous effects on the education of Indian children." Local schools seemed more interested in taking federal funds than in helping Indian students. They, too, had failed "to understand or adapt to, and in fact often denigrate, cultural differences." Nor did they recognize "the importance and validity of the Indian community."

Rather than meeting the special educational needs of Native Americans, federal aid had been misdirected and misspent. The results were a "dismal record of absenteeism, dropouts, negative self-image, low achievement, and, ultimately, academic failure for many Indian children" (a situation not unlike that found by the Petersons at Grand Portage eight years earlier). Of the subcommittee's many recommendations, the most important were the inclusion of Indian culture, history, and language as part of the school curriculum; involvement of Indian parents in the education of their children; and a commitment by the federal government "to a national policy of educational excellence for Indian children"—with "new legislation and substantial increases in appropriations to achieve these goals."[47]

The first such legislation, the Indian Education Act, was signed into law three years later. Drafted by Senators Kennedy and Walter F. Mondale, it enjoyed widespread support among Indian leaders because, unlike earlier acts, it provided for Indian participation in federal educational programs. For example, it amended Public Law 81-874 to make it mandatory that Indian parents and communities be consulted whenever impact aid funds from Washington are spent. An all-Indian, fifteen-member National Advisory Council on Indian Education was created to advise the United States Office of Education on matters pertaining to federal Indian educational programs. The Advisory Council would review all applications for grants under the new Indian Education Act.[48] With similar general goals in mind, Congress's Indian Self-Determination and Education Assistance Act of January, 1975, amended the 1934 Johnson-O'Malley Act so as to forbid the secretary of the interior to enter into any contract for the education of Indians unless the school, in consultation with the parents of its Indian children, designs "an educational plan, which . . . contains educational objectives which adequately address the educational needs of the Indian students who are to be the beneficiaries of the contract and assures that the contract is capable of meeting such objectives."[49]

Minnesota exemplifies the important role a state can take to stimulate Indian involvement in education, both as designers of curriculum and consumers. In 1969, the state legislature created an Indian Education Committee (a twenty-five-member Indian advisory group) to assist the state's department of education in setting goals. Responsible for implementation of policy is the Indian-staffed Indian Education Section of the state department of education, which during the seventies initiated several special projects for Indians: library institutes, summer camps, dropout prevention programs, and teacher-aide training. Special Indian-developed educational material has also been encouraged by the state. An excellent example of what can be accomplished cooperatively is "The Ojibwe: A History Resource Unit," produced by the Ojibwe Curriculum Committee of the American Indian Studies Department of the University of Minnesota, and the Educational Services Division, Minnesota Historical Society. Designed for students in the upper elementary and junior and senior high schools, the unit includes teachers' guides and student booklets, filmstrips and records, and a resource packet of banner biographies, drawings, posters, word charts, and a reproduction of the treaty of 1837.

Other educational benefits are also available for the Indians. In 1972–73, 145 Indians attended Minnesota junior colleges, while 385 enrolled in state colleges. Most received financial assistance from the BIA and the state. Minnesota appropriated $140,000 for scholarships in 1973 and $230,000 for fiscal 1974. The Department of American Indian Studies, established in 1969 at the University of Minnesota-Minneapolis, provides unique services for Twin Cities college students, including counselors, tutors, and instruction in the Ojibwa and Dakota languages. During 1973, nearly 3,000 tribesmen in 30 communities attended Minnesota adult education classes in driver's training, as well as continuing education in vocational skills, cultural studies, and basic education. General Education Development certificates, equivalents of high school diplomas, were earned by 528 of these students between 1970 and 1973.[50]

In addition to governmental agencies and Indian parents at Grand Portage, other Chippewa leaders have become involved in educational programs and have demanded changes that would better meet their needs. They recognize that the improvement of reservation education levels will solve, in part at least, other problems, such as economic development. The Lac du Flambeau Tribal Council agreed that:[51]

A highly educated community is more likely to create a better labor market and maintain a more stable structure in terms of the ability of the people to support and better themselves economically. A lower educated population is usually less stable and creates a poorer labor market. . . .

If Indian students are to rise above the problems of poverty and master two cultures and find their own reasons to strive, they will need exceptional tools and superior ability. They will [need] support for developing self-respect and finding success experiences in the face of adversity.

To ensure Indian participation in the education of their children, the 1972 Indian Education Act required that parental advisory committees be formed and become actively involved in curriculum development and evaluation; JOM monies are also being used to hire home-school coordinators as liaisons between the schools and Indian communities. In-service teacher training is still another important avenue for improving parent-school communication. St. Croix historian Lolita Taylor writes about the significance of school attitudes:[52]

Sensitivity is needed on the part of the teacher. If educators see Indian culture as inferior and undesirable they can certainly not help the child to greater self-respect. If they do not make some effort to teach in the language of the home if it is not English they can not hope to communicate. If administrators do not screen texts for racism, however subtle, they cannot expect the Indian child to enjoy them or to learn from them.

The state of Minnesota now requires that its teachers, most of whom are white and middle class, have at least sixty hours of human relations courses. Some tribes do their own consciousness raising by inviting school teachers to visit the reservations.[53] When Bad River tried this a few years ago, the teachers from Ashland public schools seemed surprised to discover that their Chippewa students were not living in teepees![54]

Several indicators suggest that some of the desired changes in curriculum and Indian academic performance are being achieved. In 1974, for example, at Lac du Flambeau, 81 per cent of those Native Americans surveyed believed that the public schools taught relevant subjects. (Most of the remaining 19 per cent simply wanted more Chippewa culture taught.) Dropout rates have significantly declined at Keweenaw Bay, Bad River, Red Cliff, Lac du Flambeau, Mole Lake, and St. Croix. Much of the success with Lac du Flambeau students at Lakeland High School, indicated by the figures below, is attributed to the work of an Indian home-school coordinator:[55]

| Year of Graduation | Per cent Indian Dropouts | Per cent Non-Indian Dropouts |
| --- | --- | --- |
| 1961 | 64.0 | 14.2 |
| 1969 | 38.1 | 5.3 |
| 1971 | 45.8 | 6.6 |
| 1972 | 16.7 | 7.7 |
| 1973 | 9.5 | 10.4 |

Bad River residents were much pleased when only one out of 357 of their youngsters in public schools dropped out during the 1974–75 academic year. Another sign of increased interest in education is the fact that so many parents attend reservation adult education classes or nearby colleges. One of the most popular institutions on the south shore is Ashland's Northland College, founded several decades ago by a son of Leonard Wheeler. It was therefore particularly fitting when its president recently proposed to make available his faculty's services, in whatever way they could be useful, to the Bad River band. Accepting the generous offer was Raymond Maday, tribal chairman and one of the reservation's two dozen part-time Indian students at Northland.[56]

Heartening as these educational pursuits might be, barriers remain. The Indian Education Act of 1972 required that Indians be consulted about public school programs, but then left it up to the tribes to battle with school boards for specific curricula changes. The boards were unwilling to surrender power and frequently rejected any proposals from local Indian education committees. At Lac Court Oreilles, school officials postponed conferences with Chippewa planners, held meetings without notifying the Indians, or, when a joint meeting finally took place, whites with decision-making power were absent—claiming illness or out-of-town business.[57] Sandra Shabiash, home-school coordinator at Fond du Lac, encountered school districts unwilling to include cross-cultural materials, so she established American Indian rooms in various schools, and now works directly with Indian and white youngsters on an extracurricular basis. Her goal is to eliminate the ignorance and prejudice of white parents by demonstrating to their children just what Chippewa culture and people are all about—that the Chippewa is not a "dirty, black Indian, living in a shack with a dirty floor, and living tax free on the dole." Such negative stereotypes have for years bred discrimination in the schools. According to Sandra, most Fond du Lac students who drop out (their rate ranges from 60 to 80 per cent) actually are "pushed out" by this sort of prejudicial attitude.[58]

In 1973, 55 per cent of Red Cliff residents surveyed felt that teachers did not give Chippewa students enough attention and that whites harassed them. A year later, 36 per cent of the Lac du Flambeau respondents to a similar questionnaire claimed unfair treatment in the schools. For Lac du Flambeau and Red Cliff Indians who stayed in school, such discrimination, combined at times with the problems of poverty at home, inadequate parental support, and long bus rides, resulted in below-average academic performances.

When the Iowa Tests of Basic Skills (vocabulary, reading, language, work-study, mathematics) were given to Lac du Flambeau children attending grades four through eight during the spring of 1973, their performance was one school year below the national average of pupils at that level. The educational attainment of Chippewa adults also needs to be improved. Compared with a Wisconsin state average in 1973 of 12.1 years of formal schooling, Red Cliff adults had 10.0 years, with 10.1 years for married men at Lac du Flambeau.[59] Only 37 per cent of the Keweenaw Bay Indian Community had completed four or more years of high school in 1970; the Michigan average was 58 per cent. Of the adult Indians of this reservation, only 3 or 4 per cent had received any sort of post high school instruction.[60]

Although vast improvements of Chippewa education are necessary, the important first steps have been taken. More than ever before, tribal councilmen recognize that education is a key to self-determination. The striking successes of the Petersons at Grand Portage offer proof that parent-school cooperation can produce a high level of academic achievement. Supported by Washington and their state governments, reservation leaders must continue to strive for academic programs which best meet Chippewa needs.[61]

An important feature of Indian-designed educational programs and of self-determination generally is increased pride and interest in Chippewa culture. Certainly many woodland ways have already vanished as a result of the white man's century-long assault on Chippewa behavior. By the mid-1970's, knowledge of traditional religion, folklore, music, and herbal remedies was found only among a few old people. Marriage, divorce, death, and burial practices conformed to those of the dominant culture. Regarding child rearing, a St. Croix informant simply noted, "Everybody's read Spock."[62]

So much acculturation has occurred that some anthropological articles read like coroners' verdicts. "In terms of the aboriginal past," writes Harold Hickerson, "Chippewa culture is a shambles, so much have the people everywhere had to accommodate to the new conditions imposed by their relations with Euro-Americans." Bernard James, writing nearly twenty years after his New Post study, judged that "Ojibwa culture on the American reservations is . . . for all practical purposes, dead. What I mean when I say 'for all practical purposes,'" he continues,[63]

is that modern circumstances, modern employment, modern unemployment, constant interaction with the larger modern cultural environment, modern forms of communication—automobiles, radios, television, newspapers, magazines, and the like—public welfare, housing, present-day diet, schools (as well as the attitudes and beliefs encountered in connection with any one of these), interaction with non-Indians, the civil rights movement, drinking habits, and whatnot are more important in the lives of the modern Indian of Ojibwa ancestry than whatever Ojibwa cultural factors, subtle or not, may still survive.

Perhaps. Yet considerable evidence suggests the continued strength of these "cultural factors." Equally, if not more, astute observers of the Chippewas are Peterson, Crawford, and Wurr, who for years have worked closely with Indian young people. What these educators describe in *Minnesota Chippewa Indians: A Handbook for Teachers* is a disorganized, rather than a dead, culture:[64]

In this sense, present-day Chippewa life probably has no clean-cut, coherent complex of values, status systems or social norms. The old system is partially gone and the modern one seems to be more a collection of bits and pieces of the old plus some versions of items from the dominant society.

Just what "bits and pieces" have been retained? Some are personality characteristics detailed by Peterson, Crawford, and Wurr: "Anger is seldom displayed except when drunk"; "lack of demonstrativeness between people, including husbands and wives"; "considerable affinity for the extended family"; a need "to cope mostly with concrete, practical things"; reluctance to display "an inexpert performance"; a willingness to work hard "for a specific purpose and for rewards that are quite immediate."[65] Some of the outstanding examples of Chippewa arts and crafts, which still flourish at Lac Court Oreilles, St. Croix, Grand Portage, and elsewhere, will be housed at the Red Cliff Center. During the spring of 1975 this unique building was dedicated as a new "symbol of our Everlasting

Life. Our cultural heritage will live forever here; our children will have much to learn from and to live by."[66] The harvesting of woodland resources by means of hunting, trapping, fishing, berrying, and ricing is still important in the Lake Superior bands' struggle for survival on the reservations, largely because of the scarcity of jobs for unskilled Indian workers. Most who converse in the Chippewa language are elderly, but tribal leaders are encouraging native language instruction in the public schools and the response from Indian youth has been good. "The Indian never loses his identity," one is told, and today the young people's pride in that identity permeates the reservations; it is the motivating force behind the widespread effort to preserve the remnants of Chippewa traditional culture.

Pride and confidence are necessary in the drive for Indian self-determination. Ron Sherer of Grand Portage describes this phenomenon as the Indian's "inner excitement" about himself, his culture, and his past.[67] Moreover, Chippewa youth want to announce this identity and to do something about it, says "Rex" Mayotte, a Bad River Chippewa who works as a field representative for the BIA at Bemidji. This involves "getting into" Indian studies at the high school and college levels and an unwillingness to be treated as inferiors by white classmates and teachers. Most important is the group confidence that has come from individual and tribal pride. In addition to launching the tribal projects described above, another manifestation of this confidence is the fact that reservation communities no longer feel threatened when a member leaves to pursue some kind of personal development, such as formal education. Indians now actually encourage this type of action and are proud of it.[68]

In the effort to achieve such goals as the preservation of Chippewa culture, better education for the young, the improvement of living conditions, and economic development, tribal councils play a crucial role in establishing reservation priorities, designing programs, and mobilizing members. This has not always been the case. In 1973 historian Taylor recalled that if one had sat in on a St. Croix council meeting in the early sixties, he or she—[69]

would have found a rather silent group of mostly elderly Indians attending, presided over by the current Indian Agent of the Bureau of Indian Affairs. A few proposals might have been made with accompanying advice from the Agent. If the problem was, for instance, the sale of timber, the Agent advised, then sold, and supervised the cutting after the forester had given his consent and marked the trees to be cut. The supervising left something to be desired since it was often done after the cutting and sometimes after the timber had been hauled away. Ask anyone on the reservation where the money from the sale was going and how it might benefit them and many would not know. Most did not know that the money was directed to Washington and that it did not become a part of the tribal fund for a year. The fact is, the Indian was never given a chance to make a decision as to what was happening on the reservation.

Today the picture has changed. Go to any meeting involving Indian business now and you will find young Indians planning and administering their own programs. And, because of that, housing is progressing, small industry is entering the reservation, tribal halls on the reserve house offices, and council rooms are buzzing with activity.

Chippewa tribal council meetings ceased to be merely social gatherings in the mid-sixties when the new Office of Economic Opportunity (OEO) funneled additional federal monies onto the reservations and, more important, encouraged Indians for the first time to operate programs. The success of Head Start, for example, was that it not only involved parents, but also convinced tribal leaders that they had the ability to manage such a project. Additional experience came from anti-poverty legislation which emphasized locally planned housing and economic development programs. As tribal councils contracted to carry out more and more of the functions once performed by the BIA, additional jobs opened up on the reservations, tribal leaders began drawing salaries and becoming serious-minded administrators, and the Chippewas' confidence in their own abilities skyrocketed.[70]

President Nixon's message to Congress in July, 1970, underscored the administration's new commitment to Indian self-determination; he recommended that tribes like the Chippewas control federal funds allocated to public schools serving their youngsters and that loan funds available for reservation businesses be tripled.[71] Thus began the dramatic political change of which Taylor wrote. The pendulum of national Indian policy was swinging away from paternalism and toward tribal freedom from federal control (but without the relinquishment of responsibility and support from Washington).

As powerful advocates for their people, local Indian political leaders in Michigan, Wisconsin, and Minnesota formed intertribal associations to strengthen their position in dealings with state legislatures and the federal government. Since it was established in 1968, the efforts of the Inter-Tribal Council of Michigan have helped the Indian's social and economic position in several ways. A couple of the most important include winning an EDA planning grant to hire two Indian economic development specialists in 1974 and securing funds for a statewide Indian Community Action Program from the Office of Native American Programs, HEW. Generally the Inter-Tribal Council has lobbied effectively in Lansing and Washington, according to Tribal Chairman Frederick Dakota, and at the same time has permitted his Keweenaw Bay Indian Community complete control over local policies and programs.[72] In 1961, Wisconsin Indian governing bodies formed the Great Lakes Inter-Tribal Council (GLIC) for the purpose of seeking outside financial support for a variety of community programs. As a central political and administrative body, GLIC since then has fought for and won lucrative contracts with several government agencies, including OEO. Monies thus obtained are usually prorated for each reservation and have sponsored Community Action Programs, reservation economic development, education and youth development, community health projects, alcoholism treatment centers, and Indian legal services. Unquestionably, GLIC gives the Wisconsin tribes increased political clout with both state and federal authorities. Such protection and assistance are especially important to the small tribes.[73]

On the other hand, there are some complaints that this strong organization has become too bureaucratic. Like the BIA, its effectiveness is limited because it gobbles up too much money in administrative costs and designs programs for Wisconsin tribes without enough local input and fiscal control. Indeed, Councilman Sam Livingston of Bad River claims that the BIA wields too much influence over the GLIC.[74] Only time will tell whether or not the GLIC can curb this tendency (as some critics perceive it) to control Wisconsin reservations on the intertribal level, and whether or not a satisfactory balance can be preserved between local and central Indian authorities. The problem is, of course, an ageless political dilemma and by no means unique to Native Americans. The Minnesota Chippewa Tribe, organized in the 1930's, strikes a more satisfactory equilibrium with regard to decision-making powers, while at the same time becoming, like the GLIC, an important contracting agency. The tribe's constitution outlines governing powers over interband matters which are clearly defined and exercised by the tribal executive committee, composed of the chairman and secretary-treasurer of each of the six-member reservation business committees: White Earth, Leech Lake, Mille Lac, Nett Lake, Grand Portage, and Fond du Lac. Also exactly stated are the powers of the reservation business committees over local funds, licensing, and the negotiation of contracts or other agreements. Thus Grand Portage, for example, has been able to develop its own housing project, Head Start, Community Action Program, and reservation businesses. As far as Grand Portage is concerned, relations with the Minnesota Chippewa Tribe are good.[75] From the St. Paul and Washington perspectives, the Minnesota Chippewa Tribe is a political force to be reckoned with, to consult with, to contract with.

Given this tendency of tribal councils and intertribal groups toward political independence, what will the BIA's role be in future Chippewa affairs? The consensus among both reservation leaders and government personnel is that the BIA, its old authority gone and its staff greatly reduced, will probably continue to monitor the tribal contracting process, provide advice and technical assistance when requested, and retain its rather vague trusteeship over certain Indian lands and people. Meanwhile, what if the tribes should stumble in the operation of certain programs? Or lose federal funding? Some Chippewas fear that a weakened BIA could not rescue or re-instate previous services. Self-determination could lead to a termination of federal responsibility. According to one highly placed official, opposition to self-determination comes mainly from minor BIA bureaucrats and office workers, who, out of fear of losing their jobs, go to reservation meetings and stir up needless anxieties. Upper echelon BIA employees seem more inclined to encourage the Indians to run their own programs. The Chippewas, they say, are presently getting plenty of federal funds to hire their own talented technicians and business managers, whether white or Indian. Improved educational opportunities for Indians in the future will insure that the Chippewas themselves possess those needed skills.

The willingness of Duluth's urban Indians to organize and fight for their own independence and well-being serves as another illustration of the Chippewas' ability to get along without BIA services. For more than two decades, Lake Superior tribesmen have migrated in growing numbers to Midwest cities: Cleveland, Detroit, Chicago, Milwaukee, and especially to the Twin Cities and Duluth. Of Minnesota's 22,322 Indians, nearly 12,000 were in urban areas by the mid-seventies.[76] In 1966, 612 Indians resided in Duluth; nine years later the number had swelled to 2,200.[77] The Native American population of St. Paul and Minneapolis quadrupled between 1964 and 1974.[78] Concerning their motives for leaving the reservations, Nett Lake–born Ms. Veryl L. Holmes, Indian Advocate for the Hennepin County welfare department, notes, "These people have known poverty most of their lives and the hope of having a job and a stable income is deep enough to entice them into the cities across the nation."[79] For the new arrivals, accustomed mainly to isolated rural villages, the initial shock of the big city—the size of its buildings, the traffic, the necessity of dealing with bus drivers, policemen, welfare departments, employment agencies, and the like—is sometimes overwhelming. Finding work is more difficult than expected, for Indians often lack the requisite high school diploma, references, or proper skills.[80] Another barrier is discrimination. Holmes laments that many times the Indian—[81]

is not even given the opportunity to prove himself to an employer; he is often judged and rejected according to the employer's previous experience with Indians. The stereotype of the dirty, lazy, drunken Indian looms forward in the mind's eye of the employer. The Indian can usually sense what is happening but can do little to dispel the image from the employer's thinking. He may have this same experience a number of times before he is finally hired for a job. Self-concept has been shaken, however, and leaves the Indian feeling less secure about life in the city once again.

A 1972 study by the Indian Health Board of Minneapolis documented how few urban Native Americans overcome these difficulties and find profitable, steady jobs. Of the 389 households surveyed, employment provided the primary source of income for only 13 per cent; the rest survived through the help of public assistance, Social Security benefits, relatives, and work at the day labor pool. Unemployment becomes even more unpleasant when Indians discover they must settle for the worst available housing in the city, rental units "in subdivided old houses on bar-studded inner-city streets devoid of safe places for children to play."[82] Writing in 1972 from both personal experience and professional observation, Holmes again provides a vivid picture:[83]

The caretaker leads the Indian down the dingy, darkened hallway of some huge apartment building. The wallpaper is cracked, peeling and dirty and a lone lightbulb hangs suspended on a cord from the ceiling. The small apartment is sparsely furnished, often with an old, outdated stove and refrigerator, table and odd chairs. The living room often has an old double bed, chest of drawers, maybe a table with a lamp and some chairs. The bedroom will also have a bed and dresser (or maybe two beds). The absentee landlord doesn't come around very often so you may never see him. Also, the rent could very easily be over one hundred dollars a month. Recently, I visited a family in an apartment such as I have described above and the rent was $150 a month. It seems impossible for a landlord to get away with such practices, yet it goes on year after year. These buildings are dilapidated and continue to deteriorate. Most often, there is a communal bathroom down the hall that one must share with everyone else on that particular floor of the building. It is not unusual for these dwellings to be infested with mice, cockroaches and even rats. I had just such an experience of living in this sort of building upon first arriving in the metropolitan area many years ago, yet it is still happening to people today.

The same Minneapolis Indian Health Board which studied unemployment in the early seventies also concluded that the city's health delivery services were not properly organized to meet pressing Indian needs. Home visits by their outreach workers revealed that 89 per cent of the Native American households had health care needs. One out of every nine persons ought to have been hospitalized immediately. Ninety-one per cent of those over fourteen years of age had peridontal disease. Lack of educational achievement by Indian children is a consequence of these unhappy health, living, and economic conditions. Looking at data from Minneapolis once more, one finds a high dropout rate among Indian high schoolers in 1974: 30.1 per cent compared with 14.4 per cent for the general population. Only 43 per cent of the Indian adults in Hennepin County finished high school, whereas over two-thirds of the total adult population did.[84]

Improvements in Indian-white relations brought about by the Duluth Indian Action Council (DIAC) attracted many Chippewas to move there from Minneapolis and St. Paul. Comparing the two locations is like comparing "the earth and the moon," asserts Eugene Savage, the genial and proud director of DIAC. The atmosphere in the Twin Cities is too harsh. In Duluth, whites and Indians live together peacefully, the city is sensitive to Native American needs, and DIAC provides a wide range of services. Indians organized DIAC in 1966 and selected spokesmen to meet with various white groups and ask for their help. No violence erupted, and there was no confrontation. In fact, receptive whites claimed they had been waiting for the Duluth Indians to mobilize. Since then, great strides have been made, because, according to Savage, DIAC is "a hardnosed group determined to improve the lot of the unfortunate." For new arrivals in the city, DIAC provides emergency food, clothing, and shelter. In the mid-seventies its state and federal contracts were generating over a million dollars annually in wages. A state-funded alcoholic program serving Duluth, Grand Portage, Nett Lake, and Fond du Lac is sponsored by DIAC. Its Indian youth program, supported by local churches and HEW, is also active on reservations outside the city. As a result of these and other united efforts, there is little Indian crime in Duluth other than public drunkenness and disorderly conduct. Nor is there any hard drug use (even some "grass" [marijuana] which Savage confiscated was nothing more than "rhy grass and sheep shit"). Duluth's rookie policemen attend DIAC-sponsored sensitivity sessions about Indian cultures, and should a Chippewa run afoul of the law, DIAC's legal assistance program insures protection of rights.[85]

DIAC's insistence on self-determination has brought about dramatic and creative changes in Indian education. Because nearly five hundred Native American youngsters attend Duluth public schools, DIAC fought successfully to get one of its members elected to the school board and to incorporate Chippewa culture into the curriculum. In this context, DIAC asked Dave Peterson to develop his Indian Culture Kit for use in city classrooms. The teacher's manual accompanying the material summarizes nicely DIAC's whole educational thrust: to build a "communication bridge of understanding between Indians and Whites from which both cultures may derive benefit." The dropout rate remains as high in Duluth as many other public schools with Indian populations, yet Savage discerns some improvement. In 1966, no Native Americans graduated from high school; during the 1974–75 academic year, twenty-nine received their diplomas, one graduated from college, and ninety-two were registered at the University of Minnesota-Duluth.

As an alternative school for dropouts and those reservation and city Chippewa children whom the public schools have labeled severe academic or disciplinary problems, DIAC established *Bizindun* within its downtown headquarters building in 1972. Its enrollment increased from four to thirty students within three years. It operates like an open school—"a big family"—with students in grades seven through twelve helping each other and the three teachers working with individual students as much as possible. Working with these students requires an acute sensitivity to their personal needs but also a willingness to use physical punishment at times, especially with the new boys who seem to need discipline. Besides standard school subjects, the staff teaches American Indian music and dance, Indian crafts, Chippewa language, and Indian costume making. Indian academic achievement at *Bizindun* is considered to be quite satisfactory. The highlight of each school year is a long field trip in a bus. In past years it has taken them to Albuquerque, Seattle, and the Dakotas. On commencement day, Indian graduates dressed in buckskins each receive a miniature canoe to symbolize their trip through life, along with DIAC's hope that it will be a peaceful journey—and that "they won't tip the canoe!" Later they don caps and gowns to join with their public school counterparts for a traditional white graduation ceremony.[86]

The power of self-determination to improve the plight of the Indian in Duluth is representative of events across Kitchigami land, from Grand Portage to Keweenaw Bay. Eugene Savage aptly calls it the story of "grass roots people saying 'let's do something.'"[87] During the last decade, with government aid, they have achieved many advances: Chippewa economic development projects such as the Radisson Inn at Grand Portage, the Red Cliff Arts and Crafts Center, and Lac du Flambeau's Wa-Swa-Gon Park; reservation housing programs; tribally administered health contracts; the establishment of politically powerful tribal councils and intertribal associations; a renewed pride and confidence in the Indian's heritage—and future; new approaches to the education of Chippewa children, as pioneered by the Petersons at Grand Portage. Each *Bizindun* graduate who crosses the commencement stage exemplifies this progress. Once considered severe and perpetual problem cases, these young people, with the help of DIAC, proved they could master many of the white man's skills and work within the dominant society without abandoning their Indian heritage. With diplomas in hand, clad both in buckskins and in cap and gown, they face what all must hope will be a brighter tomorrow.

# 10. How They Endured: Some Conclusions and a Look at the Future

Without question, the major trend in Lake Superior Chippewa history during the last three hundred years has been their domination by whites—fur traders, miners, lumbermen, farmers, townbuilders, missionaries, BIA bureaucrats—who showed little respect for the integrity of Chippewa culture or the Indians' right to be consulted about policies and programs affecting them. Whatever sociopolitical independence the Chippewas retained in their dealings with French, English, and American fur traders ended in 1854; the BIA assigned the bands to small reservations and launched a full-scale war against Chippewa culture for the purpose of "civilizing" them and training them to become self-supporting farmers, capable of assimilation into the mainstream of American society.

Several themes are evident in Chippewa economic affairs. Since the prosperous days of the fur trade, tribesmen have been dependent on the white man. Before 1854, they needed his superior tools, weapons, utensils, and other manufactured goods. After the Chippewas were on reservations, they relied heavily on annuities from Washington, lumbermen to clear their land, BIA money managers, and off-reservation employment. Such New Deal agencies as the CWA, CCC-ID, and WPA helped them survive the depression years of the 1930's. For two decades following World War II, white businessmen, white tourists, and white bureaucrats (federal, state, and local) continued to dominate tribal economies. Chippewa poverty and maladjustment to the prevailing economic system went hand-in-hand with such dependence, as attested by the Meriam Report, James's study of New Post, federal field surveys in the mid-sixties, and the BIA's April, 1975, data on high Indian unemployment and low earning power. In part, Washington's goal of self-sufficiency failed because of still another economic theme: failure to consult the bands about developmental programs. In 1906, Superintendent Campbell judged the Indians too financially inexperienced to be trusted with their own money, but stated that the "proper thing to do is to teach them gradually how to handle it, and how to make themselves self-supporting."[1] Nevertheless, with the exception of the Collier years, the BIA persisted with its suffocating financial paternalism well into the 1960's.

Chippewa economic self-determination during the last decade has finally begun to disprove the old notion of Indian incompetence. The Indian Self-Determination and Education Assistance Act of 1975 guarantees the tribes an effective voice in economic program planning and implementation. Although Chippewa reservation developers still face century-old problems of poverty and dependence on government grants, they are now charting their own course toward free enterprise. Jim Hull is hopeful about the EDA tourist complex at Grand Portage, writing, "this development will be only the first of several which will ultimately cause the phaseout of public subsidies and the establishment of a sound, permanent, self-sustaining community."[2]

Until the mid-1960's, Chippewa living conditions showed little improvement. Tribesmen settling on their allotments in the late nineteenth century forsook the birch-bark wigwam for permanent log and frame dwellings which housed one to three families each. The persistence of poverty and the Indians' reluctance to move to better town sites resulted in the situation found by 1913 at Odanah: rotted sidewalks, odorous outhouses, backyards covered with stagnant water and refuse, and floodwaters which annually spread raw sewage from open privies throughout the town.[3] Twenty-five years later, Odanah's turn-of-the-century homes were even more deteriorated (a four or five-room frame dwelling was valued at $325) and still overcrowded (1.62 families per home).[4] By 1966, living conditions remained shockingly substandard at Odanah and elsewhere. Such houses offered "shelter, but little of the dignities or comforts of modern life."[5] Thanks to HIP, HUD, and the Public Health Service-Indian Division, many of the shelters have been replaced by modern ranch-style houses which meet minimal federal standards for comfort and safety. Moreover, tribal leaders demanded and now play a greater role in reservation housing programs. Gone are the days when passive Chippewas settled for a "take it or leave it" house of poor design built by a low-rent housing contractor with inferior materials. Though a few families still live in dilapidated houses along the Bad River, it is the modern town of New Odanah, a few miles away, which symbolizes the great change in Chippewa living conditions.

Crowded, unsanitary, and poorly ventilated homes nurtured communicable diseases. By 1900, quarantines and vaccinations reduced smallpox epidemics, but tuberculosis and venereal infections raged unchecked on all reservations. At Bad River, 130 of the 898 persons there had tuberculosis in 1915. Shortly after the turn of the century, hereditary syphilis killed nearly one-fifth of all Chippewa children before they were six months old.[6] The BIA battled these conditions as well as Indian alcoholism (a legacy of the fur trade era) with inadequate facilities and understaffed and underpaid health care personnel. Widespread Indian misery due to illness and a low standard of living was noted by the Meriam Report in 1928:[7]

The survey staff found altogether too much evidence of real suffering and discontent to subscribe to the belief that the Indians are reasonably satisfied with their condition. The amount of serious illness and poverty is too great to permit of real contentment.

During the New Deal and postwar decades, the rate of tuberculosis and venereal infection dropped significantly. Infants were innoculated against smallpox and diptheria, BIA contract doctors periodically examined and immunized school age Indian children, and Chippewa adults received free medical care. Nevertheless, because of persistently poor living conditions, dietary deficiencies, neglect of personal hygiene, wariness of white medical personnel, and transportation difficulties, those Chippewas living at New Post, for example, continued to suffer from a high incidence of tooth decay, dental infections, pregnancy and birth complications, and infant mortality. By the 1970's, better housing coupled with modern water and sanitary systems markedly brightened the Chippewa health picture, though little progress has been made in the fight against alcoholism and youthful suicides. As was the case with economic development and housing programs, tribal leaders played an important part in improving the delivery of services via CHRs and reservation health clinics. The Indian-managed facility at Keweenaw Bay, which provides "preventative, curative and rehabilitative services,"[8] thus represents both the progress made in Indian health care over the last century and the power of Chippewa self-determination.

Chippewa education also has improved noticeably since the early days of white contact when missionaries and Indian agents designed curriculums to "civilize" Native American youngsters and prepare them for assimilation. "Put into the hands of their children the primer and the hoe," the House Committee on Indian Affairs predicted in 1818,[9]

and they will naturally, in time, take hold of the plough, and, as their minds become enlightened and expand, the Bible will be their book, and they will grow up in habits of morality and industry, leave the chase to those whose minds are less cultivated, and become useful members of society.

Indian parents refused to support the programs thrust at them; thus, educators in mission, government boarding, and public schools were plagued for decades with irregular attendance, many dropouts, and low scholastic achievement. Chippewa families must have been pleased when New Deal BIA educators downplayed assimilation and encouraged cross-cultural education and vocational training for rural life both on and off the reservations.

Then World World II intervened, and the postwar era returned to a coercive assimilation strategy with total disregard for both the Indians' cultural heritage and his right to be included in educational decision making. Predictably, the results were disastrous: a "dismal record of absenteeism, dropouts, negative self-image, low achievement, and, ultimately, academic failure for many Indian children," as the Kennedy Report described it.[10] To remedy the situation Senate investigators recommended an approach first advocated by New Dealers and already employed successfully by the Petersons at Grand Portage, the involvement of Indian parents in the education of their children and the inclusion of Indian culture, history, and language in public school curriculums.

Since 1969, the Indian Education Act and the Indian Self-Determination and Education Assistance Act have underscored the federal government's commitment to a national policy of educational excellence for Indian children. Equally appreciative of the fact that education for young and old alike is an important key to self-determination, Chippewa parents are now deeply involved in designing programs to meet the special needs of their children—be it advising the Minnesota State Department of Education, producing classroom materials like "The Ojibwe: A History Resource Unit," acting as home-school coordinators or instructing at DIAC's *Bizindun*. Likewise, Chippewa children have responded positively, as evidenced by the recent dramatic decline in high school dropout rates and the improvements in their academic performance.

The revitalization of tribal councils, also fostered by federal self-determination legislation in the 1970's, is a significant departure from the politically submissive posture which Chippewas had assumed since the seventeenth century, when they were economically dependent on powerful French, British, and American fur traders and needed their leadership. Following the halcyon days of the *voyageur* and *coureur de bois,* the Lake Superior Chippewas sold their hunting grounds, and federal Indian agents took on many of the traders' political and economic functions. By 1900 the bands were as much the wards of Washington as they had once been of the American Fur Company—financially reliant, politically powerless, disorganized, and out of touch with each other. The word used most frequently by BIA bureaucrats to describe them was "incompetent." Finally, in the 1930's, when Washington altered its entire approach to Native American affairs, the Indian Reorganization Act encouraged the Chippewas to assume limited self-government, charter tribal organizations as federal corporations—generally to take the initiative in establishing and implementing reservation policies and programs.

Though important first steps toward political independence, these movements languished until the mid-1960's because of inadequate federal funding, the persistence of BIA paternalism, misdirected educational thrusts, and the debilitation of poverty. Then, thanks to OEO and other antipoverty programs, federal monies flowed onto the reservations with the understanding that the tribesmen would operate the new projects themselves. Early successes boosted Chippewa confidence; tribal councils contracted to carry out more and more BIA functions; local Indian political leaders became powerful advocates for their people. "Go to any meeting involving Indian business now," St. Croix historian Lolita Taylor proudly wrote in 1973,[11]

and you will find young Indians planning and administering their own programs. And, because of that, housing is progressing, small industry is entering the reservation, tribal halls on the reserve house offices, and council rooms are buzzing with activity.

Political power on the local, state, and national levels was further strengthened by the formation of DIAC, GLIC, and the Inter-Tribal Council of Michigan. No longer anyone's wards, the Lake Superior bands, brimful of self-determination, have come of age politically.

In summary, there is little question that the long war waged by white Americans against traditional Lake Superior culture has succeeded in many areas. Only a handful of tribesmen on each reservation practice the old ways of living, constructing homes, curing the sick, educating the young, and worshiping the supreme being. Only bits and pieces of a woodland way of life remain.

On the other hand, the federal government has failed miserably in its numerous and costly attempts to make the reservations economically self-supporting and their Chippewa inhabitants ready for assimilation into the American mainstream. Ironically, when this was fully recognized in the early 1930's, the BIA viewed what was left of Chippewa culture—language, arts and crafts, distinct personality characteristics, tribal cohesiveness, a close spiritual bond with Kitchigami land, a strong sense of ethnic identity—as a great source of strength for Indian people which ought to be nurtured if the bands were to survive and prosper. The resistant remnants of a shattered culture have assumed great importance. They are the firm foundation upon which rest the plans of present-day tribal leaders for economic development, better living conditions, a more efficient delivery of health services, cross-cultural education for all ages, and self-government. For the first time in three hundred years, white domination is no longer the major theme of Chippewa life. The chains of BIA paternalism have been broken. The possessors of many federal and state contracts, confident in their administrative ability, proud of their Indian heritage, and organized politically, the Lake Superior bands are determined to chart their own courses.

Most leaders talk optimistically about the future. Economically, the Chippewas are better off than ever before, claims Darrell Blacketter of Fond du Lac, and life will improve, thanks to self-pride and self-determination. Rex Mayotte of Bad River feels that the Chippewas are on the verge of an era of tremendous development and are learning how to play a more meaningful role in white society. Whatever the outcome, there is no question in the mind of Minnesota Chippewa author Don Bibeau that his people will endure:[12]

It is hard to be an Indian during these times and to bring together our yesterday with what we are today. There is pain of memory which cuts through the quick of our lives and makes it difficult to love. We are still Indian in spite of a thousand treaties and missionaries with their black frocks. There is nothing and no one who will keep us from our ways and our songs. We have endured and will yet endure....

... We will endure because we are Indian. And being Indian is not simply living in the forest, or mountains or plains, or skin, features, or beads, or sense of history, or language or song: it is living in peace within the great cycles of nature which the Great Spirit has bestowed upon his children, and it is living within the tribal fold. What some others may call "community." And it is good! It is good to live within the Tribe here on this reservation in these lands of our fathers. And so it has been from the most ancient of times.

# Abbreviations

AR   Annual Report.

BIA   Bureau of Indian Affairs, Record Group 75. Located in the National Archives unless otherwise indicated.

CCF   Central Classified Files.

CIA   Annual Report, Commissioner of Indian Affairs, NCR Microcard Edition.

FOR   Field Office Records.

FRC   Federal Records Center.

LR   Letters Received.

LS   Letters Sent.

PI   Personal Interview.

WNRC   Washington National Records Center.

# Notes

## PREFACE

1. Hull, PI at Grand Portage Reservation, June 19, 1975.
2. Dakota, PI at Keweenaw Bay Reservation, June 30, 1975.
3. Kenneth R. Philp, "John Collier and the American Indian," in *Essays on Radicalism in Contemporary America,* ed. by Leon Borden Blair, 63, 65-67.
4. Lolita Taylor, "Ojibwa, the Wild Rice People," (mimeographed, 1973), ii.

## CHAPTER 1

1. Manypenny to Herriman, August 10, 1854; Manypenny to Gilbert, August, 11, 12, 14, 1854, BIA, LS, vol. 49.
2. Gilbert to Manypenny, October 17, 1854, BIA, Documents Relating to the Negotiation of Ratified and Unratified Treaties with Various Indian Tribes, 1801-1869: Treaty with the Chippewas, September 30, 1854.
3. Otto Skolla, "Father Skolla's Report on His Indian Missions," *Acta et Dicta* 7 (October, 1936):232-34; P. Chrysostomus Verwyst, *Life and Labors of Rt. Rev. Frederic Baraga, First Bishop of Marquette, Mich ...,* 290-91.
4. Henry R. Schoolcraft, *Schoolcraft's Expedition to Lake Itasca: the Discovery of the Source of the Mississippi,* ed. Philip P. Mason, 11.
5. Gilbert to Manypenny, October 17, 1854, BIA, Documents Relating to the Negotiation of Ratified and Unratified Treaties.
6. *Ibid.;* U.S., *Statutes at Large,* 10:1109-15. See also Charles J. Kappler, comp. and ed., *Indian Affairs: Laws and Treaties,* 2:648-52.
7. U.S., *Statutes at Large,* 10:1109-10.
8. *Ibid.,* 1110.
9. *Ibid.,* 1110-11. Since the St. Croix and Sakaogon (Mole Lake) bands were not signatories of the La Pointe treaty, they remained "Lost Tribes" until the 1930's when the government recognized them as Chippewa bands and set aside lands in northern Wisconsin for their use. Carolissa Levi, *Chippewa Indians of Yesterday and Today,* 95-99.
10. Hamilton Nelson Ross, *La Pointe-Village Outpost,* 116-17; U.S., *Statutes at Large,* 10:1115.

## CHAPTER 2

1. Grace Lee Nute, *Lake Superior,* 145-46; Harlan Hatcher, *The Great Lakes,* 27; George Irving Quimby, *Indian Life in the Upper Great Lakes, 11,000 B.C. to A.D. 1800,* 1-5; Federal Writers' Project, *Minnesota: A State Guide,* 236-37.

2. Federal Writers' Project, *Wisconsin: A Guide to the Badger State,* 12; Federal Writers' Project, *Minnesota,* 18; Quimby, *Indian Life,* 1–4.

3. Carrie Alberta Lyford, *The Crafts of the Ojibwa (Chippewa),* ed. Willard W. Beatty, 12; Frances Densmore, *Chippewa Customs,* 5.

4. Supt. Alexander Ramsey to Commissioner of Indian Affairs Luke Lea, October 21, 1850, in CIA, 1850, pp. 52–53; Howard Peckham, *Pontiac and the Indian Uprising,* 1–2; William V. Kinietz, *Chippewa Village; the Story of Katikitegan,* 13–14.

5. Harold Hickerson, *The Chippewa and Their Neighbors: A Study in Ethnohistory,* 71; John R. Swanton, *The Indian Tribes of North America,* 263; Hickerson, "The Chippewa of the Upper Great Lakes: A Study in Sociopolitical Change," in Eleanor B. Leacock and Nancy O. Lurie, eds., *North American Indians in Historical Perspective,* 171–72.

6. Hickerson, *The Southwestern Chippewa: An Ethnohistorical Study,* 2.

7. Swanton, *Indian Tribes,* 264.

8. Emerson F. Greenman, "The Indians of Michigan," *Michigan History,* 45 (March, 1961):2–4.

9. Densmore, *Chippewa Customs,* 22–23; Quimby, *Indian Life,* 124; M. Inez Hilger, *Chippewa Child Life and Its Cultural Background,* 136–38, 141.

10. Densmore, *Chippewa Customs,* 28–30.

11. Hilger, *Chippewa Child Life,* 129; Densmore, *Chippewa Customs,* 30–31, 38–39.

12. Henry Colin Campbell *et al., Wisconsin in Three Centuries, 1634–1905,* 1:58–59; Quimby, *Indian Life,* 124; Hilger, *Chippewa Child Life,* 115–16.

13. Hickerson, *Chippewa and Their Neighbors,* 13; Densmore, *Chippewa Customs,* 135; Benjamin G. Armstrong, *Early Life Among the Indians....,* 113–14.

14. Hickerson, *Chippewa and Their Neighbors,* 13; Victor Barnouw, *Acculturation and Personality Among the Wisconsin Chippewa,* 15; Ramsey to Lea, October 21, 1850, CIA, 1850, pp. 59–60; William Whipple Warren, *History of the Ojibwa Nation,* 42–45.

15. Greenman, "Indians of Michigan," *Michigan History,* 45 (March, 1961):3; Campbell, *Wisconsin,* 1:37; Densmore, *Chippewa Customs,* 137; Hickerson, *Chippewa and Their Neighbors,* 16; Armstrong, *Early Life,* 176–77, 205.

16. Ruth Landes, *The Ojibwa Woman,* 1–2; Hilger, *Chippewa Child Life,* 103; Quimby, *Indian Life,* 123–24; Densmore, *Chippewa Customs,* 123; Diamond Jenness, *The Indians of Canada,* 280.

17. Landes, *Ojibwa Woman,* 1–2; Hilger, *Chippewa Child Life,* 103; Robert E. and Pat Ritzenthaler, *The Woodland Indians of the Western Great Lakes,* 17; Densmore, *Chippewa Customs,* 124–25; Alexander Henry, *Travels and Adventures in Canada and the Indian Territories, between the Years 1760 and 1776,* 55.

18. Henry R. Schoolcraft, *Narrative Journal of Travels from Detroit Northwest through the Great Chain of American Lakes to the Sources of the Mississippi River in the Year 1820,* 172–73.

19. Hilger, *Chippewa Child Life,* 103; Quimby, *Indian Life,* 123; Densmore, *Chippewa Customs,* 39, 127–128.

20. Hilger, *Chippewa Child Life,* 103, 147–148; Densmore, *Chippewa Customs,* 128; Lolita Taylor, "Ojibwa, the Wild Rice People," 14.

21. Hilger, *Chippewa Child Life,* 103, 119–24; Landes, *Ojibwa Woman,* 1–2.

22. Hilger, *Chippewa Child Life,* 39, 44, 55–58.

23. Landes, *Ojibwa Woman,* 10; Henry R. Schoolcraft, *Historical and Statistical Information Respecting . . . the Indian Tribes of the United States. . . ,* 5:150; William H. Keating, *Narrative of an Expedition to the Source of St. Peter's River,* 2:152.

24. Densmore, *Chippewa Customs,* 70–71; Ritzenthaler, *Woodland Indians,* 35.

25. Armstrong, *Early Life,* 103–104; Landes, *Ojibwa Woman,* 39; Hilger, *Chippewa Child Life,* 156–58; Densmore, *Chippewa Customs,* 72.

26. Hilger, *Chippewa Child Life,* 161; Landes, *Ojibwa Woman,* 66.

27. Landes, *Ojibwa Woman,* 85–86; Hilger, *Chippewa Child Life,* 162; Peter Jones, *History of the Ojebway Indians . . . ,* 80.

28. Jones, *Ojebway Indians,* 68.

29. Densmore, *Chippewa Customs,* 73–75; Carolissa Levi, *Chippewa Indians,* 179; Thomas L. McKenney, *Sketches of a Tour of the Lakes, of the Character and Customs of the Chippeway Indians . . . ,* 306.

30. McKenney, *Lake Tour,* 292; Jones, *Ojebway Indians,* 100–01; Densmore, *Chippewa Customs,* 77–78.

31. Harold Hickerson, "The Feast of the Dead Among the Seventeenth Century Algonkians of the Upper Great Lakes," *American Anthropologist,* 62 (February, 1960):87.

32. Jones, *Ojebway Indians,* 102; Henry, *Travels and Adventures,* 151–52; Warren, *Ojibway Nation,* 73.

33. Ritzenthaler, *Woodland Indians,* 87; Landes, *Ojibwa Woman,* 1.

34. Kinietz, *Chippewa Village,* 151, 160–61; Campbell, *Wisconsin,* 1:47; Ritzenthaler, *Woodland Indians,* 87; Jones, *Ojebway Indians,* 85, 88.

35. Ritzenthaler, *Woodland Indians,* 88; Hickerson, *Chippewa and Their Neighbors* 16.

36. Jones, *Ojebway Indians,* 96; Densmore, *Chippewa Customs,* 124.

37. Ritzenthaler, *Woodland Indians,* 98–99.

38. Densmore, *Chippewa Customs,* 78–79; Landes, *Ojibwa Woman,* 6.

39. Jenness, *Indians of Canada,* 281; Warren, *Ojibway Nation,* 68.

40. Densmore, *Chippewa Customs,* 46–48; Robert E. Ritzenthaler, *Chippewa Preoccupation with Health; Change in a Traditional Attitude Resulting from Modern Health Problems,* 190.

41. "Journal of Douglas Houghton," August 16, 1832, in Schoolcraft, *Schoolcraft's Expedition to Lake Itasca,* ed. Philip P. Mason, 281; Levi, *Chippwa,* 177–78.

42. Densmore, *Chippewa Customs,* 107.

43. Ritzenthaler, *Chippewa Preoccupation with Health,* 190; Densmore, *Chippewa Customs,* 44; Levi, *Chippewa,* 194.

44. Hickerson, *Chippewa and Their Neighbors,* 52–57.

45. Densmore, *Chippewa Customs,* 86–87; Frances Densmore, *Chippewa Music,* 20.

46. Quimby, *Indian Life,* 126; Densmore, *Chippewa Customs,* 88; Bernard Coleman, *Ojibwa Myths and Legends,* 118.

47. Warren, *Ojibway Nation,* 100, 265; Hilger, *Chippewa Child Life,* 63, 67; Coleman, *Ojibwa Myths and Legends,* 115ff.

48. Henry R. Schoolcraft, *Personal Memoirs of a Residence of Thirty Years With the Indian Tribes on the American Frontiers . . . ,* 196–97; Densmore, *Chippewa Customs,* 97; Warren, *Ojibway Nation,* 56; Ritzenthaler, *Woodland Indians,* 137–38. Wenebojo is the Chippewa name for this Algonquian culture hero. Other spellings include Winabojo, Nanabozho, Manabozho, and Misabos.

49. Densmore, *Chippewa Customs,* 100–101.

50. Ritzenthaler, *Woodland Indians,* 55, 69.

51. Densmore, *Chippewa Music,* 1ff; Densmore, *Chippewa Customs,* 107.

52. Jenness, *Indians of Canada,* 277–78; Campbell, *Wisconsin,* 1:39; George Copway, *The Traditional History and Characteristic Sketches of the Ojibway Nation,* 140; Kinietz, *Chippewa Village,* 84–85.

53. Densmore, *Chippewa Customs,* 132; Copway, *Traditional History,* 137–38; Kinietz, *Chippewa Village,* 78; Quimby, *Indian Life,* 125; Jones, *Ojebway Indians,* 105, 107.

54. Landes, *Ojibwa Woman,* 133; Hickerson, *Southwestern Chippewa,* 13, 27–28.

55. Jones, *Ojebway Indians,* 130; Quimby, *Indian Life,* 124; Densmore, *Chippewa Customs,* 132, 134.

56. Warren, *Ojibway Nation,* 249–50; Ritzenthaler, *Woodland Indians,* 53; Jenness, *Indians of Canada,* 278–79.

57. "Journal of Lieutenant James Allen," July 10, 1832, in Schoolcraft, *Schoolcraft's Expedition to Lake Itasca,* ed. Philip P. Mason, 202; Densmore, *Chippewa Customs,* 135.

## CHAPTER 3

1. Reuben Gold Thwaites, ed., *The Jesuit Relations and Allied Documents. Travels and Explorations of the Jesuit Missionaries in New France, 1610–1791,* 23:209–25.

2. Thwaites, *Jesuit Relations,* 23:225–27.

3. Schoolcraft, *Personal Memoirs of a Residence of Thirty Years with the Indian Tribes,* 114; Ross, *La Pointe,* 18.

4. W. Vernon Kinietz, *The Indians of the Western Great Lakes, 1615–1760,* 318–20.

5. Ross, *La Pointe,* 11–13; Hickerson, *The Southwestern Chippewa,* 67.

6. Hickerson, *Southwestern Chippewa,* 67.

7. Harold Hickerson, *The Chippewa and Their Neighbors,* 37; George Irving Quimby, *Indian Culture and European Trade Goods,* 5.

8. Reuben Gold Thwaites, ed., "Radisson and Groseilliers in Wisconsin," *Collections of the State Historical Society of Wisconsin,* 11 (1888):64–96; Alice E. Smith, *The History of Wisconsin, Vol. 1. From Exploration to Statehood,* 19–20.

9. Reuben Gold Thwaites, "The Story of Chequamegon Bay," *Collections of the State Historical Society of Wisconsin,* 13 (1895):405–06.

10. Nicolas Perrot, "Memoirs on the Manners, Customs, and Religion of the Savages of North America," ed. Jules Tailhan, in *The Indian Tribes of*

*the Upper Mississippi Valley,* ed. Emma H. Blair, 1:22–25.

11. Louise Phelps Kellogg, *The French Regime in Wisconsin and the Northwest,* 209–17.

12. *Ibid.,* 242.

13. Hamilton Nelson Ross, *The Apostle Islands,* 7–11.

14. Kellogg, *French Régime,* 173–74.

15. Larry Gara, *A Short History of Wisconsin,* 17–21; Ross, *La Pointe,* 32.

16. Kellogg, *French Régime,* 172–76.

17. Gara, *Short History of Wisconsin,* 22–23; Kellogg, *French Régime,* 177.

18. Gara, *Short History of Wisconsin,* 8–10.

19. *Ibid.,* 4–6; Kellogg, *French Régime,* 137–38.

20. Ross, *La Pointe,* 48.

21. Lawrence Henry Gipson, *Zones of International Friction: The Great Lakes Frontier, Canada, the West Indies, India, 1744-1754,* vol. 5, *The British Empire Before the American Revolution,* 50–53.

22. Ross, *La Pointe,* 46.

23. Densmore, *Chippewa Customs,* 140–41; Barnouw, *Acculturation and Personality,* 42.

24. Barnouw, *Acculturation and Personality,* 62; Gara, *Short History of Wisconsin,* 23–24.

25. Barnouw, *Acculturation and Personality,* 42; Warren, *Ojibway Nation,* 133.

26. Barnouw, *Acculturation and Personality,* 62; Hickerson, "The Chippewa of the Upper Great Lakes," 170–71.

27. Hickerson, "The Feast of the Dead," 100; Hickerson, *Chippewa and Their Neighbors,* 11–12.

28. William T. Hagan, *The Sac and Fox Indians,* 4–5; Warren, *Ojibway Nations,* 190–93, 299.

29. Hickerson, *Southwestern Chippewa,* 71.

30. Felix M. Keesing, *The Menomini Indians of Wisconsin: A Study of Three Centuries of Cultural Contact and Change,* 13–15.

31. Richard R. Elliot, "The Chippewas of Lake Superior," *American Catholic Quarterly Review,* 21 (April, 1896):354.

32. Perrot, "Memoirs," 179–81.

33. Elliot, "Chippewas of Lake Superior," 354; "Journal of the Reverend William Boutwell," entry for June 7, 1832, in Schoolcraft, *Schoolcraft's Expedition to Lake Itasca,* ed. Philip P. Mason, 308.

34. Kellogg, *French Régime,* 222, 267–68.

35. James Taylor Dunn, *The St. Croix: Midwest Border River,* 10–11.

36. Hickerson, *Southwestern Chippewa,* 65–67; George E. Hyde, *Indians of the Woodlands: From Prehistoric Times to 1725,* 224n., 243.

37. Hickerson, *Southwestern Chippewa,* 69–70; Hickerson, "Chippewa of the Upper Great Lakes," 179–80.

38. Hickerson, *Southwestern Chippewa,* 70; La Ronde to governor of Canada Marquis de Beauharnois, July 22, 1738, in *Collections of the State Historical Society of Wisconsin,* 18 (1906):278.

39. Roy W. Meyer, *History of the Santee Sioux: United States Indian Policy on Trial,* 13; William Watts Folwell, *A History of Minnesota,* 1:81; Bernard Coleman, *Where the Water Stops: Fond du Lac Reservation,* 4.

40. Warren, *Ojibway Nation,* 127.

41. Meyer, *Santee Sioux,* 13.

42. *Ibid.,* 14.

43. Hickerson, "Feast of the Dead," 98–100.

44. Ross, *La Pointe,* 49.

45. *Ibid.*

46. Smith, *Wisconsin,* 51–53; Eugene H. Roseboom and Francis P. Weisenburger, *A History of Ohio,* 24.

47. Peckham, *Pontiac and the Indian Uprising,* 44; Kellogg, *French Régime,* 425ff; Warren, *Ojibway Nation,* 194–95.

48. Smith, *Wisconsin,* 49, 53–54.

49. Wilber R. Jacobs, *Dispossessing the American Indian: Indians and Whites on the Colonial Frontier,* 153; Kellogg, *French Régime,* 290; Quimby, *Indian Culture,* 158.

## CHAPTER 4

1. Lawrence Henry Gipson, *The Triumphant Empire: The Rumbling of the Coming Storm, 1766–1770,* vol. 11 of *The British Empire Before the American Revolution,* 429–31; Gipson, *The Triumphant Empire: New Responsibilities Within the Enlarged Empire, 1763–1766,* vol. 9 of *The British Empire Before the American Revolution,* 88.

2. For a more detailed analysis of the Pontiac uprising, see Gipson, *The Triumphant Empire: New Responsibilities,* 90–96.

3. Henry, *Travels and Adventures,* 44.

4. J[onathan] Carver, *Travels Through the Interior Parts of North America, in the Years 1766, 1767, and 1768,* p. 18; Henry, *Travels and Adventures,* 39–40; Etherington to Major Henry Gladwyn, June 12, 1763, quoted in Francis Parkman, *The Conspiracy of Pontiac and the Indian War After the Conquest of Canada,* 2:336.

5. Parkman, *Conspiracy of Pontiac,* 1:338–39.

6. Etherington to Gladwyn, June 12, 1763, quoted in Parkman, *Conspiracy of Pontiac,* 2:336.

7. Henry, *Travels and Adventures,* 80–81.

8. Etherington to Gladwyn, June 12, 1763, quoted in Parkman, *Conspiracy of Pontiac,* 2:336–37; Parkman, *ibid.,* 1:366–67; Gipson, *The Triumphant Empire: New Responsibilities,* 100–101.

9. Warren, *Ojibway History,* 210–12; Captain Daniel Claus to Sir William Johnson, August 6, 1763, *Collections of the State Historical Society of Wisconsin* 18 (1908):257–58.

10. Henry, *Travels and Adventures,* 165–66.

11. Johnson to Cadwallader Colden, August 23, 1764, in Alexander C. Flick, ed., *The Papers of Sir William Johnson* (6 vols., Albany, 1925), 4:511–12.

12. "A Conference With Chippewas," in Flick, *Papers of Johnson,* 4:478–79.

13. Johnson to Colden, August 23, 1764, in Flick, *Papers of Johnson,* 4:511–12; Gipson, *The Triumphant Empire: New Responsibilities,* 119.

14. Gara, *Short History of Wisconsin,* 27–28; Louise Phelps Kellogg, *The*

*British Régime in Wisconsin and the Northwest,* 40; Henry, *Travels and Adventures,* 192.

15. Henry, *Travels and Adventure,* 192–93; Ross, *La Pointe,* 60.

16. Henry, *Travels and Adventures,* 195.

17. *Ibid.,* 195–96, 198.

18. *Ibid.,* 196, 198–99.

19. *Ibid.,* 203–04.

20. Ross, *La Pointe,* 61; Kellogg, *British Régime,* 102–04.

21. Smith, *Wisconsin,* 72; Kellogg, *British Régime,* 135–39; Gara, *Short History of Wisconsin,* 28.

22. Kellogg, *British Régime,* 188–89.

23. Smith, *Wisconsin,* 73–74; Kellogg, *British Régime,* 198–99; Ross, *La Pointe,* 63.

24. Kellogg, *British Régime,* 237–39.

25. Warren, *Ojibway History,* 379.

26. Reuben Gold Thwaites, ed., "Papers from the Canadian Archives—1767–1814," *Collections of the State Historical Society of Wisconsin,* 12 (1892):76–78.

27. *Ibid.,* 78–82.

28. Johnson to Dease, October 1, 1786, *ibid.,* 83–84; Jean Baptiste Perrault, "Narrative of Travels and Adventures of a Merchant Voyageur in the Savage Territories of Northern America ... ," ed. John Sharpless Fox, *Historical Collections and Researches Made by the Michigan Pioneer and Historical Society* 37 (1909–10):545; Smith, *Wisconsin,* 74–75.

29. Kellogg, *British Régime,* 239; Smith *Wisconsin,* 80–81.

30. Malhiot, "A Wisconsin Fur Trader's Journal, 1804–05," *Collections of the State Historical Society of Wisconsin* 19 (1910):209–10.

31. *Ibid.,* 204.

32. U.S., *Statutes at Large,* 7:49–54.

33. George Dewy Harmon, *Sixty Years of Indian Affairs, Political, Economic and Diplomatic, 1789–1850,* 100.

34. Quoted in Ora Brooks Peake, *A History of the United States Indian Factory System, 1795–1822,* 75–76.

35. Kellogg, *British Régime,* 250–51.

36. Pike to General James Wilkinson, September 23, 1805, quoted in Zebulon Montgomery Pike, *The Journals of Zebulon Montgomery Pike, With Letters and Related Documents,* ed. Donald Jackson, 1:237–42.

37. Pike to Chippewa, February 16, 1806, Pike, *Journals,* 1:262–65.

38. Pike, *Journals,* 1:216–17.

39. Kellogg, *British Régime,* 258.

40. Reginald Horseman, *The Causes of the War of 1812,* 158.

41. *Ibid.,* 165.

42. Warren, *Ojibway History,* 321–22.

43. *Ibid.,* 322–23; Kellogg, *British Régime,* 273.

44. John Tanner, *A Narrative of the Captivity and Adventures of John Tanner (U.S. Interpreter at the Saut de Ste. Marie) During Thirty Years Residence Among the Indians in the Interior of North America,* 147.

45. Quoted in Levi, *Chippewa,* 282.

46. Warren, *Ojibway History,* 368–69; Smith, *Wisconsin,* 85–86.

47. Smith, *Wisconsin,* 90–94; Kellogg, *British Régime,* 329.

## CHAPTER 5

1. U.S., *Statutes at Large,* 7:131.

2. Smith, *Wisconsin,* 95–96.

3. U.S., *Statutes at Large,* 3:332–33.

4. *Ibid.,* 679–80.

5. Kenneth W. Porter, *John Jacob Astor: Business Man* 2:717–18; Smith, *Wisconsin,* 111–12, 115–17.

6. Warren, *Ojibway History,* 382; Solon J. Buck, "The Story of Grand Portage," *Minnesota History,* 5 (February, 1923):24–25; Smith, *Wisconsin,* 506.

7. Coleman, *Where the Water Stops,* 5; Warren, *Ojibway History,* 382–84.

8. Ross, *La Pointe,* 73–74; Subagent Daniel P. Bushnell to Governor Henry Dodge, June 19, 1837, quoted in John Porter Bloom, comp. and ed., *The Territorial Papers of the United States.* vol. 27, *The Territory of Wisconsin: Executive Journal, 1836–1848; Papers, 1836–1839,* 800; Smith, *Wisconsin,* 502.

9. Smith, *Wisconsin,* 502.

10. Ross, *La Pointe,* 114.

11. Smith, *Wisconsin,* 501, 504–06.

12. Entry for June 14, 1832, "Journal of Lieutenant James Allen," in Schoolcraft, *Schoolcraft's Expedition to Lake Itasca,* 173–74.

13. *Ibid.,* entry for June 21, 1832, pp. 186–87, and Allen to Alexander Macomb, November 25, 1833, p. 238. Other federal officials observed the Chippewa's economic dependence on fur traders. See, for example: Dodge to Commissioner of Indian Affairs T. Hartley Crawford, October 18, 1839, BIA, FOR, Wisconsin Superintendency, LS, 1:134; Bushnell to Supt. James D. Doty, September 30, 1841, BIA, FOR, Wisconsin Superintendency, II LR from Agents, 164–65.

14. U.S., *Statutes at Large,* 7:536–38, 591–95; Smith, *Wisconsin,* 504.

15. Barnouw, *Acculturation and Personality,* 12–13, 30–34, 74–75.

16. Entry for June 23, 1832, "Allen Journal," in Schoolcraft, *Schoolcraft's Expedition to Itasca,* 191; Ramsay Crooks to Crawford, October 17, 1843, BIA, LR, La Pointe Agency; Porter, *Astor,* 2:794–95.

17. Warren, *Ojibway History,* 304; Minnesota Governor and Superintendent of Indian Affairs Willis A. Gorman to Commissioner of Indian Affairs George W. Manypenny, September 30, 1854, CIA, 1854, p. 50.

18. Minnesota Governor and Superintendent of Indian Affairs Alexander Ramsey to Commissioner of Indian Affairs Luke Lea, November 3, 1851, CIA, 1851, p. 153; Schoolcraft, *Schoolcraft's Expedition to Itasca,* 110.

19. Warren, *Ojibway History,* 187.

20. *Ibid.,* 304.

21. Schoolcraft to Elbert Herring, September 21, 1831, quoted in Schoolcraft, *Schoolcraft's Expedition to Itasca,* 117–18.

22. Hickerson, *Chippewa and Their Neighbors,* 76–77; Folwell, *A History of Minnesota,* 1:150.

23. Ayer to Secretary of War, August 24, 1840, CIA, 1840, pp. 381–82; Bushnell to Doty, July 20, 1841, BIA, FOR, Wisconsin Superintendency, 2 (LR from Agents):158.

24. Bushnell to Doty, September 30, 1842, BIA, LR, La Pointe Agency.

25. Schoolcraft, *Schoolcraft's Expedition to Itasca,* xiii.

26. Quoted in Meyer, *Santee Sioux,* 39.

27. U.S., *Statutes at Large,* 7:272–77; Clark and Cass to Secretary of War James Barbour, September 1, 1825, BIA, Documents Relating to the Negotiation of Ratified and Unratified Treaties with Various Indian Tribes, 1801–1869: Treaty with the Sioux, Chippewa . . . , August 19, 1825; Alexander Ramsey to Commissioner of Indian Affairs, CIA, 1849, p. 94. For more detailed discussions of the conference, see Meyer, *Santee Sioux,* 39–41, and Smith, *Wisconsin,* 122–24.

28. U.S., *Statutes at Large,* 7:290–95; Cass to Barbour, May 19, 1826, BIA, LR, Michigan Superintendency.

29. Schoolcraft, *Schoolcraft's Expedition to Itasca,* xiv; Dunn, *The St. Croix,* 13.

30. Snelling to General H. Atkinson, May 31, 1827, quoted in Clarence E. Carter, comp. and ed., *The Territorial Papers of the United States:* Vol. 11, *The Territory of Michigan, 1820–1829,* 1082–83.

31. Entry for July 17, 1832, "Allen Journal," in Schoolcraft, *Schoolcraft's Expedition to Itasca,* 208–09; *ibid.,* xiv–xv, xxi.

32. Dodge to Crawford, October 18, 1839, CIA, 1839, p. 484; Meyer, *Santee Sioux,* 61, 105.

33. Ramsey to Lea, October 26, 1852, CIA, 1852, p. 37.

34. Cass to Schoolcraft, August 21, 1826, BIA, LR, Michigan Superintendency.

35. Edward E. Hill, *Historical Sketches for Jurisdictional and Subject Headings Used for the Letters Received by the Office of Indian Affairs, 1824–80,* "Sault Ste. Marie Agency" and "La Pointe Agency"; Smith, *Wisconsin,* 103.

36. Bushnell to Commissioner of Indian Affairs, September 30, 1841, 330; Personnel Statement of Bushnell, enclosed in Acting Superintendent W. B. Slaughter to Commissioner of Indian Affairs Carey A. Harris, June 7, 1838, BIA, LR, La Pointe Agency; Personnel Statement of Bushnell, enclosed in Dodge to Crawford, November 12, 1839, *ibid.*

37. Bushnell to Doty, May 10, 1842, BIA, FOR, Wisconsin Superintendency.

38. Personnel Statement of Hays, included in Hays to Doty, September 30, 1844, BIA, LR, La Pointe Agency.

39. Census of Subagent Alfred Brunson, September 1843, enclosed in Brunson to Doty, September 30, 1843, *ibid.*

40. U.S., *Statutes at Large,* 10:227.

41. Densmore, *Chippewa Customs,* 138–39.

42. Ross, *La Pointe,* 106; Brunson to Doty, January 10, 1843, enclosed in Doty to Crawford, February 23, 1843, BIA, LR, La Pointe Agency.

43. Hays to Doty, September 30, 1844, BIA, LR, La Pointe Agency; Hays to Dodge, September 15, 1847, CIA, 1847, p. 93; Subagent John S. Livermore to Commissioner of Indian Affairs Orlando Brown, September 15, 1849, CIA, 1849, p. 210; Herriman to Minnesota Governor and Superintendent of Indian Affairs W. A. Gorman, October 26, 1854, CIA, 1854, p. 54; Brunson to Doty, August 1, 1843, CIA, 1843, pp. 437–38.

44. Quoted in Smith, *Wisconsin,* 150–51.

45. Schoolcraft, *Schoolcraft's Expedition to Itasca,* 51.

46. Ross, *La Pointe,* 88–90; Baraga to Bishop Fred. Résé, June 25, 1835, Frederic Baraga Papers, Clarke Historical Library.

47. See Verwyst, *Life and Labors of Rt. Rev. Frederic Baraga,* and Maksimilijan Jezernik, *Frederick Baraga. A Portrait of the First Bishop of Marquette Based on the Archives of the Congregatio de Propaganda Fide.*

48. Ross, *La Pointe,* 91, 96–97.

49. Nancy L. Woolworth, "The Grand Portage Mission," *Minnesota History,* 39 (Winter, 1965):304–07.

50. Bishop Peter P. Lefevre to Acting Superintendent of Indian Affairs William A. Richmond, September 30, 1846, enclosed in Richmond to Commissioner of Indian Affairs, October 30, 1846, BIA, LR, Michigan Superintendency; "Father Skolla's Report on His Indian Mission," *Acta et Dicta,* 7 (October, 1936):227.

51. Jezernik, *Baraga,* 83.

52. "Leonard H. Wheeler," Life Memoranda, 1820–1896, American Board of Commissioners for Foreign Missions Papers, Houghton Library, Harvard University, Cambridge, Massachusetts; John N. Davidson, "Missions on Chequamegon Bay," *Collections of the State Historical Society of Wisconsin,* 12 (1892):447.

53. Ross, *La Pointe,* 75; Smith, *Wisconsin,* 156–57; Stephen R. Riggs, "Protestant Missions in the Northwest," *Collections of the Minnesota Historical Society,* 6 (1894):135.

54. Hall to David Greene, September 28, 1832, Dakota Mission, 1831–1883, American Board of Commissioners for Foreign Missions Papers.

55. Ross, *La Pointe,* 106–07; entry for June 27, 1832, "Boutwell's Journal" in Schoolcraft, *Schoolcraft's Expedition to Itasca,* 320.

56. Smith, *Wisconsin,* 156; Hall to Bushnell, September 1, 1840, enclosed in Bushnell to Dodge, September 20, 1840, BIA, LR, La Pointe Agency; Sproat School Report for Male School, Summer of 1844, Ojibwa, Pawnee and Stockbridge Mission, 1844–71, American Board of Commissioners for Foreign Missions Papers.

57. Wheeler to David Greene, September 5, 1844, Ojibway, Pawnee and Stockbridge Mission, American Board of Commissioners for Foreign Missions Papers; Gilbert to Manypenny, November 9, 1854, CIA, 1854, p. 30; Ross, *La Pointe,* 102, 110–11.

58. Davidson, "Missions on Chequamegon Bay," 447–49.

59. Riggs, "Protestant Missions in the Northwest," 150–51.

60. Hall to Greene, October [?], 1838, Dakota Mission, 1831–1883, American Board of Commissioners for Foreign Missions Papers.

61. Ross, *La Pointe,* 86.

62. Gilbert to Manypenny, November 9, 1854, CIA, 1854, pp. 29–30; Subagent James Ord to Acting Superintendent William A. Richmond, November 7, 1848, CIA, 1848, p. 558.

63. Ramsey to Lea, October 21, 1850, CIA, 1850, pp. 53–54; Gilbert to Manypenny, November 9, 1854, CIA, 1854, p. 30.

64. U.S., *Statutes at Large,* 7:536–38; Dodge to Commissioner of Indian Affairs, August 7, 1837, BIA, Documents Relating to the Negotiation of

Ratified and Unratified Treaties with Various Indian Tribes, 1801–1869: Ratified Chippewa Treaty of July 29, 1837.

65. Smith, *Wisconsin,* 148; Schoolcraft, *Personal Memoirs of a Residence of Thirty Years with the Indian Tribes on the American Frontiers . . . ,* 573.

66. U.S., *Statutes at Large,* 7:591–95; Smith, *Wisconsin,* 148–49.

67. Medill to J. A. Verplanck and Charles E. Mix, June 4, 1847, and Verplanck to Medill, August 2, 1847, BIA, Documents Relating to the Negotiation of Ratified and Unratified Treaties with Various Indian Tribes, 1801–1869: Unratified Chippewa Treaty of August 2, 1847.

68. "Petition of the Head Chiefs of the Chippewa Tribe of Indians on Lake Superior," February 7, 1849, in U.S., Congress, *House Miscellaneous Document* no. 36, 30th Cong., 2d sess., 1–2 (Serial 544).

69. Warren to Ramsey, January 21, 1851, enclosed in Ramsey to Lea, January 28, 1851, BIA, LR, Sandy Lake Agency.

70. Hall to S. B. Treat, December 30, 1850, enclosed in Treat to Lea, February 15, 1851, BIA, LR, Sandy Lake Agency.

71. Treat to Lea, January 21, 1851, BIA, LR, Sandy Lake Agency; Joint Resolution of the Legislature of the State of Michigan, January 29, 1853, BIA, LR, Mackinac Agency; Gilbert to Manypenny, December 10, 1853, BIA, LR, Mackinac Agency.

72. Levi, *Chippewa,* 60; Benjamin G. Armstrong, *Early Life Among the Indians,* 28–31.

73. CIA, 1854, pp. 4–5.

## CHAPTER 6

1. L. H. Wheeler to Agent C. K. Drew, 1859, CIA, 1859, p. 77; Federal Writers' Project, *Wisconsin,* 445. The 1854 treaty also assigned to the Bad River band 200 acres on the northern tip of Madeline Island for a fishing ground.

2. Charles C. Royce, comp., "Indian Land Cessions in the United States," *Eighteenth Annual Report of the Bureau of American Ethnology,* 797; Agent M. A. Leahy to Commissioner of Indian Affairs Thomas J. Morgan, September 10, 1891, CIA, 1891, p. 468.

3. Leahy to Morgan, September 10, 1891, CIA, 1891, pp. 466–67; BIA, "Indians of the Great Lakes Agency," unpaged pamphlet, 1968.

4. Gilbert to Manypenny, April 10, 1855, BIA, LR, Mackinac Agency; Agent D. C. Leach to Commissioner of Indian Affairs William P. Dole, October 17, 1863, CIA, 1863, p. 375.

5. Leahy to Morgan, September 10, 1891, CIA, 1891, pp. 469–70.

6. Royce, "Indian Land Cessions," 797, 841, 904; Leahy to Morgan, September 10, 1891, CIA, 1891, pp. 468–69; Federal Writers' Project, *Minnesota,* 346.

7. Mahan to Commissioner of Indian Affairs John Q. Smith, October 2, 1877, BIA, LR, La Pointe Agency.

8. Mahan to Commissioner of Indian Affairs Edward P. Smith, August 29, 1874, CIA, 1874, p. 190.

9. Leahy to Morgan, July 29, 1889 and April 20, 1891, BIA, FOR, La Pointe Agency, LS, FRC-Chicago.

10. Patterson to Agent S. W. Campbell, October 22, 1899, BIA, FOR, La Pointe Agency, LR, FRC-Chicago; Agent W. A. Mercer to Commissioner of Indian Affairs Daniel M. Browning, April 21, 1894, BIA, FOR, La Pointe Agency, LS, FRC-Chicago.

11. CIA, 1898, p. 602; Leahy to Morgan, August 29, 1892, CIA, 1892, p. 515.

12. Agent John H. Knight to Commissioner of Indian Affairs Ely S. Parker, October 3, 1870, CIA, 1870, p. 309.

13. J. M. Dodd, "Ashland Then and Now," *Wisconsin Magazine of History,* 28 (December, 1944):189–96; Federal Writers' Project, *Wisconsin,* 391–93.

14. Agent Isaac L. Mahan to Commissioner of Indian Affairs Ezra A. Hayt, September 1, 1878, CIA, 1878, pp. 145–46; Levi, *Chippewa,* 73.

15. Agent George W. Lee to Commissioner of Indian Affairs Roland E. Trowbridge, September 1, 1880; CIA, 1880, p. 102; Leahy to Morgan, September 10, 1891, CIA, 1891, p. 468.

16. Mahan to Hayt, September 1, 1878, CIA, 1878, p. 147; Leahy to Morgan, September 10, 1891, CIA, 1891, p. 469.

17. Mahan to Hayt, September 1, 1878, CIA, 1878, p. 147; Agent W. R. Durfee to Commissioner of Indian Affairs Hiram Price, August 31, 1882, CIA, 1882, p. 176.

18. U.S., *Statutes at Large,* 11:66–67.

19. U.S., *Statutes at Large,* 30:937. An economic grievance of the Chippewas in the decades following 1854 sprang from the BIA's defaulting on treaty Article IX, in which the United States agreed that "an examination shall be made, and all sums that may be found equitably due to the Indians, for arrearages of annuity or other thing, under the provisions of former treaties, shall be paid as the chiefs may direct." In 1867, Chippewa chiefs sought authorization for a conference in Washington, D.C., to deal with Article IX and compensation due for Civil War annuities paid in devalued greenbacks rather than in specie or coin, as required by the terms of their treaties.

The Commissioner of Indian Affairs vetoed the talks. He pointed out through the acting commissioner that cities were a bad moral influence for Indians and that the presentation of claims against the government could be made without traveling to Washington.

The stubborn chiefs met frequently during the 1870's and 1880's, reiterating the bad faith of Uncle Sam and urging that he pay his debts. Had not President Lincoln solemnly promised Chippewa envoys in 1865 that their claims would be adjusted? Did they not possess official documents certifying that a balance of $120,000 was due? One administration after another denied them an audience. The Senate Committee on Indian Affairs examined the Treasury Department records and reported in April, 1892, that the United States indeed owed these Indians $81,702.61 in annuity arrearages and $10,600.08 for the difference between coin and the greenbacks paid in 1863 and 1864—a total of $92,302.69. "The breach of faith to these unfortunate people," wrote the committee, "is a greater reproach to the Government by reason of the fact that, while so many tribes and bands of the western Indians have resorted to war in their exasperation, the Chippewas have been uniformly faithful and friendly." But federal statute books for the 1890's give no indication that Congress appropriated this recommended sum. See U.S., *Statutes at Large,* 10:1111; Agent L. E. Webb to Commissioner of Indian Affairs Nathaniel G. Taylor, October 12, 1867, BIA, LR, La Pointe Agency; Acting Commissioner of Indian Affairs Charles E. Mix to Webb, November 13, 1867, BIA, LR, La Pointe Agency; Agent S. N. Clark to Parker, March 27, 1871, BIA, LR, La Pointe Agency; U.S. Congress, *Senate Report* no. 571, 52d Cong., 1st sess., 3:2–4 (Serial 2913).

20. Supt. Francis Huebschmann to Manypenny, October 15, 1856, CIA, 1856, p. 39; Webb to Supt. Clark W. Thompson, October 1, 1863, CIA, 1863, p. 301.

21. Clark to Commissioner of Indian Affairs Francis A. Walker, February 1 and November 18, 1872, BIA, LR, La Pointe Agency; Walker to Secretary of the Interior Columbus Delano, February 14, 1872, U.S., Congress, *House Executive Document* no. 162, 42d Cong., 2d sess., 10 (Serial 1513); U.S., *Statutes at Large,* 17:190–91; Royce, "Indian Land Cessions." p. 851.

22. Webb to Dole, November 10, 1864, CIA, 1864; p. 418; Webb to Dole, February 6, 1862, enclosed in C. G. Wykoff to Dole, February 27, 1862, BIA, LR, La Pointe Agency; Agent Asaph Whittlesey to Taylor, November 1, 1868, CIA, 1868, pp. 378–79; Webb to Taylor, December 10, 1867, BIA, LR, La Pointe Agency.

23. Commissioner of Indian Affairs John D. C. Atkins to Hon. Tom Wall, December 9, 1887, enclosed in Atkins to James T. Gregory, December 17, 1887, BIA, FOR, La Pointe Agency, LR, FRC-Chicago.

24. Campbell to Commissioner of Indian Affairs William A. Jones, August 25, 1900, CIA, 1900, p. 409.

25. Atkins to Gregory, March 23, 1886 and December 16, 1887, BIA, FOR, La Pointe Agency, LR, FRC-Chicago.

26. CIA, 1895, pp. 592–95; CIA, 1898, pp. 618–19.

27. Leahy to Morgan, August 29, 1892, CIA, 1892, p. 515; Campbell to Jones, August 25, 1900, CIA, 1900, p. 409.

28. CIA, 1884, pp. liii–liv.

29. Charles E. Twining, "Plunder and Progress: The Lumbering Industry in Perspective," *Wisconsin Magazine of History,* 47 (Winter, 1963–64):117–19; Robert F. Fries, *Empire in Pine: The Story of Lumbering in Wisconsin, 1830–1900,* 4–7.

30. Secretary of the Interior William F. Vilas to United States Senate, February 19, 1889, U.S., Congress, *Senate Executive Document* no. 128, 50th Cong., 2d sess., 4–5 (Serial 2612).

31. Acting Commissioner of Indian Affairs A. B. Upshaw to Gregory, August 24, 1886, BIA, FOR, La Pointe Agency, LR, FRC-Chicago; Vilas to Senate, February 19, 1889, U.S., Congress, *Senate Executive Document* no. 128, 50th Cong., 2d sess., 5 (Serial 2612).

32. CIA, 1895, pp. 50–51.

33. Bad River Business Committee to Indian Agent, May 31, 1895, BIA, FOR, La Pointe Agency, LR, FRC-Chicago.

34. CIA, 1884, pp. liii–liv; CIA, 1888, pp. xl–xlii; Levi, *Chippewa,* 73, 240–41.

35. Gregory to Atkins, June 15, 1886 and August 23, 1888, BIA, FOR, La Pointe Agency, LS, FRC-Chicago; Vilas to Senate, February 19, 1889, U.S., Congress, *Senate Executive Document* no. 128, 50th Cong., 2d sess., 7–8 (Serial 2612).

36. CIA, 1888, pp. xl–xlii; Gregory to Atkins, June 15, 1886, BIA, FOR, La Pointe Agency, LS, FRC-Chicago.

37. "Relief of Chippewa Indians of Lake Superior," U.S., Congress, *House Executive Document* no. 99, 51st Cong., 1st. sess., pp. 1–4 (Serial 2741); U.S., *Statutes at Large,* 26:669; Morgan to Leahy, February 18, 1890, BIA, FOR, La Pointe Agency, LR, FRC-Chicago.

38. U.S., *Statutes at Large,* 25:166.

39. U.S., *Statutes at Large,* 10:1110.

40. "Chippewa Half-Breeds of Lake Superior," U.S., Congress, *House Executive Document* no. 193, 42d Cong., 2d sess., (Serial 1513); Folwell, *A History of Minnesota,* 1:470–78.

41. CIA, 1895, pp. 580–81; CIA, 1898, pp. 602–603.

42. Campbell to Jones, August 25, 1900, CIA, 1900, p. 409.

43. CIA, 1895, pp. 592–95; CIA, 1898, pp. 618–19.

44. Robert E. Ritzenthaler, *Chippewa Preoccupation with Health,* 225.

45. Dr. James H. Spencer to Commissioner of Indian Affairs Daniel M. Browning, August 31, 1894, CIA, 1894, p. 335; CIA, 1895, pp. 580–81; CIA, 1898, pp. 602–603.

46. Spencer to Browning, August 31, 1894, CIA, 1894, p. 335; Agency Physician to Browning August 20, 1895, BIA, FOR, La Pointe Agency, LS, FRC-Chicago; CIA, 1895, pp. 580–81.

47. "Rules in Regard to Attendance of Indian Youth at School," BIA Circular, October 30, 1891, enclosed in Morgan to Leahy, November 12, 1891, BIA, FOR, La Pointe Agency, LR, FRC-Chicago; Campbell to Jones, August 1, 1898, BIA, FOR, La Pointe Agency, LS, FRC-Chicago.

48. Wheeler to Hon. G. E. H. Day, December 5, 1861, Ojibwa, Pawnee, and Stockbridge Mission, American Board of Commissioners for Foreign Missions Papers; Leahy to Morgan, August 29, 1892, p. 518.

49. "Inculcation of Patriotism in Indian Schools," BIA Circular, December 10, 1889, BIA, FOR, La Pointe Agency, LR, FRC-Chicago.

50. Mercer to Browning, May 26, 1894, BIA, FOR, La Pointe Agency, LS, FRC-Chicago.

51. Wheeler to S. B. Treat, August 11, 1860, Ojibwa, Pawnee, and Stockbridge Mission, American Board of Commissioners for Foreign Missions Papers.

52. "Rules in Regard to Attendance of Indian Youth at School," BIA Circular, October 30, 1891, enclosed in Morgan to Leahy, November 12, 1891, BIA, FOR, La Pointe Agency, LR, FRC-Chicago.

53. Mercer to Browning, April 1, 1895, BIA, FOR, La Pointe Agency, LS, FRC-Chicago; Leahy to Morgan, August 29, 1892, CIA, 1892, p. 518.

54. CIA, 1898, pp. 602–603.

55. CIA, 1895, pp. 580–81.

56. Wheeler to S. B. Treat, March 6, 1862, and January 17, 1867, Ojibwa, Pawnee, and Stockbridge Mission, American Board of Commissioners for Foreign Missions; Ross, *La Pointe,* 125.

57. *Ashland Daily News,* January 2, 1892.

58. Leahy to Morgan, October 14, 1891, BIA, FOR, La Pointe Agency, LS, FRC-Chicago; see, for example, *Ashland Daily News,* July 6, 1888, and July 3, 1890.

59. CIA, 1895, pp. 580–81; Leahy to Morgan, September 10, 1891, CIA, 1891, p. 468; Mahan to Hayt, September 1, 1878, CIA, 1878, pp. 144–45; William R. Durfee to Commissioner of Indian Affairs Hiram Price, August 19, 1884, CIA, 1884, pp. 179–80.

60. CIA, 1895, pp. 580–81; Durfee to Price, August 31, 1882, CIA, 1882, p. 175; Durfee to Price, August 15, 1883, CIA, 1883, p. 159.

61. Durfee to Price, April 2, 1884, BIA, FOR, La Pointe Agency, LS, FRC-Chicago; CIA, 1895, pp. 580–81; Leahy to Morgan, September 10, 1891, CIA, 1891, p. 406.

62. CIA, 1895, pp. 580–81; Leahy to Morgan, September 10, 1891, CIA, 1891, p. 469.

63. CIA, 1895, pp. 580–81.

## CHAPTER 7

1. AR, Supt. E. W. Jermark, February 13, 1931, BIA, Narrative and Statistical Reports, Lac du Flambeau Agency.

2. Staff list for La Pointe Agency, enclosed in BIA Circular No. 444, June 15, 1910, BIA, FOR, La Pointe Agency, LR, FRC-Chicago; Edward E. Hill, comp., *Preliminary Inventory of the Records of the Bureau of Indian Affairs* 1:8.

3. AR, Everest, June 26, 1913, BIA, Narrative and Statistical Reports, La Pointe Agency, 1, 17–18.

4. Supt. P. R. Wadsworth to Commissioner of Indian Affairs Charles H. Burke, December 21, 1922, BIA, CCF: 99161-1922-100 Consolidated Chippewa Agency; AR, Balmer, 1917, BIA, Narrative and Statistical Reports, Lac du Flambeau Agency, 12.

5. Asst. Commissioner of Indian Affairs William Zimmerman, Jr. to Supt. Louis E. Baumgarten, November 20, 1933, BIA, CCF: 46810-1933-054 Lac du Flambeau Agency; AR, Supt. S. W. Campbell, July 25, 1910, BIA, Narrative and Statistical Reports, La Pointe Agency, 43.

6. AR, Campbell, July 25, 1910, BIA, Narrative and Statistical Reports, La Pointe Agency, 46; AR, Supt. W. N. Sickels, August 1, 1910, BIA, Narrative and Statistical Reports, Lac du Flambeau Agency, 18.

7. AR, Everest, July 1, 1928, BIA, Narrative and Statistical Reports, Lac du Flambeau Agency; AR, Wadsworth, June 30, 1925, BIA, Narrative and Statistical Reports, Consolidated Chippewa Agency.

8. AR, Supt. William A. Light, 1913, BIA, Narrative and Statistical Reports, Hayward.

9. AR, Everest, June 30, 1914, BIA, Narrative and Statistical Reports, La Pointe Agency, 16, 18; Inspector H. S. Traylor to Commissioner of Indian Affairs Cato Sells, August 2, 1915, BIA, CCF: [?]-1915-150 La Pointe Agency; Inspector Heber M. Creel to Commissioner of Indian Affairs Charles H. Burke, January 9, 1923, BIA, CCF: 3751-1923-126 La Pointe Agency.

10. Campbell to Jones, August 20, 1904, CIA, 1904, pp. 376–77; AR, Supt. G. W. Cross, 1912, BIA, Narrative and Statistical Reports, Fond du Lac; AR, Supt. W. N. Sickels, August 13, 1913, BIA, Narrative and Statistical Reports, Lac du Flambeau, 8.

11. Campbell to Hon. M. E. Clapp, April 19, 1906, BIA, FOR, La Pointe Agency, LS, FRC-Chicago; AR, Campbell, September 1, 1911, BIA, Narrative and Statistical Reports, La Pointe Agency, 34–36; Campbell to Jones, August 27, 1903, CIA, 1903, p. 352.

12. Campbell to Jones, August 27, 1903, CIA, 1903, p. 352; *Ashland Daily News,* February 25, 1908; Starr *v.* Campbell, *United States Supreme Court Reports,* 208:602–06 (1908).

13. Campbell to Clapp, April 19, 1906, BIA, FOR, La Pointe Agency, LS, FRC-Chicago.

14. BIA, CCF: 40156-1930-339 Consolidated Chippewa Agency.

15. Everest to Commissioner of Indian Affairs Robert C. Valentine, April 22, 1913, BIA, CCF: 21852-1913-047 La Pointe Agency; AR, Campbell, July 25, 1910, BIA, Narrative and Statistical Reports, La Pointe Agency.

16. *The Daily Press,* March 16, 1910; Traylor to Sells, BIA, CCF: [?]-1915-150 La Pointe Agency; AR, Everest, June 26, 1913, BIA, Narrative and Statistical Reports, La Pointe Agency, 11; AR, Everest, June 30, 1918, BIA, Narrative and Statistical Reports, La Pointe Agency, 29.

17. Everest to Sells, October 8, 1913, BIA, CCF: 21852-1913-047 La Pointe Agency; Odanah Indian Fair Booklet, enclosed in Everest to Sells, September 22, 1919, BIA, CCF: 81835-1919-047 La Pointe Agency; AR, Everest, June 30, 1922, BIA, Narrative and Statistical Reports, La Pointe Agency, 24.

18. AR, Everest, June 30, 1918, BIA, Narrative and Statistical Reports, La Pointe Agency, 30; J. F. Wojta, "Indian Farm Institutes in Wisconsin," *Wisconsin Magazine of History,* 29 (June, 1916):428–30.

19. Traylor to Sells, August 2, 1915, BIA, CCF: [?]-1915-150 La Pointe Agency; Campbell to Commissioner of Indian Affairs Francis E. Leupp, August 20, 1906, CIA, 1906, p. 395; AR, Everest, June 30, 1924, BIA, Narrative and Statistical Reports, La Pointe Agency; AR, Everest, June 30, 1927, BIA, Narrative and Statistical Reports, La Pointe Agency, 9.

20. AR, Supt. R. S. Buckland, 1910, BIA, Narrative and Statistical Reports, Mackinac Agency; AR, Buckland, August 16, 1915, BIA, Narrative and Statistical Reports, Mackinac Agency, 2–3; Report of Creel, December 22, 1922, BIA, CCF: 101389-1922-900 Mackinac Agency.

21. AR, Everest, June 30, 1927, BIA, Narrative and Statistical Reports, La Pointe Agency; AR, Everest, June 30, 1922, BIA, Narrative and Statistical Reports, La Pointe Agency.

22. AR, Balmer, 1922, BIA, Narrative and Statistical Reports, Lac du Flambeau; AR, Balmer, July 7, 1920, BIA, Narrative and Statistical Reports, Lac du Flambeau, 8–10; AR, Everest, July 1, 1928, BIA, Narrative and Statistical Reports, Lac du Flambeau; Supt. E. Reel to Leupp, August 14, 1908; BIA, CCF: 30438-1908-150 La Pointe Agency.

23. Reel to Leupp, August 14, 1908, BIA, CCF: 30438-1908-150 La Pointe Agency; AR, Supt. William A. Light, 1913, BIA, Narrative and Statistical Reports, Hayward; Wojta, "Indian Farm Institutes," 431–32.

24. Report of Field Representative Charles H. Berry, BIA, CCF: 44751-1932-150 Consolidated Chippewa Agency; AR, Supt. A. A. Bear, BIA, Narrative and Statistical Reports, Fond du Lac.

25. AR, Jermark, February 13, 1931 and March 14, 1932, BIA, Narrative

and Statistical Reports, Lac du Flambeau Agency; Report of Berry, BIA, CCF: 44751-1932-150 Consolidated Chippewa Agency.

26. Agency Physician to Jones, July 30, 1903, BIA, FOR, La Pointe Agency, LS, FRC-Chicago.

27. Report of Dr. L. F. Michael, enclosed in Sells to Everest, August 7, 1913, BIA, FOR, La Pointe Agency, LR, FRC-Chicago; Everest to Sells, September 2, 1913, BIA, FOR, La Pointe Agency, LR, FRC-Chicago; AR, Campbell, July 25, 1910, BIA, Narrative and Statistical Reports, La Pointe Agency, 24–26.

28. Agency Physician to Jones, July 30, 1903, BIA, FOR, La Pointe Agency, LS, FRC-Chicago.

29. Traylor to Sells, August 2, 1915, BIA, CCF: [?]-1915-150 La Pointe Agency; Report of Berry, BIA, CCF: 44751-1932-150 Consolidated Chippewa Agency.

30. Agency Physician to Jones, July 30, 1903, BIA, FOR, La Pointe Agency, LS, FRC-Chicago; Traylor to Sells, August 2, 1915, BIA, CCF: [?]-1915-150 La Pointe Agency; AR, Superintendent, 1926, BIA, Narrative and Statistical Reports, Lac du Flambeau.

31. AR, Campbell, July 25, 1910, BIA, Narrative and Statistical Reports, La Pointe Agency, 24–26; Campbell to Jones, September 1, 1902, CIA, 1902, pp. 378–79.

32. Everest to Sells, October 13, 1916, BIA, CCF: 109187-1916-047 La Pointe Agency; AR, Superintendent, 1916, BIA, Narrative and Statistical Reports, Lac du Flambeau, pp. 4–5; AR, Superintendent, 1926, BIA, Narrative and Statistical Reports, Lac du Flambeau Agency.

33. Report of Creel, December 22, 1922, BIA, CCF: 101390-1922-700 Mackinac Agency; Report of Medical Supervisor Robert Needberne, February 11–12, 1920, BIA, CCF: 13556-1920-150 Mackinac Agency.

34. Medical Director, District No. 1, to Supt. of Indian Affairs Charles J. Rhoads, September 13, 1932, BIA, CCF: 44555-1932-150 Consolidated Chippewa Agency; Report of Berry, BIA, CCF: 44751-1932-150 Consolidated Chippewa Agency.

35. Courtright to Commissioner of Indian Affairs John Collier, August 24, 1933, BIA, CCF: 33227-1933-126 Lac du Flambeau Agency.

36. Campbell to Jones, June 25, 1902, BIA, FOR, La Pointe Agency, LS, FRC-Chicago; Supervisor L. F. Michael to Sells, April 25, 1915, BIA, CCF: [?]-1915-150 Mackinac Agency; AR, W. N. Sickels, August 28, 1911, BIA, Narrative and Statistical Reports, Lac du Flambeau Agency, 1–2.

37. AR, Everest, June 30, 1914, BIA, Narrative and Statistical Reports, La Pointe Agency, 4–6; Deputy Special Officer J. C. LeMarr to Chief Special Officer H. A. Larson, April 11, 1917, BIA, CCF: 40965-1917-126 La Pointe Agency; Report of Creel, January 9, 1923, BIA, CCF: 3751-1923-126 La Pointe Agency.

38. Report of Inspector W. H. Gibbs, July 1916, BIA, CCF: [?]-1916-[?] La Pointe Agency; AR, Everest, June 30, 1916, BIA, Narrative and Statistical Reports, La Pointe Agency, 5.

39. *The Daily Press,* January 3, 1911; AR, Campbell, September 1, 1911, BIA, Narrative and Statistical Reports, La Pointe Agency, 5–7.

40. AR, Campbell, July 25, 1910, BIA, Narrative and Statistical Reports,

La Pointe Agency, 28; AR, Light, 1913, BIA, Narrative and Statistical Reports, Hayward, 4–5.

41. Report of Gibbs, July 1916, BIA, CCF: [?]-1916-[?] La Pointe Agency; Courtright to Collier, August 24, 1933, BIA, CCF: 33227-1933-126 Lac du Flambeau Agency.

42. Report of Creel, December 22, 1922, BIA, CCF: 101396-1922-806 Mackinac Agency.

43. Report of Dean, August 15, 1931, BIA, CCF: 47641-1931-806 Lac du Flambeau Agency.

44. BIA, FOR, La Pointe Agency, LR, FRC-Chicago.

45. AR, Everest, June 30, 1924, BIA, Narrative and Statistical Reports, La Pointe Agency; Report of Creel, December 22, 1922, BIA, CCF: 101396-1922-806 Mackinac Agency; Supt. C. H. Gensler to Helen E. Beach, April 1, 1925, BIA, CCF: 33843-1925-003 Lac du Flambeau Agency; AR, Bear, 1910, BIA, Narrative and Statistical Reports, Fond du Lac.

46. Gensler to Beach, April 1, 1925, BIA, CCF: 33843-1925-033 Lac du Flambeau Agency; Reel to Leupp, August 14, 1908, BIA, CCF: 30438-1908-150 La Pointe Agency; AR, Campbell, July 25, 1910, BIA, Narrative and Statistical Reports, La Pointe Agency, pp. 18–20; AR, Sickels, August 1, 1910, BIA, Narrative and Statistical Reports, Lac du Flambeau, 8–9.

47. AR, Campbell, July 25, 1910, BIA, Narrative and Statistical Reports, La Pointe Agency, 23.

48. Report of Dean, August 15, 1931, BIA, CCF: 47641-1931-806 Lac du Flambeau.

49. Courtright to Collier, August 24, 1933, BIA, CCF: 33227-1933-126 Lac du Flambeau Agency.

50. AR, Campbell, July 25, 1910, and September 1, 1911, BIA, Narrative and Statistical Reports, La Pointe Agency.

51. AR, Everest, July 1, 1930, BIA, Narrative and Statistical Reports, Lac du Flambeau Agency; AR, [?], February 21, 1919, BIA, Narrative and Statistical Reports, Mackinac Agency, 3–4.

52. AR, Campbell, September 1, 1911, BIA, Narrative and Statistical Reports, La Pointe Agency, 16; AR, Everest: June 30, 1916; June 30, 1919; 1920; June 30, 1922, BIA, Narrative and Statistical Reports, La Pointe Agency.

53. AR, Everest, June 30, 1922, BIA, Narrative and Statistical Reports, La Pointe Agency; Report of Creel, January 9, 1923, BIA, CCF: 3760-1923-130 La Pointe Agency.

54. AR, James W. Balmer, 1923, BIA, Narrative and Statistical Reports, Lac du Flambeau, 1; Gensler to Beach, April 1, 1925, BIA, CCF: 33843-1925-033, Lac du Flambeau Agency; AR, Supt. S. R. Hammitt, July 13, 1925, BIA, Narrative and Statistical Reports, Lac du Flambeau, 1.

55. AR, Supt. P. R. Wadsworth, June 30, 1925, BIA, Narrative and Statistical Reports, Consolidated Chippewa Agency; District Supt. Peyton Carter to Burke, November 29, 1928, BIA, CCF: 4853-1929-150 Consolidated Chippewa Agency.

56. Lewis L. Meriam, *et al., The Problem of Indian Administration. Report of a Survey Made at the Request of Honorable Hubert Work, Secretary of the Interior, and Submitted to Him, February 21, 1928.* Institute of Government Research, Studies in Administration, vii, 56–77.

57. Meriam, *Problem of Indian Administration,* viii–ix.

58. *Ibid.,* 7.

59. *Ibid.,* 8.

60. *Ibid.,* 4–6.

61. *Ibid.,* 6.

62. *Ibid.,* 9–10.

63. *Ibid.,* 11–14.

64. *Ibid.,* 16, 3.

65. Randolph C. Downes, "A Crusade for Indian Reform, 1922–34," *Mississippi Valley Historical Review,* 32 (December, 1945):331–54; CIA, 1935, p. 114; Kenneth R. Philp, "John Collier," 68–69.

66. Philp, "John Collier," 63, 65–67.

67. *Ibid.,* 71.

68. U.S., *Statutes at Large,* 48, Pt. 1, 984–88; CIA, 1935, p. 114; "Indian Tribes, Bands and Communities which Voted to Accept or Reject the Terms of the Indian Reorganization Act, the Dates when Elections were Held, and the Votes Cast," BIA, Tribal Relations Pamphlet No. 1A.

69. Meriam, *Problem of Indian Administration,* 51.


# CHAPTER 8

1. Quoted in William Zimmerman, "The Role of the Bureau of Indian Affairs Since 1933," *Annals of the American Academy of Political and Social Science,* 311 (May, 1957):34.

2. *Constitution and Bylaws of the Bad River Band of the Lake Superior Tribe of Chippewa Indians of the State of Wisconsin.*

3. *Constitution and Bylaws of the Minnesota Chippewa Tribe, Minnesota.*

4. *Corporate Charter of the Bad River Band of Chippewa Indians of the Bad River Reservation, Wisconsin.*

5. BIA, CCF: 9513-E-1936-054 Great Lakes Agency.

6. Cavill to Asst. to the Commissioner of Indian Affairs F. H. Daiker, March 22, 1941, BIA, CCF: 15342-1938-054 Great Lakes Agency.

7. Cavill to Collier, August 9, 1940, BIA, CCF: 9626-1936-066 Great Lakes Agency.

8. William E. Leuchtenburg, *Franklin D. Roosevelt and the New Deal, 1932–1940,* 121.

9. Baumgarten to Collier, May 3, 1934, BIA, CCF: 55703-1933-345 Lac du Flambeau Agency.

10. Leuchtenburg, *Roosevelt and the New Deal,* 122–23.

11. Asst. to the Commissioner of Indian Affairs John Herrick to Cavill, February 15, 1936, BIA, CCF: 76040-1942-[?] Great Lakes Agency.

12. Vigeant to Acting Supt. Mark L. Burns, June 7, 1939, BIA, CCF: 76020-P-1-a Consolidated Chippewa Agency.

13. Acting Director of Extension and Industry R. S. Bristol to Cavill, August 31, 1942, BIA, CCF: 76040-1942-[?] Great Lakes Agency.

14. Calvin W. Gower, "The CCC Indian Division: Aid for Depressed Americans, 1933–1942," *Minnesota History,* 43 (Spring, 1972):5–7; John A. Salmond, *The Civilian Conservation Corps, 1933–1942: A New Deal Case Study,* 33.

15. Analysis of IECW and CCC-ID Expenditures by Form 7 Classification and by Reservations from April 1, 1933 to December 31, 1938, BIA, CCF: 20431-1933-344 Consolidated Chippewa Agency.

16. Great Lakes Indian Agency [Report], May 1, 1937, BIA, CCF: 76040-P-2 Great Lakes Agency.

17. Gower, "CCC Indian Division," 8.

18. *Ibid.*, 13.

19. Great Lakes Indian Agency [Report], May 1, 1937, BIA, CCF: 76040-P-2 Great Lakes Agency. That the CCC-ID and WPA helped get the Chippewas through the depression was confirmed by James Blacketter, Sr., Darrel Blacketter, Alvina Tiessen, Bill Lyons, PI held at Fond du Lac Reservation, June 21, 1975; Mrs. Raymond E. Mayotte and Mandy Manypenny, PI held at Bad River Reservation, June 23, 1975; Edward H. Roy, PI held at Red Cliff Reservation, June 24, 1975.

20. McKinsey and Mani, An Economic Survey of the Bad River Reservation, Odanah, Wisconsin, BIA, CCF: 41453-1937-910 Great Lakes Agency.

21. Individual Loan Summary and Narrative Report, BIA, CCF: 46036-1939-031 Great Lakes Agency.

22. Wood, How Credit Funds have Assisted in Improving the Economic Status of a Member of the Bad River Band of Chippewa Indians, enclosed in Cavill to Collier, August 1, 1941, BIA, CCF: 41453-1937-910 Great Lakes Agency.

23. Individual Loan Summary and Gordon's Narrative Report of September 17, 1941, BIA, CCF: 44194-1938-031 Great Lakes Agency.

24. Margaret Szasz, *Education and the American Indian; the Road to Self-Determination, 1928-1973,* 61-67, 81-88, 89, 105; U.S., *Statutes at Large,* 48:596.

25. Donald L. Parman, "The Indian and the CCC," *Pacific Historical Review,* 40 (February, 1971):48-50; Gower, "The CCC Indian Division," 11.

26. McKinsey, An Economic Survey of the Keweenaw Bay Indian Community Consisting of L'Anse, Lac Vieux Desert, and Ontonagon Indian Reservations in Michigan, 1937, BIA, Narrative and Statistical Reports, Great Lakes Agency, 3.

27. McKinsey, Economic Survey of Keweenaw Bay, 30-31.

28. District Medical Director J. F. Worley to Collier, October 12, 1942, BIA, CCF: 44937-1942-770 Great Lakes Agency, WNRC.

29. McKinsey, Economic Survey of Keweenaw Bay, 2, 35-36.

30. *Ibid.*, 37-38. Many of the above statistics include two splinter groups of the Keweenaw Bay Indian Community: the Ontonagon band and the Lac Vieux Desert band. Located just west of the Keweenaw peninsula, the Ontonagon reservation had been reduced from its original 2,551.35 acres in 1854 to 724.35 acres by 1937. A lone Chippewa man inhabited the tract, sustaining himself with $96.00 in relief funds per year and $84.00 from a home he rented. Seventy-two members of the Lac Vieux Desert band resided near Watersmeet, Michigan, on eighty-six acres of land purchased by their chiefs in 1865 and 1870. Although the treaty of 1854 assigned them to the L'Anse reservation, many returned to their original home near the Wisconsin border. They rejected reorganization under the IRA. In 1937 the average annual income of the twenty-one families was a shockingly low $379.70,

derived largely from WPA wages. Living conditions were "very mean and entirely inadequate for even an average standard of living." For a detailed study of this band during the New Deal era see Kinietz, *Chippewa Village*.

31. McKinsey and Mani, Economic Survey of Bad River, 1, 3.

32. *Ibid.*, 24–25, 27, 29.

33. *Ibid.*, 35, 38–39; Cavill, Narrative and Statistical Report on General Education Program, Great Lakes Indian Agency, 1942–43, BIA, CCF: 42840-1936-800 Great Lakes Agency.

34. McKinsey and Mani, Economic Survey of Bad River, 33–34; District Medical Director Frank F. Thweat, Jr. to BIA Director of Health J. G. Townsend, September 8, 1939, BIA, CCF: 58855-1939-770 Great Lakes Agency; Worley to Collier, October 12, 1942, BIA, CCF: 44937-1942-770 Great Lakes Agency, WNRC.

35. McKinsey and Mani, Economic Survey of Bad River, 30–31.

36. *Ibid.*, 40–41.

37. *Ibid.*, 14, 39.

38. Forest Supervisor W. N. Robinson, Annual Forestry and Grazing Report, Fiscal Year 1937, BIA, CCF: 48377-1937-031 Great Lakes Agency; Statistical Report for Great Lakes Indian Agency, May 1, 1937, BIA, CCF: 76040-P-2 Great Lakes Agency; Narrative Extension Report for 1938, Great Lakes Indian Agency, BIA, CCF: 4840-1939-031, Great Lakes Agency.

39. School Reports for Great Lakes Agency, 1942–43, BIA, CCF: 42840-1936-800 Great Lakes Agency.

40. Worley to Collier, October 12, 1942, BIA, CCF: 44937-1942-770 Great Lakes Agency, WNRC.

41. Hallowell, *Culture and Experience*, 339.

42. *Ibid.*, 340–41.

43. Narrative and Extension Report for 1938, Great Lakes Indian Agency, BIA, CCF: 4840-1939-031 Great Lakes Agency; Statistical Report for Great Lakes Indian Agency, May 1, 1937, BIA, CCF: 76040-P-2 Great Lakes Agency.

44. School Reports for Great Lakes Agency, 1942–43, BIA, CCF: 42840-1936-800 Great Lakes Agency; Thweatt to Collier, November 15, 1938, BIA, CCF: [?]-1938-770 Great Lakes Agency; Worley to Collier, October 12, 1942, BIA, CCF: 44939-1942-770 Great Lakes Agency, WNRC.

45. Hallowell, *Culture and Experience*, 342–43.

46. *Ibid.*, 349–64.

47. Ritzenthaler, *Chippewa Preoccupation with Health*, 177.

48. *Ibid.;* Statistical Report for Great Lakes Indian Agency, May 1, 1937, BIA, CCF: 76040-P-2 Great Lakes Agency; School Reports for Great Lakes Agency, 1942–43, BIA, CCF: 42840-1936-800 Great Lakes Agency.

49. Worley to Collier, October 12, 1942, BIA, CCF: 44937-1942-770 Great Lakes Agency, WNRC.

50. Annual Report of Extension Workers, Report of Fond du Lac, from December 1, 1934 to November 30, 1935, BIA, CCF: 6149-1936-031 Consolidated Chippewa Agency.

51. *Ibid.*, Annual Report of Extension Workers, Report of Grand Portage; Charles Wilson, Report on the Great Lakes Chippewas, BIA, Narrative and Statistical Reports, Great Lakes Agency, 1936, 20–22.

52. Annual Report of Extension Workers, Report of Grand Portage, from December 1, 1934 to November 30, 1935, BIA, CCF: 6149-1936-031 Consolidated Chippewa Agency; Thweatt to Townsend, September 9, 1939, BIA, CCF: 58854-1939-770 Consolidated Chippewa Agency.

53. Annual Report of Extension Workers, Report of Nett Lake, from December 1, 1934 to November 30, 1935, BIA, CCF: 6149-1936-031 Consolidated Chippewa Agency.

54. Joyce M. Erdman, *Handbook of Wisconsin Indians,* 24, 27.

55. McKinsey and Mani, An Economic Survey of the Mole Lake Indian Band . . . , BIA, CCF: 20125-1939-910 Great Lakes Agency; Worley to Collier, October 12, 1942, BIA, CCF: 44937-1942-770 Great Lakes Agency, WNRC.

56. Wilson, Report on the Great Lakes Chippewas, 1936, BIA, Narrative and Statistical Reports, Great Lakes Agency; Statistical Report for Great Lakes Indian Agency, May 1, 1937, BIA, CCF: 76040-P-2 Great Lakes Agency; School Reports for Great Lakes Agency, 1942–43, BIA, CCF: 42840-1936-800 Great Lakes Agency.

57. *Indians at Work,* 9 (April, 1942):11.

58. *Ibid.,* 11 (September–October, 1943):15.

59. Szasz, *Education and the American Indian,* 107–108.

60. *Indians at Work,* 11 (September-October, 1943):16–18; Blacketter *et al.,* PI; Mayotte and Manypenny, PI; Roy, PI.

61. *Ibid.; Indians at Work,* 11 (January–February, 1944):17.

62. *Indians at Work,* 10 (July–September, 1942):7.

63. William A. Brophy, Sophie Aberle, *et al.,* comp., *The Indian: America's Unfinished Business. Report of the Commission on the Rights, Liberties, and Responsibilities of the American Indian,* 21.

64. Quoted in Gower, "CCC Indian Division," 12–13.

65. Armstrong, "Set the American Indians Free!" *Reader's Digest,* 47 (August, 1945):47–52.

66. See Szasz, *Education and the American Indian,* chapters nine through fourteen.

67. For an appraisal of the relocation program see Ruth Mulvey Harmer, "Uprooting the Indians," *Atlantic Monthly,* 197 (March, 1956):54–57.

68. Agency Annual Report, Branch of Forestry, Calendar Year of 1954, BIA, CCF: 4539-1955-031 Great Lakes Consolidated Agency, WNRC.

69. Agency Annual Report, Branch of Forestry, Calendar Year 1958, BIA, CCF: 2240-1959-031 Minnesota Agency, WNRC; Agency Annual Report, Branch of Forestry, Calendar Year 1959, BIA, CCF: 2511-1960-031 Great Lakes Consolidated Agency, WNRC.

70. Agency Annual Report, Branch of Land Operations, Range & Wildlife Management, Calendar Year 1958, BIA, CCF: 2110-1959-031 Minnesota Agency, WNRC.

71. Agency Annual Report, Branch of Land Operations, Range & Wildlife Management, Calendar Year 1960, BIA, CCF: 964-1961-031 Great Lakes Consolidated Agency, WNRC.

72. Individual Loan Summary, Bad River Band, BIA, CCF: 11563-1957-031 Great Lakes Consolidated Agency, WNRC.

73. Annual Report, Industrial Development, Calendar Years 1961 and

1962, BIA, CCF: 17115-1958-032 Minneapolis Area Office, WNRC.

74. Ritzenthaler, "Impact of Small Industry on an Indian Community," *American Anthropologist,* 55 (January, 1953):143–48.

75. This as well as subsequent paragraphs about New Post are based on James, "An Analysis of an American Indian Village. A Situational Approach to Community Study," Ph.D. dissertation.

76. Lac Court Oreilles Reservation, BIA, CCF: 7269-1964-076 Great Lakes Consolidated Agency, WNRC.

77. Ten-year reports for these reservations have the following file numbers: BIA, CCF: 7269-1964-076 Great Lakes Consolidated Agency and 7270-1964-076 Minnesota Agency, WNRC.

78. *Ibid.*

## CHAPTER 9

1. U.S., *Statutes at Large,* 88:2203, 2206–207.

2. Amy D. Chosa and H. James St. Arnold, "Overall Economic Development Plan for the Keweenaw Bay Indian Community," May, 1974 (mimeographed report on file at Tribal Community Center, Baraga, Michigan), 11.

3. Arie DeWaal, "Overall Economic Development Plan for the Chippewa Lac du Flambeau Band, Lac du Flambeau Reservation," June, 1974 (mimeographed report on file at Tribal Community Center, Lac du Flambeau, Wisconsin), 13.

4. Peter De Fault, PI held at Fond du Lac Reservation, June 21, 1975.

5. League of Women Voters of Minnesota, *Indians in Minnesota,* 141.

6. Mandy Manypenny, PI held at Bad River Reservation, June 23, 1975.

7. BIA, Great Lakes Agency, Report of Labor Force, April, 1975 (on file at agency, Ashland, Wisconsin).

8. Asst. Supt. of the Great Lakes Agency Edmund Manydeeds, PI held at Ashland, Wisconsin, June 23, 1975.

9. For detailed descriptions of the development goals of three tribes, see Chosa and St. Arnold, "Overall Economic Development Plan for the Keweenaw Bay Indian Community," De Waal, "Overall Economic Development Plan for the Chippewa Lac du Flambeau Band," De Waal, "Overall Economic Development Plan for the Chippewa Red Cliff Band," (mimeographed reports on file at Tribal Arts and Crafts Center, Red Cliff, Wisconsin).

10. League of Women Voters, *Indians in Minnesota,* 130–33; Chosa and St. Arnold, "Plan for the Keweenaw Bay Indian Community," 3–4.

11. Dakota, PI; Chosa and St. Arnold, "Plan for the Keweenaw Bay Indian Community," 15, 18–19, 21–25; Vilican-Leman & Assoc., Inc., "Report Number 3, Comprehensive Development Plan, Keweenaw Bay Indian Community, Michigan, and Watersmeet Indian Community, Michigan, May 1974," (report on file at Tribal Community Center, Baraga, Michigan).

12. "Apostle Islands National Lakeshore, Wisconsin" (National Park Service Brochure: 1973-515-985/114); De Waal, "Plan for the Chippewa Red Cliff Band," 52, 61.

13. Buffalo, PI held at Red Cliff Reservation, June 24, 1975.

14. "Program, Dedication and Ribbon Cutting Ceremonies, Wa-Swa-Gon

Park Campground and Tribal Fish Hatchery, June 7–8, 1975" (on file at Tribal Community Center, Lac du Flambeau, Wisconsin); Tribal Councilwoman Evangeline Valliere, PI held at Lac du Flambeau Reservation, June 30, 1975.

15. Tribal Chairman Raymond Maday, PI held at Bad River Reservation, June 24, 1975.

16. Larson, PI held at Lac Court Oreilles Reservation, June 25, 1975; *Christian Science Monitor,* September 3, 1971.

17. Angeline Johnson, Hazel Taylor, and Fred Arbuckle, PIs held at St. Croix Tribal Headquarters, June 25, 1975.

18. League of Women Voters, *Indians in Minnesota,* 134.

19. De Fault, PI.

20. Hull, PI; League of Women Voters, *Indians in Minnesota,* 133.

21. Sherer, PI held at Grand Portage Reservation, June 19, 1975.

22. Hull to League of Women Voters of Minnesota, September 17, 1970, League of Women Voters, *Indians in Minnesota,* 137, 139.

23. De Waal, "Plan for the Chippewa Red Cliff Band," 1.

24. *Ibid.,* 24.

25. League of Women Voters, *Indians in Minnesota,* 119–20.

26. Erdman, *Handbook on Wisconsin Indians,* 16, 59.

27. League of Women Voters, *Indians in Minnesota,* 120–22.

28. Vilican-Leman, "Comprehensive Development Plan for Keweenaw Bay," 16.

29. Councilman Sam Livingston, PI held at Bad River Reservation, June 24, 1975.

30. Sherer, PI.

31. Livingston, PI; Taylor, "Native American Contributions to Progress," 11.

32. Larson, PI.

33. Housing Authority member Naomi Ackley, PI held at Mole Lake, June 27, 1975.

34. Larson, PI.

35. Vilican-Leman, "Comprehensive Development Plan for Keweenaw Bay," 24–25, 27.

36. League of Women Voters, *Indians in Minnesota,* 122.

37. Vilican-Leman, "Comprehensive Development Plan for Keweenaw Bay," 28; Hull, PI.

38. Public Health Nurse Susan Milman of the Public Health Service-Indian Division, PI held at Bemidji, Minnesota, June 16, 1975.

39. Chosa and St. Arnold, "Plan for the Keweenaw Bay Indian Community," 19; Dakota, PI.

40. Milman, PI; League of Women Voters, *Indians in Minnesota,* 108–09.

41. Livingston, PI.

42. Chosa and St. Arnold, "Plan for the Keweenaw Bay Indian Community," 20.

43. League of Women Voters, *Indians in Minnesota,* 108.

44. David and Andrea Peterson, PI held at Duluth, Minnesota, June 26, 1975.

45. Crawford, Peterson, and Wurr, *Minnesota Chippewa Indians. A Handbook for Teachers,* 49.

46. David and Andrea Peterson, PI.

47. "Indian Education: A National Tragedy—A National Challenge, 1969 Report of the Committee on Labor and Public Welfare, United States Senate, Made by Its Special Subcommittee on Indian Education . . . ," U.S., Congress, *Senate Report* no. 501, 91st Cong., 1st sess. (Serial 12836-1).

48. The so-called Indian Education Act was actually Title IV of the Education Amendments Act of 1972. U.S., *Statutes at Large,* 86:334-345.

49. U.S., *Statutes at Large,* 88:2213.

50. League of Women Voters, *Indians in Minnesota,* 67–81; Ojibwe Curriculum Committee et al., "The Ojibwe: A History Resource Unit," *Minnesota Historical Society* (1973).

51. De Waal, "Plan for Chippewa Lac du Flambeau Band," 49–51.

52. Taylor, "Native American Contributions to Progress," 35.

53. League of Women Voters, *Indians in Minnesota,* 61.

54. Ron Maday, PI held at Bad River Reservation, June 24, 1975.

55. De Waal, "Plan for the Chippewa Lac du Flambeau Band," 51, 53.

56. Mrs. Raymond E. Mayotte and Mandy Manypenny, PI; Ron Maday, PI.

57. Larson, PI.

58. Shabiash, PI held at Fond du Lac Reservation, June 21, 1975.

59. De Waal, "Plan for the Chippewa Red Cliff Band," 29–31; De Waal, "Plan for the Chippewa Lac du Flambeau Band," 49, 51, 58.

60. Chosa and St. Arnold, "Plan for the Keweenaw Bay Indian Community," 8–9.

61. For more detailed discussions on Indian education in the sixties and seventies, see Szasz, *Education and the American Indian,* chapters eleven through the epilogue; and Donald H. Anderson, "Communication Linkages between Indian Communities and School Districts in Wisconsin," Ph.D. dissertation, University of Minnesota-Minneapolis, 1972.

62. Johnson, Taylor, and Arbuckle, PI.

63. Hickerson, *Chippewa and Their Neighbors,* 17; James, "Continuity and Emergence in Indian Poverty Culture," *Current Anthropology,* 11 (October-December, 1970):439.

64. *Ibid.,* 28.

65. *Ibid.,* 23–28.

66. "Program, Dedication of Red Cliff Center of Arts and Crafts, May 30–June 1, 1975" (on file at Arts and Crafts Center, Red Cliff, Wisconsin).

67. Sherer, PI.

68. Mayotte, PI held at Bemidji, Minnesota, June 16, 1975.

69. Lolita Taylor, "Ojibwa, the Wild Rice People," 78–79.

70. Manydeeds, PI.

71. "Indian Affairs, The President's Message to Congress, July 8, 1970," *Weekly Compilation of Presidential Messages,* 6 (July 13, 1970):894–905.

72. Chosa and St. Arnold, "Plan for the Keweenaw Bay Indian Community," 4; Dakota, PI.

73. *Great Lakes Indian Community Voice,* November 9, 1972; Buffalo, PI.

74. Livingston, PI.

75. Tribal Chairman James Hendrickson, PI held at Grand Portage, June 19, 1975.

76. Veryl Holmes, PI held at Hennepin County Welfare Department, Minneapolis, Minnesota, July 10, 1974.

77. Eugene Savage, PI held at Duluth, June 26, 1975.

78. League of Women Voters, *Indians in Minnesota,* 39.

79. Holmes, "Trail of Tears: A Study of Contemporary Urbanization of American Indians," bachelor's honors thesis, University of Minnesota-Minneapolis, 1972, 33.

80. League of Women Voters, *Indians in Minnesota,* 95.

81. Holmes, "Trail of Tears," 42.

82. League of Women Voters, *Indians in Minnesota,* 39, 87.

83. Holmes, "Trail of Tears," 38–39.

84. League of Women Voters, *Indians in Minnesota,* 110–11; Community Health and Welfare Council of Hennepin County, Minn., "A Study of the Delivery System of Social Services to the American Indian in the Greater Minneapolis Area," (April, 1974), 11.

85. Savage, PI.

86. *Ibid.;* David L. Peterson, "The Chippewa Indians of Minnesota: A Teachers Guide (for Upper Elementary Grades)," iii; Duluth Indian Action Council, "Bizindun."

87. Savage, PI.

## CHAPTER 10

1. Campbell to Clapp, April 19, 1906, BIA, FOR, La Pointe Agency, LS, FRC-Chicago.

2. Hull to League of Women Voters of Minnesota, September 17, 1970, League of Women Voters, *Indians in Minnesota,* 137, 139.

3. Report of Dr. L. F. Michael, enclosed in Sells to Everest, August 7, 1913, BIA, FOR, La Pointe Agency, LR, FRC-Chicago; Everest to Sells, September 2, 1913, BIA, FOR, La Pointe Agency, LR, FRC-Chicago; AR, Campbell, July 25, 1910, BIA, Narrative and Statistical Reports, La Pointe Agency, 24–26.

4. McKinsey and Mani, Economic Survey of Bad River, 30–31.

5. Erdman, *Handbook on Wisconsin Indians,* 16, 59.

6. Traylor to Sells, August 2, 1915, BIA, CCF: [?]-1915-150 La Pointe Agency.

7. Meriam, *Problem of Indian Administration,* 6.

8. Chosa and St. Arnold, "Plan for the Keweenaw Bay Indian Community,"

9. Quoted in Smith, *Wisconsin,* 150-51.

10. "Indian Education: A National Tragedy—A National Challenge," *Senate Report* no. 501, 91st Cong., 1st sess. (Serial 12836-1).

11. Taylor, "Ojibwa, the Wild Rice People," 79.

12. Quoted in "The Land of the Ojibwe," 47, a student booklet enclosed in "The Ojibwe: A History Resource Unit," *Minnesota Historical Society* (1973).

# Bibliography

## I. PRIMARY SOURCES

**Personal Interviews**
Ackley, Naomi. Mole Lake Reservation, June 27, 1975.
Blacketter, James; Blacketter, Darrel; Tiessen, Alvina; Lyons, Bill. Fond du Lac Reservation, June 21, 1975.
Buffalo, Henry. Red Cliff Reservation, June 24, 1975.
Dakota, Frederick. Keweenaw Bay Reservation, June 30, 1975.
DeFault, Peter. Fond du Lac Reservation, June 21, 1975.
Hendrickson, James. Grand Portage Reservation, June 19, 1975.
Holmes, Veryl. Hennepin County Welfare Department, Minneapolis, Minnesota, July 10, 1974.
Hull, James. Grand Portage Reservation, June 19, 1975.
Johnson, Angeline; Taylor, Hazel; Arbuckle, Fred. St. Croix Tribal Headquarters, June 25, 1975.
Larson, Pete. Lac Court Oreilles Reservation, June 25, 1975.
Livingston, Sam. Bad River Reservation, June 24, 1975.
Maday, Raymond. Bad River Reservation, June 24, 1975.
Maday, Ron. Bad River Reservation, June 24, 1975.
Manydeeds, Edmund. Ashland, Wisconsin, June 23, 1975.
Manypenny, Mandy. Bad River Reservation, June 23, 1975.
Mayotte, R. W. Bemidji, Minnesota, June 16, 1975.
Mayotte, Mrs. R. W., Sr. and Manypenny, Mandy. Bad River Reservation, June 23, 1975.
Milman, Susan. Bemidji, Minnesota, June 16, 1975.
Peterson, David and Andrea. Duluth, Minnesota, June 26, 1975.
Roy, Edward H. Red Cliff Reservation, June 24, 1975.
Savage, Eugene. Duluth, Minnesota, June 26, 1975.
Shabiash, Sandra. Fond du Lac Reservation, June 21, 1975.
Sherer, Ron. Grand Portage Reservation, June 19, 1975.
Valliere, Evangeline. Lac du Flambeau Reservation, June 30, 1975.

**Private Papers and Tribal Documents**
American Board of Commissioners for Foreign Missions. Papers. Houghton Library, Harvard University, Cambridge, Massachusetts.
Baraga, Frederic. Papers. Clarke Historical Library, Central Michigan University, Mt. Pleasant, Michigan.
Chosa, Amy D. and St. Arnold, H. James. "Overall Economic Development Plan for the Keweenaw Bay Indian Community." Report on file at the Tribal Community Center, Baraga, Michigan, 1974.
DeWaal, Arie. "Overall Economic Development Plan for the Chippewa Lac du Flambeau Band, Lac du Flambeau Reservation." Report on file at the Tribal Community Center, Lac du Flambeau, Wisconsin, 1974.

————. "Overall Economic Development Plan for the Chippewa Red Cliff Band, Red Cliff Reservation, Red Cliff, Wisconsin." Report on file at the Arts and Crafts Center, Red Cliff, Wisconsin, 1973.

"Program, Dedication of Red Cliff Center of Arts and Crafts, May 30–June 1, 1975." On file at the Arts and Crafts Center, Red Cliff, Wisconsin.

"Program, Dedication and Ribbon Cutting Ceremonies, Wa-Swa-Gon Park Campground and Tribal Fish Hatchery, June 7–8, 1975." On file at the Tribal Community Center, Lac du Flambeau, Wisconsin.

Vilican-Leman & Associates, Inc. "Report Number 3, Comprehensive Development Plan, Keweenaw Bay Indian Community, Michigan, and Watersmeet Indian Community, Michigan." On file at the Tribal Community Center, Baraga, Michigan, 1974.

**Bureau of Indian Affairs Records (Unpublished), in the National Archives, Washington**

Central Classified Files.
  Consolidated Chippewas Agency.
  Great Lakes Agency.
  Lac du Flambeau Agency.
  La Pointe Agency.
  Mackinac Agency.
Documents Relating to the Negotiation of Ratified and Unratified Treaties with Various Indian Tribes.
Field Office Records.
  Wisconsin Superintendency.
Hill, Edward E. Historical Sketches for Jurisdictional and Subject Headings Used for the Letters Received by the Office of Indian Affairs, 1824–80.
Letters Received.
  La Pointe Agency.
  Mackinac Agency.
  Michigan Superintendency.
  Sandy Lake Agency.
Letters Sent.
Narrative and Statistical Reports.
  Consolidated Chippewas Agency.
  Fond du Lac Agency.
  Great Lakes Agency.
  Hayward Agency.
  Lac du Flambeau Agency.
  La Pointe Agency.
  Mackinac Agency.

**Bureau of Indian Affairs Records (Unpublished), in the Federal Records Center, Chicago.**

Field Office Records.
  La Pointe Agency.

**Bureau of Indian Affairs Records (Unpublished), in the Washington National Records Center, Suitland, Maryland.**

Central Classified Files.
    Great Lakes Agency.
    Minneapolis Area Office.
    Minnesota Agency.

**Bureau of Indian Affairs Records (Unpublished) in the Great Lakes
    Agency, Ashland, Wisconsin.**
Report of the Labor Force, April 1975.

**Federal Documents (Published).**

1. General.
    Annual Report of the Commissioner of Indian Affairs to the Secretary
        of the Interior. National Cash Register Microfiche Edition, 1969.
    Bloom, John Porter, comp. and ed. *The Territorial Papers of the United
        States.* **Vol. 27,** *The Territory of Wisconsin: Executive Journal,
        1836–1848; Papers, 1836–1839.* Washington: National Archives,
        1969.
    Carter, Clarence Edwin, comp. and ed. *The Territorial Papers of the
        United States.* **Vol. 11,** *The Territory of Michigan, 1820–1829.*
        Washington: Government Printing Office, 1943.
    Kappler, Charles J., ed. *Indian Affairs: Laws and Treaties.* 2 vols. 2nd
        ed. Washington: Government Printing Office, 1904.
    Royce, Charles C., comp. "Indian Land Cessions in the United States,"
        *Eighteenth Annual Report of the Bureau of American Ethnology.*
        Washington: Government Printing Office, 1899.
    *United States Statutes at Large,* 3, 10, 17, 25, 26, 30, 48, 86, 88.
    *United States Supreme Court Reports,* 208. (Starr *v.* Campbell), 527–34.

2. Special.

    Bureau of Indian Affairs. "Indians of the Great Lakes Agency." Wash-
        ington: Government Printing Office, 1968.
    _____. *Tribal Relations Pamphlet No. 1A: Indian Tribes, Bands and
        Communities which Voted to Accept or Reject the Terms of the
        Indian Reorganization Act, the Dates when Elections were Held,
        and the Votes Cast.* Washington: Government Printing Office,
        1946.
    *Constitution and Bylaws of the Bad River Band of the Lake Superior
        Tribe of Chippewa Indians of the State of Wisconsin (Approved
        June 20, 1936).* Washington: Government Printing Office, 1936.
    *Constitution and Bylaws of the Minnesota Chippewa Tribe, Minnesota.*
        Washington: Government Printing Office, 1936.
    *Corporate Charter of the Bad River Band of Chippewa Indians of the
        Bad River Reservation, Wisconsin (Ratified May 21, 1938).*
        Washington: Government Printing Office, 1938.
    *House Miscellaneous Documents.*
        No. 36, 30th Cong., 2d sess. (Serial 544).
    *House Executive Documents.*
        No. 162, 42d Cong., 2d sess. (Serial 1513).
        No. 193, 42d Cong., 2d sess. (Serial 1513).

No. 99, 51st Cong., 1st sess. (Serial 2741).

"Indian Affairs, The President's Message to Congress, July 8, 1970,"
    *Weekly Compilation of Presidential Messages,* 6 (July 13, 1970):
    894–905.

*Senate Executive Documents.*
    No. 128, 50th Cong. 2d sess. (Serial 2612).

*Senate Reports.*
    No. 571, 52d Cong., 1st sess. (Serial 2913).
    No. 501, 91st Cong., 1st sess. (Serial 12836-1).

## Books (Firsthand Accounts)

Armstrong, Benjamin G. *Early Life Among the Indians. Reminiscences from
    the Life of Benj. G. Armstrong. Treaties of 1835, 1837, 1842, and 1854.
    Habits and customs of the red men....* Dictated to and written by
    Thomas P. Wentworth. Ashland, Wisconsin: Press of A. W. Bowron,
    1892.

Carver, J.[onathan] *Travels Through the Interior Parts of North America, in
    the Years 1766, 1767, and 1768.* Facsimile of 3d ed. Minneapolis: Ross
    and Haines, Inc., 1956.

Copway, George. *The Traditional History and Characteristic Sketches of the
    Ojibway Nation.* Boston: Benjamin B. Mussey & Company, 1851.

Crawford, Dean A.; Peterson, David L.; Wurr, Virgil. *Minnesota Chippewa
    Indians. A Handbook for Teachers.* St. Paul: Upper Midwest Regional
    Educational Laboratory, 1967.

Henry, Alexander. *Travels and Adventures in Canada and the Indian Ter-
    ritories, between the years 1760 and 1776.* Facsimile of 1809 ed. Ann
    Arbor: University Microfilms, Inc., 1966.

Johnson, William, Sir. *The Papers of Sir William Johnson.* Edited by Alex-
    ander C. Flick. 6 vols. Albany: University of the State of New York,
    1925.

Jones, Peter, *History of the Ojibway Indians: with Special Reference to the
    Conversion to Christianity.* London: A. W. Bennett, 1861.

Keating, William Hypolitus. *Narrative of an Expedition to the Source of St.
    Peter's River....* 2 vols. London: G. B. Whittaker, 1825.

McKenney, Thomas Lorainne. *Sketches of a Tour of the Lakes, of the
    Character and Customs of the Chippewa Indians, and of Incidents
    Connected with the Treaty of Fond du Lac....* Baltimore: F. Lucas,
    Jr., 1827.

Meriam, Lewis L. *et al. The Problem of Indian Administration. Report of a
    Survey Made at the Request of Honorable Hubert Work, Secretary of
    the Interior, and Submitted to Him, February 21, 1928.* Institute for
    Government Research, Studies in Administration. Baltimore: Johns
    Hopkins Press, 1928.

Pike, Zebulon. *The Journals of Zebulon Montgomery Pike, Letters and Re-
    lated Documents.* Edited by Donald Jackson. 2 vols. Norman: Univer-
    sity of Oklahoma Press, 1966.

Schoolcraft, Henry R. *Historical and Statistical Information, Respecting the
    History, Condition and Prospects of the Indian Tribes of the United
    States: Collected and Prepared under the Direction of the Bureau of
    Indian Affairs, Per Act of Congress of March 3d, 1847.* 6 vols.

Philadelphia: Lippincott, Grambo & Company, 1851.

_____. *Narrative Journal of Travels from Detroit Northwest through the Great Chain of American Lakes to the Sources of the Mississippi River in the Year 1820.* Albany: E. & E. Hosford, 1821.

_____. *Personal Memoirs of a Residence of Thirty Years with the Indian Tribes on the American Frontiers....* Philadelphia: Lippincott, Grambo, and Company, 1851.

_____. *Schoolcraft's Expedition to Lake Itasca: the Discovery of the Source of the Mississippi.* Edited by Philip P. Mason. East Lansing: Michigan State University Press, 1958.

Tanner, John. *A Narrative of the Captivity and Adventures of John Tanner (U.S. Interpreter at the Saut de Ste. Marie) during Thirty Years Residence Among the Indians in the Interior of North America.* Edited by Edwin James. Facsimile of 1830 ed. Minneapolis: Ross and Haines, Inc., 1956.

Thwaites, Reuben Gold, ed. *The Jesuit Relations and Allied Documents....* 73 vols. New York: Pageant Book Company, 1959.

Warren, William Whipple. *History of the Ojibway Nation.* Minneapolis: Ross and Haines, Inc., 1957.

## Articles (Firsthand Accounts)
Dodd, J. M. "Ashland Then and Now." *Wisconsin Magazine of History* 28 (December, 1944): 188–96.

Malhiot, Francois Victor. "A Wisconsin Fur-Trader's Journal, 1804–05." *Collections of the State Historical Society of Wisconsin* 19 (Madison, 1910): 163–233.

Perrault, Jean Baptiste. "Narrative of the Travels and Adventures of a Merchant Voyageur in the Savage Territories of Northern America Leaving Montreal the 28th of May 1783 (to 1820)." Edited by John Sharpless Fox. *Historical Collections and Researches made by the Michigan Pioneer and Historical Society* 37 (Lansing, 1909–10): 508–619.

Perrot, Nicolas. "Memoir on the Manners, Customs, and Religion of the Savages of North America." Edited by Jules Tailhan, S.J. In *The Indian Tribes of the Upper Mississippi Valley,* edited by E. H. Blair. 2 vols. Cleveland, Arthur H. Clark Company, 1911.

Skolla, Otto. "Father Skolla's Report on His Indian Missions." *Acta et Dicta* 7 (October, 1936): 217–68.

Thwaites, Reuben Gold, ed. "Papers from the Canadian Archives—1767–1814." *Collections of the State Historical Society of Wisconsin* 12 (Madison, 1892): 23–132.

_____. ed. "Radisson and Groseilliers in Wisconsin." *Collections of the State Historical Society of Wisconsin* 11 (Madison, 1888): 64–96.

Wojta, J. F. "Indian Farm Institutes in Wisconsin." *Wisconsin Magazine of History* 29 (June, 1946): 423–34.

## Brochures.
Duluth Indian Action Council. "Bizindun."
Community Health and Welfare Council of Hennepin County. "A Study of

the Delivery System of Social Services to the American Indian in the Greater Minneapolis Area." April, 1974.

## II. SECONDARY SOURCES

**Books.**

Barnouw, Victor. *Acculturation and Personality Among the Wisconsin Chippewa.* Memoir Series of the American Anthropological Association, no. 72 (October, 1950).

Brophy, William A. and Aberle, Sophie, *et al. The Indian: America's Unfinished Business. Report of the Commission on the Rights, Liberties, and Responsibilities of the American Indian.* Norman: University of Oklahoma Press, 1966.

Campbell, Henry Colin, *et al. Wisconsin in Three Centuries, 1634–1905.* 5 vols. New York: The Century History Company, 1906.

Coleman, Bernard, Sister. *Ojibwa Myths and Legends.* Minneapolis: Ross and Haines, Inc., 1962.

———. *Where the Water Stops: Fond du Lac Reservation.* Duluth: College of Saint Scholastica, 1967.

Densmore, Frances. *Chippewa Customs.* Smithsonian Institution Bureau of American Ethnology Bulletin, no. 86. Washington: Government Printing Office, 1929.

———. *Chippewa Music.* Smithsonian Institution Bureau of American Ethnology Bulletin, no. 45. Washington: Government Printing Office, 1910.

Dunn, James Taylor. *The St. Croix: Midwest Border River.* New York: Holt, Rinehart and Winston, 1965.

Erdman, Joyce M. *Handbook on Wisconsin Indians.* Madison: Governor's Commission on Human Rights, State of Wisconsin, 1966.

Federal Writers' Project. *Minnesota: A State Guide.* New York: Hastings House, 1938.

———. *Wisconsin: A Guide to the Badger State.* New York: Duell, Sloan, and Pearce, 1941.

Folwell, William Watts. *A History of Minnesota.* 4 vols. rev. ed. St. Paul: Minnesota Historical Society, 1956.

Fries, Robert F. *Empire in Pine: The Story of Lumbering in Wisconsin, 1830–1900.* Madison: State Historical Society of Wisconsin, 1951.

Gara, Larry. *A Short History of Wisconsin.* Madison: State Historical Society of Wisconsin, 1962.

Gibson, Lawrence Henry. *The British Empire Before the American Revolution.* 15 vols. New York: Alfred A. Knopf, 1936–1970.

———. *The Triumphant Empire: New Responsibilities Within the Enlarged Empire, 1763–1766.* Vol. 9 of *The British Empire Before the American Revolution.* New York: Alfred A. Knopf, 1956.

———. *The Triumphant Empire: The Rumbling of the Coming Storm, 1766–1770.* Vol. 11 of *The British Empire Before the American Revolution.* New York: Alfred A. Knopf, 1965.

———. *Zones of International Friction: The Great Lakes Frontier, Canada, the West Indies, India, 1744–1754.* Vol. 5 of *The British Empire Before the American Revolution.* New York: Alfred A. Knopf, 1942.

Hagan, William T. *The Sac and Fox Indians*. Norman: University of Oklahoma Press, 1958.

Hollowell, A. Irving. *Culture and Experience*. Philadelphia: University of Pennsylvania Press, 1955.

Harmon, George Dewey. *Sixty Years of Indian Affairs, Political, Economic, and Diplomatic,* 1789-1850. Chapel Hill: University of North Carolina Press, 1941.

Hatcher, Harlan. *The Great Lakes.* New York: Oxford University Press, 1944.

Hickerson, Harold. *The Chippewa and Their Neighbors: A Study in Ethnohistory.* New York: Holt, Rinehart and Winston, Inc., 1970.

———. *The Southwestern Chippewa: An Ethnohistorical Study.* American Anthropological Association Memoir, no. 92, vol. 64 (June, 1962).

Hilger, M. Inez, Sister. *Chippewa Child Life and Its Cultural Background.* Smithsonian Institution Bureau of American Ethnology Bulletin, no. 146. Washington: Government Printing Office, 1951.

Hill, Edward E., comp. *Preliminary Inventory of the Records of the Bureau of Indian Affairs.* 2 vols. Washington: National Archives, 1965.

Horseman, Reginald. *The Causes of the War of 1812.* Philadelphia: University of Pennsylvania Press, 1962.

Hyde, George. *Indians of the Woodlands: from Prehistoric Times to 1725.* Norman: University of Oklahoma Press, 1962.

Jacobs, Wilbur R. *Dispossessing the American Indian: Indians and Whites on the Colonial Frontier.* New York: Charles Scribner's Sons, 1972.

Jenness, Diamond. *The Indians of Canada.* National Museum of Canada Bulletin, no. 65. 6th ed. Ottawa: 1963.

Jezernik, Maksimilijan. *Frederick Baraga. A Portrait of the First Bishop of Marquette Based on the Archives of the Congregatio de Propaganda Fide.* New York: Studia Slovenica, 1968.

Kellogg, Louise Phelps. *The British Régime in Wisconsin and the Northwest.* Madison: State Historical Society of Wisconsin, 1935.

———. *The French Régime in Wisconsin and the Northwest.* Madison: State Historical Society of Wisconsin, 1925.

Keesing, Felix M. *The Menomini Indians of Wisconsin: A Study of Three Centuries of Cultural Contact and Change.* Philadelphia: American Philosophical Society, 1939.

Kinietz, William Vernon. *Chippewa Village: the Story of Katikitegon.* Cranbrook Institute of Science Bulletin No. 25. Bloomfield Hills, Michigan: 1947.

———. *The Indians of the Western Great Lakes, 1615-1760.* Ann Arbor: University of Michigan Press, 1965.

Landes, Ruth. *The Ojibwa Woman.* Columbia University Contributions to Anthropology, vol. 31. New York: Columbia University Press, 1938.

League of Women Voters of Minnesota. *Indians in Minnesota.* St. Paul: North Central Publishing Company, 1974.

Leuchtenburg, William E. *Franklin D. Roosevelt and the New Deal, 1932-1940.* New York: Harper and Row Publishers, 1963.

Levi, Carolissa. *Chippewa Indians of Yesterday and Today.* New York: Pageant Press, 1956.

Lyford, Carrie Alberta. *The Crafts of the Ojibwa (Chippewa).* Edited by

Willard W. Beatty. Phoenix: Printing Department, Phoenix Indian School, 1943.

Meyer, Roy W. *History of the Santee Sioux: United States Indian Policy on Trial*. Lincoln: University of Nebraska Press, 1967.

Nute, Grace Lee. *Lake Superior*. Indianapolis: Bobbs-Merrill Company, 1944.

Parkman, Francis. *The Conspiracy of Pontiac and the Indian War after the Conquest of Canada*. 2 vols. 10th ed. Boston: Little Brown and Company, 1912.

Peake, Ora Brooks. *A History of the United States Indian Factory System, 1795-1822*. Denver: Sage Books, 1954.

Peckham, Howard H. *Pontiac and the Indian Uprising*. Princeton: Princeton University Press, 1947.

Quimby, George I. *Indian Culture and European Trade Goods*. Madison: University of Wisconsin Press, 1966.

_____. *Indian Life in the Upper Great Lakes, 11,000 B.C. to A.D. 1800*. University of Chicago Press, 1960.

Porter, Kenneth W. *John Jacob Astor: Business Man*. 2 vols. Cambridge, Massachusetts: Harvard University Press, 1931.

Ritzenthaler, Robert Eugene. *Chippewa Preoccupation with Health; Change in a Traditional Attitude Resulting from Modern Health Problems*. Public Museum of the City of Milwaukee Bulletin, Vol. 19. Milwaukee: 1953.

_____ and Ritzenthaler, Pat. *The Woodland Indians of the Western Great Lakes*. Garden City, New York: Natural History Press, 1970.

Roseboom, Eugene Holloway, and Weisenburger, Francis P. *A History of Ohio*. Columbus: Ohio Historical Society, 1967.

Ross, Hamilton N. *The Apostle Islands*. Batavia, Illinois: Batavia Herald Company, 1951.

_____. *La Pointe—Village Outpost*. St. Paul: North Central Publishing Company, 1960.

Salmond, John A. *The Civilian Conservation Corps, 1933-1942: A New Deal Case Study*. Durham, North Carolina: Duke University Press, 1967.

Smith, Alice E. *The History of Wisconsin. Vol. 1. From Exploration to Statehood*. Madison: State Historical Society of Wisconsin, 1973.

Swanton, John R. *The Indian Tribes of North America*. Smithsonian Institution Bureau of American Ethnology Bulletin, no. 145. Washington: Government Printing Office, 1952.

Szasz, Margaret. *Education and the American Indian; The Road to Self-Determination, 1928-1973*. Albuquerque: University of New Mexico Press, 1974.

Verwyst, P. Chrysostomus. *Life and Labors of Rt. Rev. Frederic Baraga, First Bishop of Marquette, Mich. . . .* Milwaukee: M. H. Wiltzius & Co., 1900.

**Articles.**

Armstrong, O. K. "Set the American Indians Free!" *Reader's Digest* 47 (August, 1945):47-52.

Buck, Solon J. "The Story of Grand Portage." *Minnesota History* 5 (February, 1923):14-27.

Davidson, John N. "Missions on Chequamegon Bay." *Collections of the State Historical Society of Wisconsin* 12 (1892):434-52.

Downes, Randolph C. "A Crusade for Indian Reform, 1922-34." *Mississippi Valley Historical Review* 32 (December, 1945):331-54.

Elliott, Richard R. "The Chippewas of Lake Superior." *American Catholic Quarterly Review* 21 (April, 1896):354-73.

Gower, Calvin W. "The CCC Indian Division: Aid for Depressed Americans, 1933-1942." *Minnesota History* 43 (Spring, 1972):3-13.

Greenman, Emerson F. "The Indians of Michigan." *Michigan History* 45 (March, 1961):1-33.

Harmer, Ruth Mulvey. "Uprooting the Indians." *Atlantic Monthly* 197 (March, 1956):54-57.

Hickerson, Harold. "The Chippewa of the Upper Great Lakes: A Study in Sociopolitical Change." In *North American Indians in Historical Perspective,* edited by Eleanor B. Leacock and Nancy O. Lurie. New York: Random House, 1971.

———. "The Feast of the Dead Among the Seventeenth Century Algonkians of the Upper Great Lakes." *American Anthropologist* 62 (February, 1960):81-107.

James, Bernard J. "Continuity and Emergence in Indian Poverty Culture." *Current Anthropology* 11 (October-December, 1970):435-52.

Parman, Donald L. "The Indian and the CCC." *Pacific Historical Review* 40 (February, 1971):39-56.

Philp, Kenneth R. "John Collier and the American Indian." In *Essays on Radicalism in Contemporary America,* edited by Leon Borden Blair. Austin: University of Texas Press, 1972.

Riggs, S. R. "Protestant Missions in the Northwest." *Collections of the Minnesota Historical Society* 6 (1894):117-88.

Ritzenthaler, Robert Eugene. "Impact of Small Industry on an Indian Community." *American Anthropologist* 55 (January, 1953):143-48.

Thwaites, Reuben Gold. "The Story of Chequamegon Bay." *Collections of the State Historical Society of Wisconsin* 13 (1895):397-425.

Twining, Charles E. "Plunder and Progress: The Lumbering Industry in Perspective." *Wisconsin Magazine of History* 47 (Winter, 1963-64): 116-24.

Woolworth, Nancy L. "The Grand Portage Mission." *Minnesota History* 39 (Winter, 1965):301-10.

Zimmerman, William. "The Role of the Bureau of Indian Affairs Since 1933." *Annals of the American Academy of Political Science* 311 (May, 1957):31-40.

**Special.**

"Apostle Islands National Lakeshore, Wisconsin." National Park Service Brochure: 1973—515—985/114.

Ojibwe Curriculum Committee *et al.* "The Ojibwe: A History Resource Unit." St. Paul: Minnesota Historical Society, 1973.

**Unpublished Studies.**

Anderson, Donald Howard. "Communication Linkages between Indian Communities and School Districts in Wisconsin." Doctoral disserta-

tion, University of Minnesota, Minneapolis, 1972.
Holmes, Veryl L. "Trail of Tears: A Study of Contemporary Urbanization of American Indians." Bachelor's honors thesis, University of Minnesota, Minneapolis, 1972.
James, Bernard. "An Analysis of an American Indian Village. A Situational Approach to Community Study." Doctoral dissertation, University of Wisconsin, Madison, 1954.
Peterson, David L. "The Chippewa Indians of Minnesota: A Teachers Guide (for Upper Elementary Grades)." Copy in author's files, 1969. (Photoduplicated.)
Taylor, Lolita. "Native American Contributions to Progress." Copy in author's files, 1974. (Photoduplicated.)
_____. "Ojibwa, the Wild Rice People." Copy in author's files, 1973. (Mimeographed.)

**Newspapers and Magazines.**
*Ashland Daily News,* 1891–1908.
*The Daily Press* (Ashland), 1910–11.
*Christian Science Monitor* (Boston), 1971.
*Great Lakes Indian Community Voice,* 1972.
*Indians at Work* (Washington), 1933–45.

# Index

Brunson, Alfred: 80–81
Buffalo, Henry: 187
Bungees (Plains Chippewas): 8
Bureau of Indian Affairs (BIA): 68,
79, 107, 111, 122–23, 129, 132–34,
137–39, 156, 164, 169, 185, 190,
203–205, 230; hurt by intertribal
warfare, 74–77; removal policy of,
87–88, 96, 157, 162, 166–67, 169;
acculturation program of, 93, 110,
211; allotment program of, 97,
111; farming program of, 98, 104,
114, 117; supervises timber industry on reservations, 100–102,
112–14, 158; health programs of,
120–21, 130–31; educational program of, 123–24, 143–44, 157,
197–98; loan and grant programs
of, 138, 149, 159, 166, 168; paternalism of, 169, 183, 216; future of,
206; its role summarized, 215
Bushnell, Daniel P.: 78

Cadotte, Jean Baptiste: 55, 57,
59–60, 189
Cadotte, Jean Baptiste, Jr.: 60, 75
Cadotte, Michel: 60, 66, 70, 75
Campbell, S. W.: 98, 112–13, 122,
126–27
Carlson, Elmer J.: 113–14
Cass, Lewis: 75–76
Cass Lake: 37
Cass Lake band: 75
Cavill, J. C.: 136–37
Chequamegon Bay, Wis.: 4, 27–30,
33, 36, 58, 66
Chippewas: background of, 7–8
Chorette, Simon: 62
Civilian Conservation Corps—
Indian Division (CCC-ID): 138–
40, 144, 149, 154, 156, 168
Civil Works Administration (CWA):
137–38, 140, 168
Clans: 10–11, 152
Clark, William: 75
Cloquet, Minn.: 95, 109, 121
Clothing: 9–10
Collier, John: 131–34, 143, 156, 168,
196

Community Action Program: 188,
205
Community Health Representative
(CHR): 193
Consolidated Chippewa Agency:
110–11, 135
Couderay, Wis.: 161
*Coureurs de bois:* 29–32, 38–39, 61
Courtright, B. G.: 121, 126
Crandon, Wis.: 154
Crawford, Dean: 195–96, 202
Crees: 33, 36–37
Crooks, Ramsay: 69, 71, 73
Culture: 8–9, 82, 201–02, 211, 216–
17; *see also* acculturation

Dakota, Frederick: 186, 205
Danbury, Wis.: 154
Dawes Severalty Act (1887): 97, 106,
131
Dean, Dorothy: 123–24, 126
Dease, John: 61
Death: 15–16
De Fault, Peter: 184
Delawares: 63, 68
DePeyster, Major Arent Schuyler:
59
Depression: impact on reservations
110, 119, 125–26, 135–36, 140–41,
146–47, 149–50, 153–54
Detroit, Mich.: 55, 60, 65–66, 68
Diphtheria: 145, 149
Dodge, Henry: 87
Downes, Randolph C.: 131
Drexel, Kate: 108
Duluth, Minn.: 206
Duluth, Sieur: 28, 36
Duluth Indian Action Council
(DIAC): 195, 208–10

Economic Development Administration (EDA): 185–86, 188–89
Economic development programs for
reservations: 110, 159–60, 185–89,
204–05
Economic Opportunity Act: 165
Education: 14–15, 105–106, 110,
123–25, 144, 157, 168, 170, 199–
201, 203, 208, 210; and accultura-

Great Lakes Inter-Tribal Council
(GLIC): 205
Gregory, James T.: 102
Groseilliers, Sieur des: 28, 39

Halfway House, Keweenaw Bay
Reservation: 194
Hall, Sherman: 83–84, 86
Hallowell, A. Irving: 150–52
Harrison, Governor William Henry:
65, 68
Hays, James P.: 78
Hayward, Wis.: 109
Hayward Indian Hospital: 145, 148,
163, 166
Head Start: 196, 204
Health: 105, 110, 130–31, 168, 208,
210; traditional practices, 15,
18–19; and housing, 104–105,
119–20; and BIA, 120–21, 130–31;
on specific reservations, 121,
144–45, 147–50, 152–54, 163,
166–68, 193; and self-
determination, 192–93, 205; his-
tory summarized, 213; see also
specific diseases
Health, Education and Welfare, Department of (HEW): 183
Henry, Alexander: 53–55, 57–61
Herriman, David B.: 3–4, 89
Hertel, Wis.: 155
Hickerson, Harold: 27, 202
Holliday, John: 69, 71
Holmes, Veryl L.: 206–208
Home Improvement Program (HIP):
190
Hopkins, Harry: 137
Housing: 9, 102, 104, 110, 119–20,
167–70, 190–93, 207, 210, 239; on
specific reservations, 115, 119–20,
145, 148, 150, 152–54, 160, 162–
63, 166, 186, 189–92; federal programs for, 190, 192; self-
determination for, 190–92; history
summarized, 212
Housing and Urban Development,
Department of (HUD): 190–91,
193
Housing Assistance Administration:
190

Howard, Captain William: 57
Hudson's Bay Company: 59
Hull, James: 189
Hunting: 13, 31, 95, 150, 152, 162,
184, 203
Hurons: 26–27, 30, 33–34, 39

Ickes, Secretary of the Interior
Harold: 132
Illinois Indians: 34
Indian Education Act (1972): 197,
199–200
Indian police and judges: 93–94,
122–23
Indian Reorganization Act of 1934
(IRA): 110, 132–34, 136–37, 144,
168–69, 238
Indian Self-Determination and Edu-
cation Assistance Act (1975): 183,
197
Institute for Government Research:
128, 131
Interior, Department of: 128, 183
Intermarriage: 127–28
Intertribal associations: 204–05, 210
Inter-Tribal Council of Michigan:
186, 204–205
Iowas: 75
Iroquois: 27–28, 31, 33–35, 56

James, Bernard: 161–62, 202
James, Reverend Woodbridge L.: 83
Jamet, Lieutenant: 54
Jay Treaty (1794): 60, 63
Jesuits: 26, 28–31, 34, 54
Jogues, Father Isaac: 26–27
Johnson, George: 77
Johnson, Sir John: 61, 73
Johnson, Sir William: 53, 55–56, 59
Johnson-O'Malley Act of 1934
(JOM): 143–44, 157, 197, 199
Jonois, Father: 54

Kaskaskias: 63
Kennedy, Senator Edward: 197–98
Kennedy Report: 196–97
Keweenaw Bay, Mich.: 28, 36, 69
Keweenaw Bay band: 71
Keweenaw Bay outfit: 70
Keweenaw Bay Reservation: 136,